BARENTS SEA
Kirkenes
Boris Gleb
Nikel
Murmansk
Ivalo
Olenogorsk
Rovaniemi
WHITE SEA
GULF OF BOTHNIA
Oulu
FINLAND
U. S. S. R.
Helsinki
Leningrad
Tallinn
Novgorod
Pskov
Riga
Moscow
N
W
E
S
Vilnius
Miles
0
100
200
POLAND
Warsaw
palacios

10-

Incident at Boris Gleb

By DeWitt S. Copp

RADIUS OF ACTION
THE PURSUIT OF "M"
THE ODD DAY
BETRAYAL AT THE UN

Incident at Boris Gleb

The Tragedy of Newcomb Mott

DeWitt S. Copp

DOUBLEDAY & COMPANY, INC.
GARDEN CITY, NEW YORK
1968

Library of Congress Catalog Card Number 67–22444

Printed in the United States of America
First Edition

For Dad

ILLUSTRATIONS

Introduction

Much has been written about our son Newcomb, most of it at the time of his trial in Murmansk, Russia, and since his death in January 1966. After reading the many fictions which have appeared, it was a relief to talk with the author of this book, who had taken an active interest in Newcomb's case from the beginning. Because he demonstrated he is a writer dedicated to seeking facts, we gave him our complete cooperation. This included our notes, correspondence, and personal recollection of events.

Part of the returns from his book will be used to augment the Newcomb Mott History Scholarship at Antioch College, Yellow Springs, Ohio. We hope that students who receive the scholarship will gain a deeper understanding of the problems one encounters when trying to communicate with peoples of a different background and culture, and whose code of ethics and motivations may be divergent from their own.

Phyllis and Howard Mott

Two Sundays ago Marty and I took a bus out to Point Place on the bay leading to Lake Erie. The ride was the usual Toledo fare, but the distance was over six miles; we really got our money's worth. While there we decided to walk down a road to see where it went; Marty wasn't too keen on it, but I convinced him of its worthiness. It became dead end as far as cars were concerned, but a path was evident. It stretched for some miles. A little more than a mile and we were able to go out on a narrow strip of beach, which curved around points for a few miles. A duck hunter in a blind equipped with decoys was on our route. We traveled on, ending up on the opposite end of a private community within a community. . . .

From a letter written by Newcomb Mott to his parents
on October 23, 1958

Boy that sounded pretty serious; I hope you're a lot better. Did you think you were a kangaroo? It's damn good you're tough. You and I seem to be accident prone, although I'm probably more so. A lot of it is undoubtedly that we take chances, not always weighing the risks sufficiently. . . .

Newcomb Mott to his brother Rusty
on November 3, 1959

Chapter One

Beyond Lake Inari the arctic terrain lost its timbered carpeting and gave way to rock land. The mountains were stone and flanking them were long stone hills. Between the mountains and the hills, stands of birch sought with thin success to capture the summits. In the flat areas birch grew thickly, and in the scattering of fields and pasture the land was russet, for in this first week of September it was coming on to *ruska aika,* the brown time, as the Finns say.

There were many ponds in the valleys and smaller ponds amid the flat stone croppings of the hills, and to the east, a short distance past the lake's end, the Pasvik River made its cut, flowing northward toward the Bökfjord and the Barents Sea.

The sky was overcast, and the grayness of cloud, complementing the grayness of rock, created a visual starkness that brushed the eyes with its harsh, provocative imagery and left a faint but disturbing feeling of human transience.

The land lying to the east of the Pasvik was Soviet and to

the west predominantly Norwegian. The Norwegian portion was but a narrow wedge forty miles long and at one point less than a mile wide. As a result the Finnair DC-3 kept to the west of the Norwegian strip, flying over Finnish territory, not crossing into Norway until shortly before making its approach to Kirkenes, its destination.

An hour before, the flight had departed Ivalo, Finland, at the southern tip of Lake Inari, and now as the pilot began his long gradual letdown to Kirkenes he was even more careful to maintain a course clear of the Pasvik River, for at one point the Soviets held a small square salient of land on the western side of the river. They called it Borisoglebsk and the Norwegians referred to it as Boris Gleb. The salient was less than three miles square, but its location and its dimensions were vastly more important to far-distant men in the Kremlin than either its size or barren aspect would indicate. It had a story to tell and purposes to serve: some present, and some for a possible future time.

On board the plane there were only three passengers. Two were Finn—Markku Rautonen, a writer, and Helge Heinonen, a photographer. They had come to Ivalo by way of Rovaniemi and were assigned by the Finnish weekly *APU* to do a series of articles on Lapland and the Norwegian cap area. While standing outside Ivalo's small barrackslike air terminal waiting for their flight to be announced, they had taken note of the third passenger. He was engrossed in a magazine and seemed oblivious to the chattering racket, churned up by a gaggle of tractors and earth movers as they busily labored along the edge of the cement tarmac, sowing the gusty air with a rain of dust. They noticed him first for his size and his reddish blond hair. He was well over six foot tall and solidly built. They could not see his face, but they could tell he was a young man, and because of his clothes and some indefinable quality that marks a stranger, they took him for a foreigner.

Once on the plane, they had had a better look at him, for

he had moved up the aisle passing them with a nod and a smile, choosing a seat just ahead of their own. He had the manner of a big and gentle man and his looks lent support to the impression. A sense of assurance went with his size, its quality further enhanced by the expression in his pale blue eyes which seemed to be musing on their own secret joke or perhaps simply on the enthusiasm with which they saw things. There were toleration and good humor and sensuality in his long, full-lipped mouth. Only the cast of his cleft chin indicated an inner stubbornness. The total effect was that of a vigorous young man on his way somewhere, literally and figuratively, quietly enjoying every moment of the journey.

In the course of the brief flight the pretty stewardess came forward and spoke to him, and then they knew for sure that he was a foreigner. His speaking in English was, of course, proof, but it was not so much that as it was his negative reply when the stewardess asked him if he wished to buy a bottle of whiskey.

As Rautonen put it: "All Scandinavians buy whiskey when they get a chance to get it at a reasonable price. In Lapland you can only buy alcohol in Rovaniemi or in Hammerfest, Norway. Only a foreigner does not know this and does not know that in Lapland alcohol is very hard to come by and very expensive. On board a plane crossing the border you get it tax-free."

Because of his refusal they thought he must be feeling ill or else he was very rich. They did not know he simply didn't drink anything stronger than beer.

When the plane started losing altitude, preparatory to landing, the young man stopped his reading and took stock of the view.

The plane descended on a northerly heading, following a long leg of land whose bony configuration formed a centerpiece between adjoining fjords and whose outer extension shaped the western wall of the harbor. Beyond its fistlike end, swinging around from the east, a darkly rising headland sought to make union with it, and from a distance gave the brief illusion of success. The impression was that here earth and water were locked in immutable conflict. The water of the fjords penetrated between the tapering cliffs with ease, deep and smooth flowing, gray velvet in the diffuse light. And in return, the earth reached out to hem in the harbor and cut off access to the sea. Or so it seemed, until the plane banked and, on reciprocal course, brought the village of Kirkenes into view.

The village was situated at the tip of a broad tongue of gently shelving land and offered a sharp contrast to the surroundings. Many of the houses had bright-colored roofs. They stood in orderly rows clustered about a scattering of buildings, with a fronting ribbon of docks and wharves, and a tiny man-made inner harbor with its boats hugging the lee side of the breakwater. And taken altogether, they swiftly erased the original impression, for one could instantly perceive that men had established this dwelling place not because some elements of nature were in conflict but because they were usable. The water was a means of transportation and of livelihood; the land was a means of livelihood, too, and of protection against crueler elements. But most of all, before passing beneath the wing, the homes and buildings of Kirkenes gave a subtle reaffirmation of life amid the barren solitude of earth and sea and sky at season's end.

The airport was a distinct rectangular patch against the granite plateau that divided the fjords. Although the field appeared empty of other aircraft and devoid of military installations, the stewardess had announced that photographs were forbidden.

The pilot set the DC-3 down on the single east-west runway with gentle expertise, and as the craft slowed it passed at intervals the cement ruins and mounded earth of what had once been revetments and gun emplacements; rubble bones that marked another time. Then the arctic air had pulsed to the sound of aircraft whose purpose was to seek out the allied convoys making the run to Murmansk, convoys which at dreadful cost brought desperately needed supplies to the beleaguered Russians. But that was another time and another world and now the all but deserted installation bore the distinction of being NATO's northeasternmost air base. In the ear-ringing silence that followed the last turn of the propellers, the distinction seemed about as meaningful as the emptiness of the scene.

The three travelers bade farewell to the stewardess and then walked the short distance across the flight line to the boxlike administration building. There was the feel and smell of rain in the gusty air. A clump of scud had made contact with a towering rock projection which appeared deceptively close to the end of the runway.

Inside the rustic wooden-beamed waiting room Markku Rautonen learned from the flight attendant that there was no bus because there were so few passengers, but a taxi was waiting to take them into Kirkenes. Rautonen and his companion hefted their bags and started toward the door when they noticed the young stranger checking over his own luggage.

"Hello, sir," Rautonen said, speaking English slowly and clearly in spite of his heavy accent. "Perhaps you would like to ride with us to town. There is no bus. We have taxi waiting."

The young man straightened up, smiling. "That's very kind of you, but I think I'll need to change some Finnish money into Norwegian first. Do you know if I can do that here?"

"No need. You can use any money and make change at bank in Kirkenes or at tourist hotel. Are you staying at tourist hotel?"

"Yes, that's right."

"Well, then, good. We go. It cost you about two marks in Finnish. I'm Rautonen. This Mr. Heinonen. He not speak English." He thrust out his hand. He was a heavily built man with an oval face and a pelt of black hair, while his companion was fair with sharper features.

"My name is Mott . . . Newcomb Mott." The young man shook hands with the two of them, and they liked the easy tone of his voice and the easy manner of his greeting. When they had their luggage stowed in the trunk of the small cab, he insisted because of his size that he sit in the front with the driver, thinking it would make the ride more comfortable for the two Finns, and laughing aside their protests.

The taxi followed a long straight finger of road to where it intersected the highway. The highway was a narrow macadam thoroughfare which wove itself in and around and up and down the massive landscape. The impression gained from the air was magnified on the ground so that land's imprint was felt physically. This was stark, wild country whose character was accentuated not through a complex contrast of opposites, but through a simple blending of honed rock around and over which vegetation fought for survival. Where the birches grew, they grew densely, but they grew low as if they knew to grow higher was to risk having their branches torn off by the winds.

Rock plains and hulking mounds of stone have in their look the same lost immensity of empty sea and sky. Men living in such a land would feel its power and give to it the gift of omniscience, drawing both strength and fear from its gods, depending on the iron whim of fate, and if it failed them, going down with the knowledge that something larger had willed it. Or so it had once been, and if the gods were gone, the land was the same, and the initial effect was the same.

"This is your first visit to Lapland, Mr. Mott?" Rautonen asked, breaking the silence.

"Ahh—yes. Yes." The traveler pulled his glance away from the scenery and swung around to face the pair. "It was one of those spur-of-the-moment things." He grinned. "I had planned to take the bus from Ivalo up to Lakslev and see the Porsanger Fjord. But just before I was to leave I went to the Finnair office in Ivalo to check on my return reservations, and the girl there told me I could come to Kirkenes much quicker and see a lot more, so I decided to do just that. The change was made so quickly I'm not sure I have a reservation at the tourist hotel. There wasn't time to confirm it. Is your friend a photographer?"

"Yes." Rautonen explained their assignment and then asked, "How long you plan to stay in Kirkenes?"

"Only two days. I've got a flight out Saturday afternoon."

"Too bad. Not enough time. You should stay week at least. Then you see all these trees and hills in red, yellow, brown, all colors of the rainbow."

"That's the way it will look in October where my home is in Massachusetts. That's in New England. . . ."

"Hey, you come to see reindeer," Rautonen interrupted, "look there!"

The reindeer, a stag, stood on a rock fell not far from the road. He made no move as the taxi proceeded past him down the hill toward a metal bridge which spanned the throat of the fjord.

"Well, what do you know, my first arctic reindeer!" Mott exclaimed. "He certainly doesn't seem to mind us."

"Maybe he bring you luck, like the ram at Saint Olaf's castle," Rautonen replied dryly.

The taxi went across the bridge and started up the long shank of hill on the other side, and they could look back and see the reindeer still standing motionless as though carved out of the leaden scenery. Even the shrill echoing whistle from one of the two fishing boats chugging down the fjord had no effect on him, and as they glanced toward the sound they could also hear the faint mewing of the gulls as they circled the vessels.

"It's rather spectacular scenery," the young American said, "not like Finland."

"Good for hunting and fishing," Rautonen said.

"How close are we to the Soviet Union?"

"Very close. Over that way beyond those hills, I think. But to really visit Russia you must go to Leningrad. Only one hour flight from Helsingfors. You should go, not too costly."

"I looked into the possibility when I was in Helsinki. All the tours were filled up, and I didn't have time to wait for a visa. It's too bad I can't see this part of Russia while I'm here, since it's so close."

"But you can," the reporter said. "There is tourist base, Boris Gleb. Anyone with passport *velkomen.*"

"Is that so! What do you mean 'tourist base'?"

"It is very tiny near the village. Really nothing, I've heard an old church and some kind of power station," Rautonen said deprecatingly. "Tourists go to buy alcohol and cheap trinkets."

"But it's in the USSR, isn't it?"

"Yes, but not things you want to see, like in Leningrad."

Mott grinned, "Maybe, but it sounds a lot easier to reach than Leningrad."

The taxi crested the hill and after traveling a long straight piece of road bordered by a lake, it swung around a curve and there, suddenly, were the tourist hotel and, gently inclining away before it to the harbor's edge, the village of Kirkenes.

It rained most of the night, but in the morning when Newcomb Mott came ambling down from his room for breakfast, the rain had stopped and the wind was punching ragged holes in the overcast, opening up patches of blue.

The girl at the desk returned his pleasant greeting, smiling up at him. Her name was Ava. She was young and fair in a typically Nordic way and her accent was an added touch of attractiveness. They discussed the weather and the good possibility that it would clear, and then after confirming that he had a room for the night, he came to the point.

"I understand there is a Russian tourist village, Boris Gleb, not far from here. Can you tell me how I can reach it? Is there a bus that goes there?"

The girl shook her head. "I'm sorry but I think it is only permitted for Scandinavian people to go there unless you have a visa."

"Oh?" The smile faded. "Are you sure? The two gentlemen I arrived with said all I needed was my passport."

"Just for Scandinavians," she repeated. "But if you like, you can check with Mr. Frydenburg, the manager. He should be here shortly." And then because she could see that he was obviously disappointed she said again, "I'm sorry."

He thanked her and went into the nearly empty dining room whose front windows looked out over the village roof tops, affording a broad view of the town, the harbor, and the distant headland which was still partly capped in cloud.

After a smorgasbord breakfast, offering everything from roast beef to cereal, Newcomb Mott left the yellow-painted tourist hotel with its neat fronting of green grass and bright flags and walked down town. In the light of morning the surrounding terrain had lost some of its bleak aspect. The houses of Kirkenes were multicolored, reds, and yellows, and blues. Their blend and neatness and snug appearance created an atmosphere which radiated inward as well as outward. The factory buildings of the Sydvaranger ironworks dominated the village from their own gray eminence on the southern fringe of the town, but their bulk did not intrude, and neither in appearance nor purpose was theirs an ugly domination. Their being was tied directly to the economic welfare of the more than four thousand citizens of Kirkenes.

The newly arrived traveler found the central shopping area of the town to be a spacious if functional esplanade with a number of buildings and side streets still in the process of construction. There were few cars, a goodly number of bicycles, and walking still seemed to be a popular method for getting from one place to the next. In such a manner he found the local Finnair office and decided to reconfirm his return reservation to Ivalo.

Martti Suomela, Finnair's Kirkenes representative, stood as tall as his visitor and was about the same age. He had a thick mop of curly black hair and the girls of the town considered him very handsome. His English was excellent and when Newcomb Mott asked him the question still uppermost in his mind, his answer, though delivered with a smile, was nevertheless direct and unequivocal.

"I am afraid not. Boris Gleb is open only to Scandinavians unless you have a visa."

And now he'd been told no twice.

When he left the Finnair office, he briefly put aside thoughts of Boris Gleb and concentrated on accomplishing his original purpose for coming to Kirkenes—to see the fjords and, if possible, the Laplanders. And by chance, or because he was now caught in a skein of fate as old as Odin, nothing worked out. At the main dock he learned that the boat to Vadso across the Varanger Fjord left at seven-fifteen in the morning, and if he took it on Saturday he would not get back in time to make his flight. The same bad timing held true for two other possible points of interest. When he found it was possible to drive forty miles southward to Skogfoss, following the Pasvik River, paralleling the Soviet border and at Svanvik see the Soviet town of Nikel, he looked into the possibility of renting a car, and decided it was too costly. In his walking about he had taken note of the modest but substantial three-story office building of the Sydvaranger ironworks. Because he was having no success in his sightseeing efforts and because it was part of his nature to be interested in many things, he went in and asked the receptionist directions to the mine itself.

In his pursuit of activity he did not realize that another factor was working against his following a routine course of action. Weekends in Kirkenes begin about Friday noon, and until Monday there was little doing to attract the non-hunting, nonfishing tourist, especially since the season was all but past. He had changed his plans on the spur of the moment and come to Kirkenes, and now he was thinking it had been a waste of time. There was really nothing to see or to do in the village, and as he walked back up the hill to the tourist hotel a plan of action was seeking root in his mind. Already he had made some notations in his pocket notebook toward its development.

At the hotel's small reception counter Newcomb Mott saw that Ava had been replaced by another young lady. "Is the manager here?" he asked.

"No, I'm sorry, Mr. Frydenburg will be back shortly. Is there anything I can do to help?"

He assumed his amused look. "Well . . . I had hoped to visit Boris Gleb, but I understand it's not open to Americans."

"That is correct."

"Suppose I had a visa, would the Russians let me in then?"

"Yes, if you had the proper visa, but otherwise, no."

And so he had heard it three times. Without a visa Boris Gleb was forbidden to Americans.

"Howcome Newcomb" his parents had dubbed him as a child. And in his twenty-seven years Howcome Newcomb had traveled much and been in many faraway places and seldom had he taken no for an answer . . . at least not right away. If his sense of assurance was a cloak, his size, his bemused expression, and his obvious sincerity also gave the same effect. These characteristics, this genuine touch of humanity, had stood him in good stead everywhere he had traveled. But there was within him an innocence easily seduced by a stubborn resolve which when exposed to the uncivilized could put him in jeopardy.

Near afternoon's end he came by bus to the Sydvaranger mining village of Bjørnevatn. The houses of the village bore the same architectural style and color tone as did those of Kirkenes, some sporting red shutters, some blue, some with fronting stands of birch and white picket fences. Newcomb Mott, walking up the street toward the mine gate past the houses of Bjørnevatn, cast a long shadow amid the snug scene—a scene that reflected both strength of purpose and an ingrained appreciation of life.

At the gate office he introduced himself and asked the guard if he could be shown the mine works. The guard spoke only a few words of English, but he understood the request, and as he indicated that the visitor should sign the guest book, he telephoned the mine's maintenance engineer, Birger Kvammen.

Kvammen lived but a stone's throw from the gate, in a solid two-story, cream-hued structure. When the call came he was not busy because the weekend had already begun for him. Moreover, when he learned that the visitor was either an American or an Englishman, he was immediately interested in meeting him, for he liked to practice speaking English every chance he got. He had learned the language in school and had gained some experience in using it during two visits to the United States.

Kvammen, of medium height and solidly built, had the coloring and look of a northlander. He wore glasses and in the gaze of his pale blue eyes, the cut of his broad, angular face and tucked-in mouth there was an air of steadiness and quiet good nature. A family man, the father of a boy and girl, he brought his son along to meet the unexpected caller.

And a fine meeting it was, for as he put it later, "We took to each other."

He found that the big American's interest in the open-pit iron mine was genuine. "He wanted to know. His enthusiasm was real . . . I liked it."

As they drove about through the moonlike plain of the mine, stopping at the huge yawning craters, pits that had been blasted and bored down into the rock, Kvammen explained the process of mining for iron ore. They paused before some of the huge earth-moving equipment and then examined and discussed the operation of the rock crusher. Kvammen learned how his visitor had had a near miss in a blasting accident in a mine in South America.

And then they came to the massive hole of the east pit and got out of the car to take a closer look. The clouds were all but gone from the sky and the blue-white texture of the sky bore the same honed look of the rock escarpment on which they stood. When they had taken stock of the dizzying depth of the pit, Kvammen's visitor turned away and looked in the opposite direction.

"Does the height bother you, Mr. Mott?"

"No, not at all. I was just wondering if we are close to the Soviet border here?"

"Right over that ridge." Kvammen pointed to a long low plain of rock marking the eastern horizon.

"That close?"

"About three or four kilometers. You see that path there?" he pointed. "It winds up through that scattering of birches."

"Yes, I see it."

"That's the way people go from here . . . to buy their vodka." Kvammen smiled. "It's nothing but a whiskey shop . . . a trick."

The visitor didn't reply at once but stood gazing at the rock hill as though measuring its distance. "Is there a wall along the border?"

"Oh no, nothing like that. Just a reindeer fence . . . a wire fence."

"What would happen if someone crossed the border by mistake?"

The engineer looked at him closely. "How do you mean?"

"Oh, I mean by accident."

"Well, I suppose if the border was open and they were Norwegians, the Russians would hold them for two or three weeks. But it wouldn't be a good thing to do."

"No, I guess not." Mott grinned. "I'd certainly like to visit Boris Gleb while I'm here."

"I assure you it is not all that much to see. An old church and a place to eat and drink and buy cheap alcohol . . . But I think if you wish, you can visit it."

"What do you mean?"

Kvammen could see that his words had excited the young American and he answered carefully. "About two weeks ago I was down in the Pasvik valley picking *moulter* berries. They're very delicious, you know. I had my transistor radio with me because I wanted to listen to the symphony. Instead, I got the Soviet station in Murmansk. It blocked out everything, and I heard part of a broadcast in Norwegian. The announcer was talking about Boris Gleb, and he said that tourists other than Scandinavians were welcome to pay a visit."

"Really! What about having a visa?"

"Nothing was said about having a visa, but you had best check this out at the tourist hotel. They can tell you better than I."

It was late afternoon when Birger Kvammen dropped Newcomb Mott off at the tourist hotel. It had been a brief and pleasant encounter, and from it Mott had received a piece of information that fell into place as the influencing factor in a course of action he had been mulling over since noon. As a result, he walked back down to the bus terminal. There he copied the schedule he sought in his notebook.

Later he ate a solitary meal, and from his window seat in the dining room he could observe the gentle flood of darkness lap the pale eventide colors from land and sea. The color ebbed slowly as though reluctant to give way. The hills became black by degrees, as did the water, and finally all that remained of day was a pink ribbon of light lying on the western headlands, and then it, too, faded and the lights of Kirkenes gleamed brightly against the night.

It was during this time of transition that he made his decision, and on the face of it, it was not a stupid or even bad decision. Since he had been given conflicting information on whether he would be permitted to visit Boris Gleb, he would go to the people who could tell him once and for all—the Russians. He would find the Soviet border control point, and he would ask the guards there, and if they said *nyet,* he would then ask them to stamp his passport to prove that he had been there and so be one up on his brother Rusty, with whom he had a running contest on countries visited. If the Soviets let him in, then all the better. But in either case he would go and inquire for himself and be back in plenty of time to catch the plane to Ivalo.

The decision was a measure of his sense of independence. Such independence is a quality becoming more difficult to recognize in a world where group thinking and group action mark the norm. There is in it a degree of carelessness because so much in society depends on interdependence, and when Mott's independence put him in the hands of hostiles, they wished to punish the quality as much as they did the act.

When he had finished his Pilsner, he left the dining room and walked back down town to take in the night life of Kirkenes. It consisted of a restaurant featuring an elderly Italian tenor and a movie theater. He chose the latter, and Markku Rautonen and Helge Heinonen, also on the town, saw his towering figure as he strode across the marketplace to the *kino* where the moviegoers of Kirkenes were being offered a double feature—*Summer Holiday* and . . . *The Running Man.*

Arctic daylight in early September arrives about 4 A.M., and at 7 A.M., when Newcomb Mott left his second-floor room and came downstairs to the hotel's central hall and reception area, the day was so fair and the light so clear it seemed to be much later.

John Frydenburg, who was working in his office just off the reception desk, heard the sound of the early riser's voice and the words "Boris Gleb." He came quickly out to the front desk. He had not met Mott before, but he recognized him because the desk girls had remarked on his size and his interest in Boris Gleb.

Frydenburg had been the Turisthotell's manager since it had been rebuilt in 1956, and he prided himself on the efficient and smooth manner with which he ran the establishment. Blond, with an oval-shaped face, wearing horn-rimmed glasses and neatly tailored clothes, he somehow gave the impression of being a schoolteacher instead of a hotel manager. He spoke English well with a pleasant accent, and now he spoke it directly and to the point.

"Mr. Mott, I understand you are anxious to visit Boris Gleb. Since you don't have the proper visa, please don't be so foolish as to attempt it."

Newcomb Mott grinned and then chuckled, looking down at the manager and the pretty desk clerk.

The reaction did not set well with Frydenburg. He was a serious man who believed that one did not laugh at serious matters.

"It is no joke, Mr. Mott," he snapped, his pale green eyes hardening. "No joke at all. I repeat, do not try to go to Boris Gleb without a visa."

"I thank you for your advice." The amused expression remained and Frydenburg felt he was being mocked. He had four sons of his own, the eldest not half this man's age, but all of them he knew would understand a direct warning better than this grown man.

"Look, Boris Gleb is nothing, a restaurant, a bar. Even those permitted to go are not permitted to visit the power dam or the village, and the Russians in the village are not permitted to visit the restaurant and fraternize with tourists. The whole thing is a snare and a delusion. None of it is really worth seeing, and particularly when there is risk involved!"

"I understand." Mott continued to smile. "I'll be careful, I'm only going to the border point and I'll be back in plenty of time to get the bus to the airport. . . . See you later." He gestured in farewell and turned away toward the main exit.

The big red-and-yellow bus bound for Jakobselv picked Newcomb Mott up at the bus stop diagonally across the street from the tourist hotel. It was seven-fifteen of a winelike September morning.

"Boris Gleb?" he said to the driver and was beckoned into the empty vehicle.

It was a longer ride than he had expected. The bus came to the crossroads where a turn to the right would have led to the airport or the route to Skogfoss. The driver drove straight on, going up an incline, having to shift gears near the top where the macadam gave way to gravel. The road curved past a pond and a scattering of farmhouses, some with late hay cuttings drying on fencelike racks. There were no passengers waiting to board the bus as it proceeded through the countryside, following a descending course and then skirting a long, still lake. Past the lake's edge the road continued to drop, and after a short time the driver began to brake. They rounded a curve where a few small dwellings stood grouped near a fork in the road. The left branch led to Elvenes and the bridge across the Pasvik River, the right fork branching off sharply going up a hill. By the side of the road there was a metal pole with a sign on it which said, *Skafferholet.*

The bus ground to a stop. The driver opened the door and turned toward his passenger, pointing at the road to the right. "Boris Gleb," he said.

"Tak," Newcomb Mott thanked him in Norwegian. Then he got off the bus, and it went on down the hill, disappearing around the bend.

Now he stood alone in an unfamiliar land. Aside from the sun, the road, and the sign, there were no real points of orientation. And since he had not bothered to acquire a map and study the territory, or better, rent a car and reconnoiter the area, he did not know where he was in relation to the border or its specific direction, for as he admitted later: "I had not asked anyone what the border crossing point or the way to it was like. . . ." The fact did not bother him, because he reasoned that all he had to do was to follow the road and it would take him to where he wanted to go. Moreover, on such a morning, in such a setting, the heart of youth—if it is a real heart—listens only to its own urging. Deceptively, earth and sky were painted in soft pastels. The green of leaf was pale and the yellow of it pure gold. The white grace of birch played a gentle counterpart to the rusting fields and even the gray rock hills appeared muted under the arching span of arctic blue.

It was all a conspiracy of prismatic colors and a warm sun to delude him and make him stride vigorously up the road. But even had the weather been foul, and no matter how bleak and forbidding the scene, he would have pushed on. He was the kind that pushed on.

For a few minutes there was nothing but the road going up, brush on each side, giving way to trees and fields. Then, suddenly, off to his right, he saw a red-painted lodgelike building. Fronting it was a pole with a Norwegian flag, waving languidly in the breeze. A dirt road led into a circular drive, and he translated the sign at the road entrance to read "Forbidden." Because of the sign, the flag and the military truck in the drive, he took the place to be a Norwegian military encampment, not knowing it was the headquarters for the Norwegian Border Commission.

He went on by, the road continuing to rise, and then ahead where it leveled a bit, he saw a sign pole and his pace quickened. Later he was to write a letter detailing his itinerary and making a long list of what he considered were his mistakes, number one being the sudden decision to change his plans and fly to Kirkenes instead of going by bus to Lakslev. Actually, he made no serious mistakes until he reached the road sign. Part of the error was due to his inability to read Norwegian; part of it to his being Newcomb Mott.

The sign said *Soviet Minnesmerke*. In English it meant "Soviet Memorial." He translated it to read "Soviet border" or "Soviet border point." Beside the sign, a wagon track angled off to the right. The trees and underbrush screened the track and the land it appeared to lead into, but along the near horizon there was a line of hills.

See him then in his moment of deliberation as he stood beside the sign pole, casting his own towering shadow. He wore a long-sleeved plaid shirt, a pull-over sleeveless sweater, gray slacks, and shoes not made for hiking. Was some invisible force abroad in the leaf-still silence of *ruska aika?* For had the sign not been there, he would have gone on up over the crest of the hill. At the crest he would have gotten a fine view of the Pasvik Valley and the metal span of the Elvenes bridge where it crossed the river. Then, because he was in a hurry, he would have followed the road down to where it swung parallel to the river, and it would have brought him to the Norwegian border post. There the friendly guards would have examined his passport and told him it was not possible for him to go farther. He would have been disappointed, but he would have accepted the rejection as final. Most probably the guards would have pointed out to him the cluster of houses about a half mile down the river on the eastern side. This, with its fronting powerhouse structure, was the village of Boris Gleb. But the sign was there. It was there because little more than twenty years past, soldiers of the Red Army had liberated the area from the Nazis, and a memorial marker had been erected to commemorate the action. Newcomb Mott, misreading the sign, took the wrong path, and in the fresh purity of a September morning made his way swiftly toward a point of no return.

The track was well worn, for the Norwegian border guards used one branch of it as a short cut from the border house to their headquarters. It passed through a tree-studded field, leading toward rougher terrain. Beside the track, amid the thick scrub, grew a profusion of blueberry bushes. It was because of the blueberries that Newcomb Mott came upon the Petersens of Bjørnevatn.

The Petersens were a vigorous elderly couple, she a fair

attractive woman, younger looking than her years, and he a bald, weather-tanned retired miner. Busy at their berrypicking, they did not hear the young man's approach until he was upon them. It was Mrs. Petersen who saw him first.

"Gud jeg skvalk!" she gasped.

Although he did not understand her exclamation—"God, you scared me!"—he understood her surprise, and he repeated the word *skvalk* with a smile.

For a moment they took him to be a fellow Norwegian, but when he pointed down the trail and said, "Boris Gleb?" they stared up at his bigness and, because of his accent, decided he was a Russian.

The Petersens had never met a foreigner near the border before, and they knew from having lived long in the area that the Soviets kept a constant watch on their own people to prevent them from crossing into Norway. They knew, too, that all Russian visits to Kirkenes had to be official or group visits, featuring musicians, singers; and once mining engineers had come to Bjørnevatn. But all had come through Storskog on the east side of the river where the official crossing point had been established and where the border commissioners held meetings. At every meeting between Norwegian and Soviet officials since the opening at Boris Gleb the Norwegians asked a standard question, "Why are there no Russian tourists coming over to visit Norway?" And the standard answer had been: "No Russian has asked for permission." It had become a well-known joke, and for a moment the Petersens thought they might have some information to change the belief.

Mr. Petersen, using sign language, indicated that the stranger should go straight ahead a short distance and then turn sharply to the left.

When Newcomb Mott thanked them in English and then with a half salute and a smile strode away, he left them even more surprised. They knew he must be English or American, but his being on the trail made even less sense to them than it did to see a Russian. They watched him for a moment, puzzling together, and then realizing there was no answer to their questions, they returned to their berrypicking. A few minutes later when they paused to see if they could still see him, he had disappeared from sight, and since the terrain in the vicinity was somewhat open, they assumed he had made the turn to the left and was hidden from view behind a flanking hill.

But he had not turned left; he had continued straight, missing the path, and because he had spotted a reindeer fence angling away in the near distance, he also missed a cut in the hills through which he could have seen the buildings of the tourist compound. He traversed rock ledge and barren earth, moving through the scattered birches toward the fence. Far behind to his right he could see the building he had taken to be an army headquarters. The path had petered out, but he figured that he could be seen from the army post, and if he was trespassing he would hear about it soon enough. What he could hear on the far side of a hill was someone hammering, and in the clear morning air it was such a homey sound he believed he must be close to his destination. At the reindeer fence he paused. Beyond lay a cleared strip of ground and then thickening tree growth extending upward to meet a jumbled tableau of hills and valleys. Parting the two strands of wire, he stepped through the fence, being careful not to tear his clothes. It was no problem to cross the cleared strip ahead and to his right he saw a yellow-painted marker. He went to it. There was a metal plate with a hammer and sickle on its face. Because in Kirkenes he had heard that Norwegian officials were not happy about having their people visit Boris Gleb, he was not surprised that the path had faded away or that he had found the yellow border marker. He reasoned that one way to prevent people from making the visit was to obscure the way. He had found it, and now all he had to do was to bear south and east and he'd come out at the proper point. He struck off into the unfamiliar maze, and the point of no return was past.

Betwixt heaven and earth, he wandered amid the mountains of the moon, or so it must have seemed to him. The land rose up and fell down, and there was nothing friendly in any of it. He was no hunter on the hill, and to his eye there was a sameness to tree and cliff and bald ridge line. He saw no one, saw no habitation, only the iron reach of naked summits. He climbed the low ones, hopeful that they would offer him an identifying clue, but they offered only more of the same. He tried to follow a southeasterly course, but in avoiding what he considered insurmountable barriers he traversed swampy ground and became totally lost. All he got from the low-swinging arctic sun was its growing warmth and a vague indication of the cardinal directions.

After a time his right knee began to act up. It had sustained two operations for cartilage removal, and although he could play a good game of tennis on it, long hiking brought pain and weakness, particularly the up-hill, down-dale type.

He kept on, slowly angling his way up the side of a heavily birched promontory, sure he was going to come out somewhere. He stopped to rest frequently and wipe the perspiration from his face and neck. He already knew he was seven kinds of a damn fool, but the realization did nothing to solve the problem, and for nearly two hours he wandered in the rock limbo. It was a long two hours before he finally stood on a broad shelf and through a screen of trees saw the land ahead dropping down to the autumn stillness of the Pasvik River.

He descended through the thick forest growth, losing sight of the river when the land sloped into a marshy depression. He traversed it carefully and began moving up an incline. Suddenly just beyond the top of the incline a small cluster of buildings came into view. The two principal ones were single-storied structures painted white. As he ascended he spotted the church with its bell tower and twin balled turrets. His spirits rose. This must be the place. And then he knew it was because in front of the main building he saw a young woman talking to two men in uniform. They appeared to be watching his approach.

He waved, pulling his passport from his pocket, and went striding up toward them. He had found Boris Gleb.

The Foreign Ministry of the Soviet Union presents its compliments to Norway and has the honor to communicate that tourists from the Scandinavian countries visiting Borisoglebsk in the future will be permitted to enter the above mentioned area without visas. . . .

From a Soviet note dated May 24, 1965,
to the Norwegian Embassy in Moscow

The Norwegian authorities will not object to the citizens of the Nordic countries—Norway, Sweden, Denmark, Finland, and Iceland—in the tourist season to pass the Norwegian-Soviet border for visits to Boris Gleb. . . . There will be established border check points at the place of crossing and the usual border control.

From the Norwegian reply to the Soviet Foreign Ministry
dated June 25, 1965

Chapter Two

Newcomb Mott did not know that the place he had come to had a story of its own to tell, a story with both political and geographic significance. This remote, thinly inhabited arctic region, in which picturesque Laplanders followed the reindeer herds, had once been a part of Finland.

Finland in 1809 became a grand duchy of the Russian Empire under Czar Alexander I. The Finns were allowed to retain much of their autonomy, and up until 1890 Finno-Russian relations were fair enough. They turned sour, however, beginning in 1890 when Czar Nicholas II began his Russification policy. In so doing, he broke the Russian-approved Finnish constitution, and overriding his granduncle's solemn declaration to honor the law of the land, attempted to set up Russian colonies on Finnish territory. One result was that Russians living in the Kola Peninsula were encouraged to go west and settle along the Pasvik River, thus establishing some degree of the Czar's suzerainty among the barrens. To comfort them in their labors, a church was already there. It had been built on the river's west bank in the early seventeenth century. The church was named Boris Gleb, in honor of two eleventh-century princes murdered by their brother, Sviatopolk, who had seized power on the death of his father and ruled by means of the traditional Russian method of terror. In 1072 Boris and Gleb were venerated by the Russian Orthodox Church and canonized as martyr princes, and many Russian churches were later named in their honor.

On December 6, 1917, the Finns proclaimed their independence, and Lenin's newly risen Bolshevik regime was the first to recognize Finland as a sovereign state. Then a few months later Trotsky's Red Army attacked in an effort to establish Finnish Reds in control.

The Finns, with allied help, quickly bloodied the Russian noses, and the war was over by the end of May 1918. A year later, in July 1919, the Finnish constitution was drafted and went into effect. Finally in 1922 the Soviets recognized the independence of Finland, and in determining the eastern boundary between the two countries, the Petsamo District in the far north was ceded to Finland.

Since the Finns were not of the Russian Orthodox faith, the church at Boris Gleb stood idle and unused. However, nearby the Finns built a tourist hotel where sportsmen came to catch salmon in the river and hunt bear and other wildlife in the mountains. A trading post was also set up, and the Norwegians visited it to buy custom-free goods, especially sugar and margarine. Newcomb Mott was not aware that the trail he had taken was known to the Norwegians as the "sugar path," so named in those better times.

Less than twenty years after the Soviets had recognized Finland's independence, they tried to end it. From November 1939 until March 1940 little Finland fought its gallant war against the might of Communist Russia. Harsh as the Soviet surrender terms were, however, they did not include the territorial annexation of the Petsamo District. Instead, the Soviets acquired fifty-year rights to the port of Petsamo and began negotiations to take over British-leased nickel mines at Nikel and elsewhere. Before this latter effort could be concluded, Hitler struck eastward and the two-year Communist-Nazi love affair came to a thunderous end. The Finns were caught in the middle.

During the Soviet-Nazi alliance, with Soviet approval, Finland had allowed three German divisions to enter and be stationed in its territory. Following the commencement of hostilities between Germany and Russia, two more divisions were swiftly added. Now the Germans wanted the Finns to join them in their fight against the Soviets, and the Finns wanted no part of either side.

When on June 25, 1941, Russian planes began indiscriminate bombing of Finnish cities and towns, the Finns had no choice but to fight back. They fought a war of only limited gains, wishing to do no more than restore their former eastern frontier. This they swiftly did, and in the north they retook the port of Petsamo and drove to the Murmansk-Leningrad rail line.

In September 1944, Finland once more was forced to capitulate before the onslaught of the Red Army. This time surrender terms included the arctic territory "voluntarily ceded to the Finns in 1920." This meant the district of Petsamo became Soviet. The port's name was changed to Pechenga. The nickel mines were confiscated, and the tiny salient of Boris Gleb on the west bank of the Pasvik was Russian once more. Now it was Norway's northern cap province of Finmark that had a forty-mile stretch of border with the USSR.

In October 1944, units of the Red Army under the command of Marshal Meretskov liberated Finmark as far west as the Tana River. Kirkenes, its houses burned to the ground, its ironworks destroyed under the Nazi's scorched-earth policy, was the first principal Norwegian village to be freed from German occupation. But most of its inhabitants were not on hand to greet the Russians, for in their retreat by sea the occupiers had put the people of the village on a prison ship and taken them to the isolation of a fjord on Norway's west coast where they remained under difficult conditions until war's end.

In November 1945, little more than a year after they had arrived, the Soviets withdrew their troops from Finmark.

When Norway joined NATO in 1949, to Soviet thinking this placed a hostile power on the exposed tip of its northwestern flank even though a short distance to the south Finland acted as a buffer. Since 1943, Kremlin strategists had designated the United States the *Glavni Vrag*—the Main Enemy. Now the main enemy was less than fifty miles from Pechenga and seventy-five from Murmansk. To the devious, determinedly aggressive, stubbornly suspicious Communists, the threat was real, and in taking steps to guard against it they turned the territory between Murmansk and Boris Gleb into a massive military bastion. This development has also been due to the fact that the USSR has so few outlets to the sea, and in the arctic their only ice-free ports are Murmansk and Pechenga. Today the two have been converted into a huge naval base, the largest in the Soviet Union.

Although Norway in joining NATO declared that no foreign troops would be based on its soil and, in 1961, that no nuclear weapons would be placed on it either, the Soviets know full well that there are some allied troops in Norway and that Polaris submarines are on station in the Barents Sea, their missiles in easy range of the Russian coast. They know, too, that to the west but a short distance beyond their frontier, there lie forty-three hundred miles of ice-free coastline, honeycombed with fjords, many of which would make excellent bases for their own submarine fleet which is the largest in the world. They would give much to possess some of this arctic real estate which they voluntarily relinquished little more than twenty years ago, for, from a naval point of view, their ships and harbor facilities are squeezed into too small a space and are extremely vulnerable to attack.

At this time the Soviet fleet at Murmansk is backed up on land by two divisions of the Red Army and one thousand aircraft of various types located east and west of the rail line running south to Leningrad, 650 miles away. And perhaps most significantly of all, somewhere in this territory between Murmansk and Boris Gleb there is a missile base. Its rockets could be aimed at the heartland of the U.S.A. or at major Scandinavian targets, or both.

In 1959, when the Soviet Ministry of Foreign Affairs gave to the U. S. State Department a map designating areas off limits to foreign travelers, only a twenty-five-kilometer strip, marking the Soviet-Norwegian-Finno frontier, was included. In its latest designation issued in July 1966, a vast territory encompassing nearly one half of the entire Kola Peninsula has been added.

After the formation of NATO, the Kremlin, knowing that a military take-over of Finmark was not in the cards, directed its efforts toward an extensive program of Communist persuasion. Secure in its domination of Finland, strongly entrenched in Norrbotten, the Swedish sector of the cap, the Kremlin launched its Kalotten Program. Kalotten literally means "the top of the head." The purpose of this old Marxian exercise was to gain influence and strong support and eventual domination without need of military control. The Kalotten Program by and large has had little success. Most of the 450 thousand Norwegians living in the rugged territory want no part of Communism or the Russians. Had it been otherwise, or should it become otherwise in some manner, fair or foul, NATO's northern defense line would be flanked. From a purely military point of view, this is no small threat. And although the Kalotten Program has not succeeded in its aims, the effort continues. Techniques of propaganda, agitation, subversion, and espionage all are utilized, and the opening of Boris Gleb as a tourist attraction in the summer of 1965 is an excellent illustration of the program at work.

Two years prior, in 1963, the Soviets built a dam across the Pasvik just south of Boris Gleb. It was constructed with Norwegian help, as were the sixteen new houses that constitute the village on the east bank of the river. The inhabitants of the village are primarily engaged in maintaining the dam, its powerhouse, and allied installations. The purpose of the dam is to provide the water for hydroelectric power, as the Soviets have made it known they wish to develop the area economically. Aside from possible iron deposits, and the nickel mines at Nikel, which has its own power dam, there is nothing much that can be developed in the general locality besides Red military strength.

Some Norwegians in Kirkenes believe that is the primary purpose of the dam, and they are critical of their countrymen who were willing to work for the Soviets, but they have no strong reply when their countrymen point out that the United States led the way by agreeing to sell wheat to the Russians.

In the spring of 1965 the church on the west side of the Pasvik was refurbished, painted, filled with old icons, and declared a museum. At the same time, the rubble of a Finnish tourist hotel, burned during the war, was cleared away and across the road from the church a small compound was built, dominated by two single-story structures, painted white. The smaller of the two was a headquarters building and a place for overnight guests, and the larger a poshly designed bar, restaurant, dance hall, and gift shop.

Markku Rautonen dubbed the place "a vodka kiosk."

While the kiosk was being readied for visitors, secret talks were taking place in Oslo between Norwegian and Soviet officials. The subject of these talks was the opening of the border at Boris Gleb to non-Russian tourists. Exactly when the talks started or how they proceeded prior to May 25 is not known, but between that date and June 27, when the border was officially opened, the agreement was worked out and approved by the Socialist government of Einar Gerhardsen. The opening celebration was well attended by Communist officials from Murmansk, including Vasiliy Fedorovich Mosin, Chairman of the City Soviet of Murmansk, and Norwegian officials from Kirkenes and elsewhere. The Norwegian Parliament had had no chance to debate the issue as is usually done. It was simply presented as a *fait accompli.*

It was a one-sided agreement, to say the least. Supposedly any Scandinavian with a valid passport was free to visit Boris Gleb. This included the vodka kiosk, the church, the dam, and the village. In reality the last two were excluded, and the only Russians the visitors were permitted to fraternize with were the special Intourist people who manned the compound. A visa was not necessary to pay a call, but a pocketful of kroner was a must, and if a visitor took a liking to the place, he could remain forty-five hours. Typically in practice, the agreement was not reciprocal; no individual Russians were allowed to visit the Norwegian side of the border. Both sides set up adjacent border crossings connected by a dirt road, a hill acting as a buffer between them, and regular border patrols continued to function along the poorly defined, badly delineated frontier.

Between June 27 and October 1, 1965, when the Norwegian Government closed the gate, 13,275 Scandinavians, nearly 12,500 of them Norwegian, visited the tourist compound at Boris Gleb. The Soviets accepted any currency but their own in exchange for inexpensive vodka and brandy. Other items, such as gasoline and American cigarettes, trucked in from Murmansk, were for sale. Estimates of how much the Soviets took in during the ninety-four-day period range from one to three million kroner or not less than $142,000. The unusual financial success of the venture had nothing to do with interest in religious antiquities, or the bettering of Scandinavian-Soviet relations. It was a matter of cheap booze.

In Oslo, in Hammerfest, in Kirkenes, and elsewhere in Norway there were those in positions both high and low who viewed the seemingly precipitous opening of the border at Boris Gleb with no enthusiasm at all. They felt that the sale of alcohol, no matter how beneficial to the strengthening of Soviet foreign currency, was but the surface motivation behind the effort. It was known that many of the visitors to Boris Gleb did not simply make their purchases and depart but stayed on in the bar, drinking up, being entertained by music from Murmansk, and attended by charming Intourist girls and their male counterparts. It is also well known that people who drink too much talk too much. It is not so well known, however, that Intourist is an appendage of the KGB, the Soviet Committee of State Security.

Those critical of the border opening reasoned that aside from serving the customers, the function of the attendants was to keep their ears open and extract information from the talkative on any subject, but with the special emphasis on NATO. Many of the customers returned frequently, and no doubt the most promising from the Soviet point of view were parted not only from their money, but also from some of their knowledge.

There was yet another source of concern, actually the most serious. Certain members of the Norwegian Intelligence believed that the Soviets planned to use Boris Gleb as an agent contact point. Before summer's end they knew it was so. Nothing was done to close down the operation because those most concerned did not wish to tip the Soviets off to their knowledge.

On December 31, 1965, the new Norwegian Government of Per Borten terminated the Boris Gleb agreement and did not seek to renew it. In this, Newcomb Mott played an invisible role. His case was not only a popular reason but also a valid excuse for the Norwegian Government to close a cul-de-sac many had never wanted opened.

Thus when Newcomb Mott made his difficult way to Boris Gleb on September 4, he was wandering about in no tourist playland but in an extremely sensitive and tricky territory. The aforementioned developments in Norway lay in the future, but all were to be influenced by what befell him. Just as he did not know the geography of the area, he did not know its politics either. No one had bothered to tell him, there was nothing about any of it in the travel folders, and few were willing to admit that tourism at Boris Gleb was but a cover for the harder realities of the Cold War. In all his travels Newcomb Mott could not have intruded into a more deceptive battleground.

It is not enough and basically it is not true to say, as so many people have said to me, that the Russian people are like people everywhere and only the Government is different.

The people, too, are different because wholly different social and political conditions have retarded and perverted their development and set them apart from other civilizations.

From an introduction written by
former U. S. Ambassador to Russia,
General Walter Bedell Smith, to the book
JOURNEY FOR OUR TIME by the Marquis de Custine

Chapter Three

The young woman whom Newcomb Mott approached stood between the two uniformed guards looking puzzled. She was blonde and lithe and bare-legged and wore a dress with a bow tied at the waist. Her name was Victoria Kochimalkin, and her multilingual talents attested not only to the fact that she was intelligent, a valued Intourist interpreter, but also to the importance of Boris Gleb to the Soviets.

A short time before, she had arrived from the village on the east side of the river where all who served the tourist compound lived. She had been in the information office when through the window she had seen Newcomb Mott step out of the bushes. Girl guide Kochimalkin knew that no foreigners were supposed to be on the premises and that there was still a half hour before the border would officially open for the day and the Saturday influx would begin. Surprised, she left the office and stepped outside to be joined by border guards Andrei Rogov and Ivan Rubenenko. The two had been passing the time of day by a wooden shack that served as check-in point.

Rogov had spotted Mott first, and he asked Rubenenko if he knew if any foreigner had stayed overnight. Rubenenko did not, and he motioned the advancing stranger to come toward them.

As he approached, Victoria noted that he looked hot and tired and that his shoes were wet. She called to him in Norwegian, *"Hej, aer du Skandinav?"*

He understood and replied, "No, my name is Newcomb Mott. I'm an American." He handed her his passport.

She quickly translated his reply to the guards and Rubenenko snapped his own query back in Russian, "What are you doing here?"

The question was put by Victoria, and he answered, beaming down at her, "I'm an American tourist."

"How did you get here?" she said.

"I wandered over the hills. I came to buy souvenirs for my father and friends . . . if the price is right. This is Boris Gleb, isn't it? I was looking for the custom's point and . . ."

Victoria translated, studying his photograph in the passport and then thumbing through the pages, explaining the pertinent facts to the guards. There was a rapid exchange among the three of them, and then she said formally, "You have trespassed on Soviet territory without a visa. It is not permitted. Please come."

At the entrance of the central building there was a marquee with the word "Welcome" in both Scandinavian and English. Curiously, on the side of the building there was also a billboard with a list of things to be seen at Boris Gleb. It, too, headlined with the word "Welcome," was written in English as well as Scandinavian.

As they entered, Rogov, on instructions from Rubenenko, turned away, heading toward the guard shack.

The interior of the tourist center was made up of an extensive restaurant, a bar, and a small information office. The décor was far fancier than the outward wooden shell would suggest; all done in a kind of people's paradise design—the wheels of technological progress decorating the drapes and the bar padded and carved in an arctic motif.

Victoria ushered him into the office where there were a small desk with a dial phone on it, several chairs, and some travel posters on the wall of Leningrad and Moscow. He realized by now that he had done something illegal and that he was in a bit of a jam, but he didn't think it was particularly serious. At the girl's suggestion he sat down, not at all unhappy to get off his feet, for his knee was throbbing painfully. She had given his passport to Rubenenko and when an officer appeared in the doorway, he held it in his hand. The newcomer, a well-built, dark-haired man with rather pleasant features was Alexander N. Mironichev, in command of the Boris Gleb border control. He looked fit and official in his uniform.

With Victoria acting as interpreter, Newcomb Mott again explained how he had come to Boris Gleb. Mironichev did not appear to be disturbed. Through Victoria he said, "It is too bad you didn't come by way of the border control point. You would have been welcomed and no visa needed. No trouble. This way complicates matters. We must search you."

The trespasser apologized for the error and while emptying his pockets said he hoped he wouldn't be detained too long since he had a plane to catch that afternoon.

Again through Victoria, who had become much less constrained, Mironichev said if all went well Mr. Mott would be returning to the Norwegian side before the day was over. In the meantime did he have some article which could be used to help the dogs trace the way by which he had come to Boris Gleb?

They settled on a piece of paper from his notebook, and the officer excused himself and left with one of the guards. Newcomb Mott relaxed. He'd made a mistake, but these were reasonable people like people anywhere. He asked if he might buy a cup of coffee, and when Victoria learned he hadn't had any breakfast she whipped him up some scrambled eggs and toast to go with the coffee. He ate the welcome meal, sitting at a table in the restaurant. Except for Victoria, who had told him to call her Vicki, and the guard standing in the entrance foyer, there was no one about, no other waitresses or attendants. He decided it was still a beautiful morning, and his only worry was that he might not get back in time to catch his plane.

When the guard at the door called and signaled to him, he thanked Victoria Kochimalkin for her hospitality and asked if he could pay for the meal. She replied it wasn't necessary, and so he bade her good-by, figuring he was about to be escorted back to the border. He was still hopeful he could get someone to stamp his passport, even if it cost money.

The two guards, their submachine guns slung on their shoulders, escorted him to their van-type jeep, a Gaz. He climbed in through the rear, with one of the guards, and the other took over the wheel. When the driver pulled out of the compound, instead of turning left in the direction of the border, he turned right and went toward the dam. Ironically, the univited guest was the first foreign tourist to view the guarded dam close up as the vehicle proceeded across its top to the east side of the river.

The dirt road descended, then leveled, and presently he could see they were headed toward the village whose houses were clumped on a bluff above a newly built hydroelectric power station and some other installations.

By the time he'd been brought to one of the houses and expeditiously taken to a second-floor room where the door had been closed and locked behind him, he knew full well that his return to Norway was not going to be all that easy. Still, he had been assured he was going to be returned that day, and since he had the ingrained faculty of taking people in authority at their word, he was confident that if his departure was not to be sooner, then it would be a bit later.

What he did not know and could not know was that Mironichev had already reported to the resident KGB chief. The order had promptly been given to take the American across the river to the village where he would be out of sight, for his Soviet hosts had no desire to have him seen or to have him make contact with the Saturday influx of legitimate visitors due to begin their pilgrimage when the red hammer and sickle flag went up at 11 A.M.

The long day passed slowly for him. By four o'clock he had become resigned to missing his flight. That was worry enough, but the two guards posted outside his door were an extra source of concern.

A short geographic distance away, but in other respects a world away, someone else had become worried about his welfare. This was John Frydenburg. It was four-fifteen when he checked with the girl on the front desk as to whether the wayward guest had returned in time to make his airport connection. Her reply was negative, and the small knot of annoyance he had been carrying toward the young man since their morning encounter was knicked by the sharp edge of fear. When he went up to room 212 and opened the door and saw Newcomb Mott's luggage, and on the table his air ticket, Frydenburg's fear became fixed. But because he was a cautious man and did not wish to risk making a fool of himself, he made no immediate move. The missing American could have gotten on the wrong bus, could have gotten lost, could have decided to stay over another day, or half a dozen other things.

However, when at six o'clock Newcomb Mott had not returned, John Frydenburg went into his office and telephoned Gunnar Haarsted, the chief of the Kirkenes police. Haarsted, in turn, notified the acting Chief of the Norwegian Border Commission, Lt. Colonel Odd Stube Aune. Before long an organized search was under way.

If the second-floor room where Newcomb Mott was being held faced northerly, as did most of the houses in the village, he could have seen clearly enough, before darkness settled in, the Norwegian border post up the river on the west bank a short distance away, and beyond it, the metal span of the Elvenes bridge. Norway and freedom were still very close, but he did not consider attempting to escape. This was because sometime between dusk and nightfall someone, possibly Victoria Kochimalkin, came and told him there had been a hitch, but they would surely be sending him back tomorrow. And so in the darkness of the brief arctic night he adjusted himself to what he must accept as an interesting if unforeseen delay in route; an experience he would take relish in relating to his parents and to his brother Rusty, whom he was looking forward to meeting in London in only a few days' time.

Wrapped in the cocoon of this comforting view, Newcomb Mott lay his six-foot-five frame down to rest and so passed his first night in the hands of his Soviet captors.

On the following day, whose clear weather was a replica of its predecessor, the resident KGB officer paid his respects.

He is a faceless man, a nameless man, who resided that summer at Boris Gleb. He may have been the only KGB man there, or one of several, or a half dozen. Perhaps he was the popular bartender who sported a Drakish beard and everyone called Alexander, or he could have been the more rotund dispenser of potato water, or quite possibly the handsome blond man with a tight smile and quick intelligent eyes. He could have been anyone of the three or even the fat, bald Intourist official from Murmansk. But if his face and name cannot be placed, at least some of his words can.

"Are you a CIA agent?"

"No, I'm what I said, a tourist."

"Do you know anyone in the CIA?"

"No, not a soul."

"Tell me how you came here."

"But I've already told you."

"Tell me again."

The KGB man was pleasant, but he was persistent, and some of his questions he repeated over and over again. "Do you work for CIA?"

Newcomb Mott had only one question: "When are you going to let me go? I have a job to get back to."

"Tell me about your job."

"But I've already told you."

"Tell me again."

At some point late in the afternoon the KGB man suggested that a little fresh air might be in order. They went out and in the soft light of the fading day walked around the house several times. Despite the unrelenting quality of the questioning, there had been nothing menacing or ugly in the interrogation or the interrogator's manner. Everything was being handled in an amicable and sensible way. The questions had to be asked, and the inconvenience and delay were too bad but simply unavoidable, and for reassurance, the point had been stated that other tourists had made similar errors, had gotten lost and strayed over the frontier, and in every case after the proper investigation they had been returned to Norway. Tomorrow most probably he would be going back.

The KGB man did not inform Newcomb Mott that just as Mironichev of the border guards, and his superior Colonel Gravrilko, could not make the decision to send him back, neither could a KGB agent in Boris Gleb, or his chief to whom he would report in Murmansk. The orders must come from someone far superior in the Kremlin; perhaps Semichastny, the Director of the KGB and a member of the Central Committee, or his superior, Presidium member Alexander Shelepin. And because it was Sunday, and in any society rank has its privileges, no orders had yet arrived concerning the disposition of the captive.

It is now apparent that such orders arrived the next day, Monday the sixth. This was the day that Newcomb Mott was interrogated by the Procurator or District Attorney for the *rayon* (area). The Procurator most probably came from Nikel whose nickel mines make it a populous point in a singularly unpopulated territory. He, too, is a nameless and faceless person. That he came to Boris Gleb was undoubtedly a result of instructions sent from Murmansk via Moscow, for in the Soviet society—as in any other—there is a form for everything. And as in any other societies this form operates on the surface of Russian life and is open for all to see. But unlike the form of democratic societies, its actions are directed by the Soviet Committee of State Security, the KGB. The KGB is, in fact, the warp and woof of Soviet society; the substance by which the society is controlled. The society is silently and fully aware of it. But this fact of Russian life is not readily seen and so is not accepted by the uninformed American tourist.

Thus to Newcomb Mott the Procurator was a legal fellow, asking legal questions because there was a legal matter—minor as it seemed—to be resolved. It did not dawn on Newcomb Mott, as it would not on millions of his fellow Americans, that the Procurator was following the form not specifically to get to the bottom of the legal matter but to carry out KGB instructions in order to reach a foregone decision. It was a decision not based on the legality of anything but on a single KGB point of substance: an American, possibly an agent but most likely a tourist, had mistakenly blundered into its hands.

The form, of course, was necessary to the substance so that on the surface a legal course of action could be followed. Investigation had shown that the American had intruded fourteen hundred meters—exactly two thirds of a mile—into Soviet territory from a point starting at the 212th border marker and leading to the area in front of the tourist compound where he had been apprehended. The investigators estimated that he had trespassed on Soviet soil between twenty and thirty minutes before being taken into custody. These conclusions had been reached through the efforts of border guard Viktor Ribekin and a comrade, who, with their tracking dogs using the piece of paper from Newcomb Mott's notebook for scent, claimed they were able to retrace his footsteps.

These were indeed remarkable dogs, a Soviet first if there ever was one, for unlike any other known species they were able to track the subject across great reaches of bare rock and swamp ground and determine that his route had been direct and to the point.

At any rate, this was what the official investigation had revealed. Furthermore, because Newcomb Mott was honest beyond measure no matter what the circumstance, Mironichev, the KGB man, and the Procurator learned that he had knowingly crossed into the Soviet Union without the proper documents.

The form fitted smoothly into considerations of the substance. Let the form continue.

Early next morning Newcomb Mott left Boris Gleb by car. He traveled with the Procurator and undoubtedly there was a guard. Even so, he must have thought with understandable relief that at long last he was going to be released. Although he had been fed and permitted to shave, he had been wearing the same clothes for the past three days, and he was eager to have a shower and a change. But of more importance, he was anxious to arrange plane reservations to London.

They drove under leaden skies, following the road south running beside the Pasvik River on whose western side lay Norway. But when they arrived in Nikel, the driver, instead of turning toward the river, drove to the railroad station where a train stood waiting.

It was an all-day ride, and because it was dark and overcast Newcomb Mott had no way by which he could tell the direction the train was traveling, and moreover its route through the mountains was circuitous. The land was much the same as the land he'd left: mountainous, barren, desolate; and everywhere an emptiness whether the earth jutted skyward or lay flat, and over it all the rain knifed down.

He'd traveled on a lot of trains but never like this. There were loudspeakers in the corridors and in the compartments. They spewed a constant cacophony of Russian music, interspersed with a male voice shouting what sounded even in Russian like a bad commercial. It was—for the announcer was selling State Socialism with all the subtlety of a pounding drum. Hot tea was served by an attendant several times during the course of the day. The seats were not comfortable. The WC had little to recommend it, a wet floor, only cold water, and the sweet, cloying smell of Russian soap.

It was a long ride and no doubt because even in such a spot his "How come?" quality could never remain dormant for long, he tried to absorb something from his surroundings and in so doing asked a good many questions. But to the two most important—"Where are we going?" and "Am I being returned to Norway today?"—he got no answer or evasions that did nothing to enlighten him or give substance to his morale. However, he was not the sort that abandoned hope easily. He possessed a capacity for believing that things would get better long before they got worse. There was a good bit of Candide in him, and many were to term his outlook naïve, but from the beginning it was not just with naïveté that he faced his ordeal but with an inner strength which is most easily defined as courage.

The train pulled into a city. He alighted in the cold, wet darkness. There was a van-type car waiting. He was instructed to get in. He could not see where he was being taken, but the drive was brief.

When he got out of the car he saw he was in a courtyard. There were high walls all about and at the ends of the walls searchlights, patiently fanning the night.

He swung about in disbelief. “Where am I!”

And now he was answered, “You are in Murmansk.”

“But what is this!”

“This is the Murmansk Oblast prison. Step this way, please.”

September 8

Department received telegram from United States Embassy Oslo that American citizen Newcomb Mott arrived in Kirkenes, Norway, September 2. Last seen 7:00 A.M.*, September 4. Had voiced interest in visiting town of Boris Gleb in USSR.*

UPI correspondent in Moscow requested background from Oslo press reports that Mott had inadvertently crossed Soviet border. First Embassy knew of incident. Embassy made inquiry to Soviet Ministry of Foreign Affairs.

Department initiated investigation. Sent biographic and passport information. Notified parents.

From official State Department Chronology
of Newcomb Mott case

Chapter Four

Sheffield, Massachusetts, whose settlement dates from 1726, lies just north of the Connecticut western border in the Housatonic Valley, and is one of a host of small New England villages through which Route 7 slices its winding way toward Canada. Sheffield has its white-spired two-hundred-year-old church, its time-worn graveyard, its restored colonial homes with clapboard siding and center chimneys, its antique shops, its quiet elm-shaded center, and to the west, the long protective haunch of the thickly timbered Berkshires. Only the traffic swishing through its heartland strikes an alien note in a snug ancestral atmosphere. It is an atmosphere created not only by what the eye perceives but also by some anterior memory, a narrowing between now and then. Sheffield is a village repeated many times in many places throughout New England so that its charm and character are not distinctively isolated but pleasantly replayed like a well-remembered theme.

Howard Mott had brought his wife and two sons to live in

Sheffield in the summer of 1956. The move had been made from Ridgewood, New Jersey, for a number of sound reasons, not the least of which was the strong attachment he and his wife Phyllis had for things past. It was in fact their business, for as book antiquarians and collectors of antiquity, their lives were immersed in the creative literary, art, and craft efforts of those who, like the early settlers of Sheffield, were long gone but had left an indelible imprint.

The home the Motts bought was a big, rambling, square-faced Federal hard by the edge of Route 7 with a fronting hemlock hedge screening it from the highway. It had been built in 1790 by George Root, and the Motts in acquiring it were the fifth family in line of possession. Here Howard Mott set up his business, moving some seventeen thousand volumes, pamphlets, pictures, and autographs from New York City, where twenty years before he had embarked in the rare-book business, a year after his graduation from Harvard.

Although the buying and selling of creative works of antiquity had not made him particularly wealthy, his activities and reputation in the field had made him well known and well respected among his colleagues and clients in the United States and abroad. Whereas moderate economic success assured the necessities of life to his talented and helpful wife and his two sons, it was the very nature of his work which inspired an influence whose benefits could be measured through the associations, contacts, and intellectual stimulation derived from the world in which the entire family dwelt and particularly to which his sons were so readily exposed.

Phyllis Mott, before she began devoting much of her time to assisting her husband, had had a career in her own right. She had been a diagnostic haematologist at the Van Wedel Laboratory of White Plains, New York, responsible for the work of several laboratories. As such, she was a registered member of the Society of Clinical Pathology. Her interests ranged far—medicine, art, music; as a young woman she had been a gifted dancer. Once she joined her husband in his work he maintained that she thought and wrote as though she were in the eighteenth century; it was, of course, a compliment.

But for all of Howard Mott's attention to the past, he was in his thinking a modern American. The friends and acquaintances and clients who came to visit the Motts in Sheffield, to do business or to spend a restful weekend in the country, were allied in similar pursuits, and these pursuits centered on interests that were current and topical but had little or nothing to do with international politics. And for all they knew as modern Americans, they knew little and possessed only surface knowledge of Communists or Communism. Sure, the Communists were difficult to deal with, but they were changing in spite of themselves, and as a member of the Grolier Club, Howard Mott was, with fifty fellow members, looking forward to a trip to the Soviet Union to be made the following summer.

However, on the morning of Wednesday September 8 he and Phyllis had another trip on their minds. In two days they were due to leave for London on business, so when the phone rang at nine-thirty they assumed the call was in connection with their intended journey.

The caller identified himself as Bernard Caughey, UPI Bureau Chief in Boston, and then without preamble he asked, "What can you tell me about your son who has been lost for the past five days up on the Norwegian-Soviet border?"

Caught off balance as he was by the query, Howard Mott replied, "Nothing. It's the first I've heard of it. What can you tell me?"

Caughey explained that the word had come from UPI's correspondent in Oslo, who had few details except that Newcomb had disappeared on the fourth and was being searched for by Norwegian border police in the vicinity of Kirkenes.

Howard Mott asked the newsman to please call again as

soon as he had additional information, and he, in turn, would see what he could find out from the State Department.

In retrospect neither of the Motts had had any premonition of bad news to come, or even after Caughey's call, that it marked for them the first stroke in a series of sledge-hammer blows that would be theirs to endure in the following months. At that moment in time, they were, of course, shaken and concerned but not frantically so. Newcomb was hardly a novice, he'd crossed a lot of borders in his day, and if he had crossed one by mistake, they were confident he would know how to handle himself. They were also confident that the State Department and allied officials abroad would immediately be able to straighten everything out. However, Howard Mott's immediate call to the State Department did nothing to reassure the couple in this belief, and it, too, was in the nature of a first.

On that initial call, the desk officer to whom Howard Mott spoke in the Security and Consular Section knew nothing about Newcomb's disappearance and when he was asked if he would please make inquiries to the proper quarters and find out what he could, he replied that a telegram of inquiry could be sent to Norway if Mr. Mott was willing to pay the charge of five dollars. This was standard practice because SCS receives literally thousands of queries on temporarily missing Americans.

"What the hell!" Howard Mott said succinctly. "I don't care what it costs, send it! . . . And would you please be good enough to let me know what you find out?"

During the remainder of the week Howard and Phyllis Mott spent a good many hours on the telephone either making calls or receiving them. In that five-day period their telephone bill was in excess of one hundred dollars.

Because Newcomb was planning to stay in London with Bill Fletcher, an old family friend and fellow book antiquarian, they called him at once on the chance that Newcomb might have slipped out of Norway and was already in

London, or if not, that Bill Fletcher had at least heard from him. In August they had sent Newcomb a birthday card and a letter asking him if he could meet them in Scotland before their originally planned reunion in London. The letter was sent to a hotel in Stockholm where they knew he would be staying. He did not receive it, for he had already left the hotel when it arrived. Later his parents realized that had he received word of their change in plans, he would have changed his own and instead of going north into Scandinavia, he would have gone north to Scotland.

Bill Fletcher had heard nothing. However, the press had heard something, not enough to offer additional information, but enough to start calling and asking questions. That same afternoon Bernard Caughey reported back and gave the couple their first bit of concrete evidence as to Newcomb's whereabouts. He was in Soviet hands, probably being held at a place called Nikel, but there was nothing more to be added. Upon receiving this chilling confirmation, Howard Mott again called the State Department's Security and Consular Section, and was informed that his son was no longer categorized as a missing person and therefore his father would not have to pay for further inquiries. The voice on the other end verified Caughey's information and said that the proper authorities were investigating, and there was "not too much to worry about" because a small border town in the area had recently been opened to tourists. It was Howard Mott's long-time friend John Slocum, Assistant Deputy Director of USIA, who suggested that he call the American Ambassador to Norway, Margaret Joy Tibbets. Because of the time difference between Sheffield and Oslo, the Motts waited until 2 A.M. of the ninth before placing the call. It was not the Ambassador to whom they finally spoke, however, but to the First Councilor. The Councilor was fully conversant with the case, but he could supply no further details, except that since Newcomb was known to be in Russian hands the Embassy in Moscow would be handling the situation. He assured the Motts that everything would be done to bring about Newcomb's release, but he saw no purpose being served by Howard Mott's coming to Oslo.

On the following morning Bernard Caughey again reported to say that it was possible that the Norwegians might give Newcomb three months in jail or require him to pay a fine for crossing the border without permission. That afternoon the AP Press Bureau confirmed that Newcomb was being held for interrogation, but no one knew exactly where or on what grounds.

At 2 P.M. on Saturday September 11, the Motts heard a CBS newscast which stated that the Soviets had agreed to allow a Consular representative from the U. S. Embassy in Moscow to visit their son who was being held in a Murmansk prison on charges of having illegally crossed the Soviet border.

Thus it had taken four somewhat nerve-racking and upsetting days for the Motts to glean these few unclarified facts about their son's disappearance and detention. This information—unsatisfactory and disturbing as it was—had been gathered through their own efforts, the aid of UPI's Bernard Caughey, and the reporting of allied news media. No one in the State Department had made any effort to contact them to offer clarification or assurance. And now they considered putting in a call to the U. S. Embassy in Moscow, for wide as their range of friends were, they knew few people in Washington from whom they could ask advice. But as they mulled it over on Sunday they suddenly thought of Tom McDade.

McDade, a friend and client, was Comptroller for General Foods Company in White Plains, but he had formerly been an FBI agent, and they thought that possibly from his Washington days he might be able to steer them.

They waited until Monday morning to make the call. McDade apologized for not having contacted them. He had heard the news but felt he would have been intruding at a trying time.

When Howard Mott explained the purpose of their call, McDade was bowled over. "For God's sake," he said, "you mean you don't know who to call in Washington! And they haven't contacted you! I'll be back to you as fast as I can."

Twenty minutes later he was back with the necessary information. He had two names, Virginia James and Carroll Woods. Both were officers in the State Department's Office of Soviet Union Affairs. Miss James headed the Political Affairs Section and since she was soon to retire, Mr. Woods was in the process of taking over her duties.

For Howard and Phyllis Mott it had been a difficult five days, but at last communication had been established with those in Washington directly involved with securing their son's release.

Miss James knew all about the case and said she would have more to report on the following day since a Consular officer from the Embassy in Moscow was meeting with Newcomb in Murmansk. The Soviet Ministry of Foreign Affairs had informed the Embassy that Newcomb was being detained for illegal border crossing and that he must remain in Murmansk until the investigation into the charges was completed. She was hopeful that if his outright release could not be arranged, he would at least be let out of prison on bail.

Virginia James sounded confident and competent, and the Motts relaxed a bit and put aside their sense of puzzlement and annoyance at the failure of the State Department's Office of Soviet Union Affairs in contacting them. After all, Newcomb had committed no great crime and the power and savvy of the United States Government should certainly be able to negotiate his swift release.

The relationship finally established with the State Department through their own efforts would in the days following go through a metamorphosis, running the gamut from admiration to frustration, sadly terminating in outright bitterness.

October 2, 1965
Murmansk

Mr. William Townsley Shinn, Junior
Consul of the United States of America
American Embassy
Moscow, USSR

Dear Mr. Shinn,

The following is an explanation of my job; *I did not have time Sept. 13th to tell you, as we had less than five minutes when you asked if I were a book salesman. I hope I'll be able to keep my job.*

I work for D. Van Nostrand Co., 120 Alexander St., Princeton, N. J., in the College Department. My position is called college traveler. My territory of colleges encompasses most of upper N.Y. State, Western Pa., and all of W. Va. In all I am responsible for somewhat over 300,000 college students. I talk to approximately 2000 professors a year. . . . My job is to call upon professors at these colleges who are teaching courses Van Nostrand has textbooks or supplementary paperbacks for. I have to discover how each professor teaches his individual courses . . . and I have to decide which books would interest him (or them) and why. . . . I see to it that the professors get free copies of the books they and I think they might like to assign to their students at some future date. Hopefully, the books and my visits will bring about an order for the professor's class. . . .

From a letter written by Newcomb Mott

Chapter Five

He had been in Soviet hands for ten days and an inmate of the prison for nearly a week when he learned that he was going to have a meeting with a U. S. Embassy official. In those few days Newcomb Mott had been lied to, had been interrogated, had been harassed and incarcerated in a grim and unnatural place. In his own mind, where fairness and compassion lay uppermost, it was inconceivable that such punishment in any way fitted the crime—if there was a crime at all.

His cell he estimated was seven and a half feet by twenty feet long. It was constructed of cement blocks and had a high ceiling. There were a metal bunk, table, and chair, all securely fastened to the floor. Out of even his tall reach a light bulb had been set into the wall; it never went out. For plumbing facilities there was a hole in the floor. The metal door to the cell had two fixtures, a peek hole and a gratelike opening through which food could be shoved. The food was as wretched as the surroundings.

On Wednesday, September 8, the interrogation was resumed. This time the KGB officer introduced himself as Captain Alexandrovitch. He was later declared to be Captain Androv. Androv was a slight, nervous man with a rasping voice and sarcastic laugh. Conversely, the interpreter, Nina Kulikova, was a very good-looking young woman who, like Vicki Kochimalkin, spoke English perfectly and let the prisoner know by look and manner that she was sympathetic to his plight. Whether she, too, was a KGB officer is not known, but whatever her position, she was under KGB direction and carried out her instructions accordingly. At the outset she represented the soft approach while Androv represented the hard.

If the Murmansk prison where Newcomb Mott was held is like other Soviet prisons, his questioning took place in a special interrogation room. It was a rather long, spacious room with a double entrance door at one end and a row of barred windows at the other. The interrogator sat at a large desk, fronted by a conference table. Behind the desk in one corner there was a large safe. On both sides of the room there were arrangements of several easy chairs around low tables. The prisoner's wooden chair was in the left-hand corner near the entrance, so that he was able to take in the entire room and the view beyond the windows which looked out over the prison walls.

The room was a study in psychological effect. The interrogator, his big desk, and the empty chairs around the conference table represented power and prestige; the safe, secrecy and security; the comfortable chairs, one of which Nina occupied, a sense of warmth and ease for those who belonged; and the scene through the windows, regardless of what it was, the world outside and freedom. The room was comfortable and heated, and the contrast between it and a cold cement cell was vast.

When the questioning began Newcomb Mott asked that the U. S. Embassy in Moscow be notified of his detention. He was assured this would be done. The questioning continued off and on for the next four days, much of it repetitive, much of it following the same pattern. But there were other questions concerning the prisoner's opinion on such subjects as Viet Nam, the treatment of Negroes in the U.S., his job, his hobbies of coin and stamp collecting, his travels, sports, his political attitudes. In all his replies he was utterly honest. He was against United States involvement in Viet Nam, and he had long been upset over what he considered ill treatment of Negroes. No doubt he told the interrogator of the time that he and some fellow students at Antioch College had picketed a barbershop which refused service to Negroes. It is now apparent that Androv and his KGB superiors misunderstood and misjudged him, possibly because they could not conceive of critical opinions of the domestic and foreign policies of one's country as simple honesty and not the roots of potential disloyalty.

He, of course, at the time had no idea that Androv's interrogation had any other than the obvious purpose, plus natural curiosity, nor would most Americans. This purpose, as noted, appeared to be following the legal form to get the facts to ascertain whether the young American was a CIA agent, and if he was not, to determine whether he had indeed broken Soviet law. But now another factor entered the case, not because it was a new thought on the KGB's part, but because in getting to know Newcomb Mott, using standard operating methods, Androv—and, as a result, his superiors—came to believe that the prisoner might be potentially usable. Any foreigner, particularly an American, who is picked up by the Soviets for whatever the reason is examined in this light, and there is much evidence to support the contention that the subsequent treatment of Newcomb Mott for at least a time shows that the KGB was operating on the basis of making him their "pigeon." What followed represents a classic case of Soviet "carrot and stick" techniques in exploring this strategic possibility at the expense of a human being.

On September 11 Androv informed Newcomb Mott that he was officially under arrest and presented him with a statement to sign. The statement recounted Mott's answers to questions about how he had come to Boris Gleb, and it declared that he had not been threatened and no force had been used against him. Androv represented the stick part of the exercise.

Under orders, prison officials and guards represented the carrot. This was not difficult duty because Newcomb Mott was a rarity in their lives, probably the first American many of them had been close to. Not only were his size and reddish hair impressive, so were his manners. He was extremely polite, yet he was also determined. He let it be known he was not about to utilize the hole in the floor. Until he was permitted to use the proper facilities he refused to eat solid food. After five days of near fasting the prison doctor had come to see him. He informed the doctor, a young man about Rusty's age, that he'd go right on dieting until such indignities were stopped. When Captain Vilkov, the Deputy Prison Commandant, informed him that he would be allowed to use the doctor's WC once a day, he gratefully accepted it as a concession on his jailors' part. This was also true when he complained about the food and was given extra rations, and when they changed the bulb in his cell to a blue one so that he could sleep better.

Fifteen minutes a day he was taken to an empty walled yard for exercise, and although he was kept isolated from other prisoners it was either during this daily period or while he was using the doctor's facilities, in which there was a window, that he saw that other prisoners had shaved heads. He protested, saying he would not permit his head to be shaved. Understandingly, his guardians agreed. But their permissiveness really surprised him when they gave him a safety razor with which to shave himself within his cell. The razor was, of course, a potential weapon.

All these concessions, however, he saw as examples of the fundamental humaneness of the prison administrators and guards with whom he came in contact. He had no idea that all extras were to be charged to the U. S. Embassy and thus to his parents, and that such generosity was simply part of a KGB-ordered charade. Their treatment also took into account the possibility that if orders came from Moscow to release him, he would go home saying no harm had come to him while in Communist hands and that he had been well treated. Such statements would add another touch of color to the "mellowed" Soviet image, particularly if reprinted in a U.S. national magazine.

However, should the word come to treat the prisoner rough, or to slay him, these same reasonable warders could as quickly subject him to all manner of torture as they could in giving him an extra blanket. They could murder him with exactly the same degree of understanding as they used in allowing him to take a shower once every twelve days; it was all a matter of orders, concealed within the prison by their actions and without by the form.

The usual legal form required that a prisoner be told within a week of his detention whether he was officially under arrest. And this was why on the eleventh Androv so informed him, but the Napoleonic Code to which the Soviets subscribe also requires that a formal act of accusation be presented to the court as well. Thus at the very time Androv was telling Newcomb Mott he was officially under arrest, Valentin I. Oberenko, Deputy Chief of the American Section of the Soviet Ministry of Foreign Affairs, was confirming to Political Councilor David E. Boster of the U. S. Embassy in Moscow that Newcomb Mott was indeed being detained in Murmansk on charges of having illegally crossed the Soviet border and that the case was under investigation.

This admission by Oberenko, the number-two man in the American Section, was in reply to a visit Boster had paid the day before. This visit marked the Embassy's initial contact with the Soviet Government on the case. Many more contacts were to follow the details of which are described in Chapter Eleven.

In that first meeting Boster stressed four points: Was Newcomb Mott being held? If so, it was hoped he had already been released or soon would be. If not, why not? And finally, the Embassy would like to have immediate Consular contact with the prisoner.

In his reply Oberenko informed Boster that Consular access would be granted on the thirteenth. Boster repeated that he hoped since Mott had been in Soviet custody for a week and seemed to be nothing more than an innocent tourist, he would be released at the meeting of the thirteenth. Oberenko had no answer.

There are two ways in which foreign travelers can reach Murmansk from Moscow. When permission is granted, which is seldom, they can take an extremely uncomfortable thirty-one-hour train ride, or they can fly via Arkangel, often remaining overnight and arriving in Murmansk the following day. There is a direct flight from Moscow but it is not for foreign use, and only rarely do the Soviets give U.S. diplomatic personnel the green light to take the train. So it was that William T. Shinn, twenty-nine-year-old U. S. Embassy Vice Consul, came to Murmansk via Arkangel and in the forenoon of September 13 paid a call on Vasiliy Fedorovich Mosin, Chairman of the Murmansk City Soviet. Mosin, a large, moon-faced functionary, informed the visitor that a noon meeting had been arranged at the office of the Regional Procurator of the Murmansk Oblast.

William T. Shinn had joined the Embassy in Moscow at the end of August but he was no stranger to Soviet life or Iron-Curtain-country living. He had attended the University of Moscow in 1959 and 1960, specializing in Soviet law, and he spoke Russian with ease. Prior to his Soviet assignment he had served for two years in the Embassy in Warsaw. He had also received his A.B. from Princeton and his M.A. from Harvard. Six foot three, blond, and straight featured, he was a young diplomat of considerable intellectual ability possessing a great deal of drive and self-containment. He fully recognized the complexity of the Russian character, harboring no illusions concerning the forces and motivations that shaped and molded it.

At noon in a small room on the second floor of the Procuracy, Newcomb Mott and Bill Shinn met. Also present were Androv and Nina Kulikova. When the two young men shook hands, it was more than a routine greeting; it was one man reaching for help from another, and in the clasp and strength of the grip a connection established.

The prisoner wore a dark blue jacket over his prison clothes, for already the weather was raw and unpleasant. To Shinn, he appeared in good health and naturally a bit nervous. Despite the tenseness of the meeting and everything having to be translated by Nina for Androv, in their hour session he told Shinn in precise detail how he had come to cross the border. At one point Androv interjected to state that the investigators already had direct evidence that the prisoner had been told he must have a visa to visit Boris Gleb. As to physical and mental condition, the prisoner said he felt all right, but he admitted he was suffering from headaches and stomach trouble. The Deputy Prison Director, he added, had seen to the improvement of his diet, to help counteract the stomach problem. In telling what had befallen him and in answering Shinn's questions, he concentrated on every point, but when he began to relate the details of his interrogation by the KGB, Androv announced via Nina that the time was up.

Shinn asked if there were any messages he could convey to those at home and Mott replied that he did not want his parents to worry. He also said he would like to have long-time family friend and former New York Police Commissioner Francis W. H. Adams, as well as James Dixon, president of Antioch College, notified of his misfortune.* He said he needed nothing because now that a representative of his own government was on the scene he naturally felt optimistic. This

* Neither Mr. Adams nor Mr. Dixon was notified by the State Department.

feeling was enhanced by his failure to understand the nature of his captors. He believed his release would be swift. They shook hands in farewell and Shinn said he'd be back as soon as he could. The prisoner was further heartened because he believed that "soon" meant very soon. Bill Shinn had given him his Embassy card, and when they took him away he had it with him as though it were a talisman.

After the prisoner had departed, Shinn remained to talk to Androv. He asked the KGB officer if a formal act of accusation had been drawn up against Newcomb Mott. Androv made no reply and Shinn let him know, that he, too, understood the legal form, reminding the captain that under Soviet law the deadline for filing the accusation had already passed. Androv then admitted the document had been filed and that the prisoner had been accused of illegal entry into the USSR under Article 83 of the Criminal Code of RSFSR (Russian Soviet Federated Socialist Republics).

The Article states: "Exit abroad, entry into the USSR or crossing the border without the requisite passport or the permission of the proper authorities shall be punished by deprivation of freedom for a term of one to three years."

Bill Shinn, of course, had known since the eleventh through the Soviet Ministry of Foreign Affairs that Newcomb Mott was being held on charges of illegal entry. But he also knew that the accusation had to be formally approved by the Procurator of the Murmansk Oblast, Stepan Lebedyuk, and that once it was, again by Soviet law, the prisoner's "rights" came under the protection of the Procurator. Therefore he was anxious to meet Lebedyuk and see if release or bail could not be arranged while the "preliminary investigation" continued.

That afternoon Shinn returned to the Procuracy and requested a meeting with Lebedyuk. He was informed that the Procurator was away on business, and that his assistant was on vacation. He then asked to see whoever was in authority. After a wait he was presented to an official who claimed to be in charge of personnel. The official curtly informed him that no interviews could be given and that all inquiries should be directed to the Ministry of Foreign Affairs in Moscow.

Patiently, Bill Shinn made his way back to Vasiliy Mosin's office, where he explained to the Murmansk Chairman that there evidently had been some kind of a misunderstanding. He pointed out that under Soviet law it was not possible for Newcomb Mott to have a defense attorney while the investigation proceeded, and therefore he wished to see the official in the Procurator's office who was responsible for guaranteeing the prisoner's rights. Mosin declared that he would look into the matter and asked Shinn to come back the next morning. The Vice Consul did so, and then was told that a meeting had been arranged at the Procurator's office.

It is a Soviet technique to keep an unwanted caller waiting, and Assistant Procurator Nadezhda Alexsandrova Ryskalina let U. S. Vice Consul William T. Shinn cool his heels for the better part of an hour before she welcomed him. Nadezhda Alexsandrova was a square-shaped matron of about fifty. She sported an official uniform and matched it with a loud staccato voice.

Shinn began the discussion by asking if it would be possible to release the prisoner during the preliminary investigation, under Article 101 of the RSFSR Code.

"Nyet!" snapped Nadezhda Alexsandrova.

Trying reason based on Soviet legality, Shinn then pointed out that Article 83 did not come under Article 96 of the Procedural Code, which lists those crimes under which the accused must be confined. However, he further suggested that Article 93 might apply to Newcomb Mott, which would require him only to appear for the investigation when needed.

Her replies to these suggestions were louder, longer, and

somewhat confused. At first she maintained that Article 93 didn't apply to the prisoner because he was a foreigner. Then realizing the error of this reasoning—for if one Article didn't apply, then none applied, not even the one he was charged under—she backwatered, retracting the statement, and announced that the law demanded the prisoner's confinement.

Shinn next asked if it was possible to set bail.

He was informed that under Soviet law there was no such thing as bail.

In reply, he presented the Assistant Procurator with a copy of Article 99, devoted entirely to the setting of bail.

Nadezhda Alexsandrova took the time to read it and then announced it did not apply to the case. She then brought the interview full circle in the style of Lewis Carroll by reiterating that Newcomb Mott was accused of intentionally violating Soviet law.

Realizing that the Assistant Procurator had had her orders, Shinn dropped the subject and asked that if the case should go to court could the prisoner have a defense attorney who spoke English.

The reply to this was that the investigating organ would appoint an attorney and it would not be necessary for him to speak English since there would also be an interpreter.

When Shinn suggested the possibility of a conditional sentence, Nadezhda Alexsandrova concluded the meeting by saying the matter was up to the court and that she would not speculate further.

U. S. Vice Consul William T. Shinn left Murmansk knowing full well that Newcomb Mott's release was not to be predicated on any form of Soviet legality and that continuing efforts to obtain the prisoner's freedom must be advanced on a higher level.

As for the prisoner, he was returned to cell number 88 heartened by his meeting with Bill Shinn, who had impressed him with his perception and air of authority. But as the days slowly passed without further contact and without any communication from home, Newcomb Mott had to fight to keep his balance. The soft voice of Nina Kulikova clucking sympathetically that it was too bad that the U. S. Government and his family had abandoned him worked its subtle effect. On September 25 and 30 he asked Androv to please get in touch with the U. S. Embassy. Androv replied that he would, but it was up to the Embassy to make the contact, failing, of course, to say anything about the Embassy's standing request for visitation rights having been submitted to the Soviet Ministry of Foreign Affairs at the outset.

Psychologists know that prolonged isolation works adversely on most humans. It is recognized that one of the biggest obstacles facing our astronauts in the exploration of space is isolation, and special training is employed to combat its effects. The KGB is expert in the use of isolation, and in Newcomb Mott's case isolation was used to build in the prisoner a sense of abandonment by government, family, and friends. Conversely, association with prison guards and officials was intended to create a feeling of friendliness. After all, his jailors were simply doing their appointed jobs. And if they could not let him go, they could at least endeavor to make his stay not quite so unbearable. Extra food, a warm coat because it was cold, a physical examination by a twenty-year-old doctor, occasional visits from prison officials such as Captain Vilkov, who spoke English and regretted there was no word from home, and the soft voice and sweet look of Nina—how could the untutored not be affected?

Although at the time he did not understand the premeditation behind his keepers' actions, he did recognize the adverse workings of isolation, and he set up his own methods to fight them. He knew that physical health was important and that he must keep his strength. The prison day started at five o'clock with the blaring of the Soviet national anthem.

Newcomb Mott began his day with push-ups. He was losing considerable weight—he was always hungry, but push-ups became a must. His cell was nine paces long, and he paced back and forth, back and forth. He had no reading material. They had left him a pencil when they divested him of his personal possessions, but he had nothing to write on, and so to stimulate mental activity he sang. Music had long been a love and his appreciation traversed the scale from symphony to the blues. But since he could not very well sing Mozart's "Jupiter" or turn his voice into a trumpet, he concentrated on folk songs.

It's seven long years since last I see you!
Ah-way, you rolling river!

His pear-shaped baritone must have surprised the guards. One doesn't usually sing in prison. Perhaps after a time his singing began to disturb them, not the quality of his voice, which was good, but the fact that he sang for long periods of time in both English and Spanish, and he sang with gusto. The rising and falling voice offered its own reply to repression, its own affirmation of the spirit in a place that was spiritless.

Of course, he could not spend all his time singing, and since the future lay in doubt, a degree of mental safety lay in reflections on the past—of home, of loved ones, of his job, of previous travels and adventures, of girls known and lost. He could remember so much of a world gone by.

"When I wrote to you from Morocco, I forgot to mention that I had also been in Gibraltar for two days. I climbed 'the Rock' by road and went into all the tunnels open to the public. I did the climb with an English girl and her mother (too bad!) I had met in Seville. . . . The rock takes up most of the land area of the colony. The inhabitants are predominately of Spanish descent but British citizens and very proud of it. They and the garrison live on the lower portion of the peninsula mostly near the water. . . . Boats travel every day between Gibraltar and Tangier. They seem to be always crowded.

"When I was in Tangier I went to an Arab night club to see belly dancing. Very interesting! One of the belly dancers there introduced me to doing the twist. When they aren't doing their acts they mix with the single men in the crowd like regular 'bar girls.' However, some of them are very pretty. After 12:30 I was the only guest there. It was quite different. Some of the girls' boy friends were there, and I talked with them and some of the girls. The illusion of sex and mystery was shattered. If the drinks weren't so expensive I would have succumbed, however, to their wiles. They would snuggle up and hold your hand. I go into such lengthy description partly, if you haven't guessed, because I completely fell for the illusion.

"Also in Tangier, I walked all over the Kasbah and in other parts of the city with a 12-year-old guide. The country is expensive in many ways and there are many poor people which accounts partially for the aggressive storekeepers, the pimps, the insistent shoeshine boys, and the more insistent boys and men who demand almost to guide you somewhere. Their money-seeking attitude occasionally put me on edge.

"After leaving Morocco, I spent four days in Torremolinos on the Casta del Sol and two days in Valencia. I will be here in Mallorca until Sunday (a total of two weeks). The Palma area of Mallorca is crowded with many English, French, and Swedes. The beaches are nice. I will spend a day or two in Barcelona, a week in Switzerland, and probably the week before Italy in Austria, rather than Denmark. . . ."

That was the way it had been a summer ago. The clean hard imminence of "the Rock" and, as you went up, the breeze coming in off the water to cool you. The crowded, tourist-filled ship moving across the narrow throat of sea toward the haze-shrouded hump of land. The marvelous sensuality of the dancing girls, gyrating in timeless unison to a discordant yet demanding beat; the cluttered, heat-filled streets, awash with a babel of unwashed humanity. Warm sun above, hot sand underfoot, the surf curling in, and tomorrow another day . . . another day to explore.

A year ago, a hundred years ago, that was the way of it before he had returned home to his job with the D. Van Nostrand Company. He had gone to work for the publishing firm in the fall of 1963, and as he paced his cell and sang his songs and thought of the past he began to worry more about losing his job than any other thing.

Despite all the traveling he had done, the places and people observed on three continents, his job represented a base of stability and a point of reality in which he could see a future. It was totally unlike a physical journey, which might offer information about his fellow man but did not in itself offer a sense of permanence or anything that was soundly meaningful. Isolated in a prison cell, cut off from all contact with family and friends, fed a constant stream of lies by direction, the future a stone wall and a blue light that never went out, his anxiousness grew about being unable to report to his company on September 20 as scheduled. It may be that concentrating on his job also helped him believe that his imprisonment would end one day soon and there was a place of business to which he could return. He had known many girls and he had liked many girls, but he was not married, nor in love, and thus the thought of wife or fiancée could not sustain him; it was only the job.

Androv saw this by what was said, but he was interested in seeing it in writing and so on September 30, when the prisoner again mentioned contacting the Embassy, he suggested, through Nina, that it might help if Mott wrote to Bill Shinn and set down the details of his position. They gave him paper and his pen with red ink and on October 2 he was permitted to write his first letter from Murmansk. He used his meeting with Shinn as an introduction.

Oct. 2, 1965
Murmansk

Mr. William Townsley Shinn, Junior
Consul of the United States of America
American Embassy
Moscow, USSR

Dear Mr. Shinn,

The following is an explanation of my job; *I did not have time Sept. 13th to tell you, as we had less than five minutes when you asked if I were a book salesman. I hope I'll be able to keep my job.*

I work for D. Van Nostrand Co., 120 Alexander St., Princeton, N.J., in the College Department. My position is called college traveler. My territory of colleges encompasses most of upper N.Y. State, Western Pa., and all of W. Va. In all I am responsible for somewhat over 300,000 college students. I talk to approximately 2000 professors a year [*84* colleges]. *This should give you an idea of how much I have to cover in terms of total colleges. Naturally, the* full school year *is necessary to cover them all. I was supposed to report in Princeton Sept. 20th.*

I work on a straight salary. My job is to call upon professors at these colleges who are teaching courses Van Nostrand has textbooks or supplementary paperbacks for. I have to discover how each professor teaches his individual courses, if there is a committee to decide a course adoption (book order) for a large introductory course and I have to decide which books (*we have hundreds*) *we have would interest him* (*or them*), *and* why. *For example, we have six introductoy biology texts and four beginning calculus books. We also have an engineering mechanics text with vectors in two volumes, and a one volume one using matrices and tensors, short-shrifting the statics portion. Our political science texts are, for the most part, institutional in approach; if a professor is behavioral in orientation, our books (with few exceptions) won't do. These things, too, I have to take into account.*

I see to it that the professors get free copies of the books they and I *think they* might *like to assign to their students at* some *future date. Hopefully, the books and my visits will bring about an order for the professor's class. The professor gives the order to the college bookstore (not to me); the store orders the books from Princeton; and the students then have to purchase them.*

Van Nostrand publishes books for many disciplines, so I have to talk with professors of: mechanical engineering, civil engineering, political science, history, sociology, architecture, philosophy, economics, geography, accounting, physics, biology, chemistry and mathematics to name some.

I must report to the company any criticisms (intelligent ones) of our books or a competitor's. I report course changes or curriculum changes; the latter is of especial interest at good institutions like Cornell University and Carnegie Tech. because it might set a trend in education. Therefore, the textbooks would have to reflect it in the future. Now and then a new textbook *causes revamping of courses at better colleges around the country. Last year the Van Nostrand College Dept. published two distinctly new textbooks which have affected the way courses are taught. One was Reed-Hill's* Physical Metallurgy Principles *and the other was Mendelson's* Introduction to Mathematical Logic (*used now at MIT, Cornell, Pitt., and Carnegie Tech for examples*). *Van Nostrand's* college dept. *publishes about 70 books a year. We have to know pretty much all the books the company publishes because sometimes a reference book or a trade book fits a college course.*

The company expects me to report the chances our individual books have at each college, particularly the forthcoming and recent books, so they have an idea of what I'm doing out there by myself, *whether the book is good or bad, whether it will sell, and whether they should have it reprinted.*

Another very important responsibility I have is to discover and report in detail *interesting books that I think Van Nostrand might like to publish. This last school year I reported about 110 books being written, quite a lot. They included books on: personality, Japanese, prefectual politics (a comparative, behavioral study, which has never been done before), cross cultural societal analysis, money and banking, criminology, urban geography, comparative study of the state politics (all 50) of the U.S.A., contemporary philosophy, machine design (M.E.), thermodynamics (M.E.), applied linear algebra, molecular biology, advanced calculus, marriage and the family, a history of Africa and plant growth and development.*

That about *sums up what my job entails. You can see it is one I like, and that I am quite happy with Van Nostrand Co., and my territory. If I stay here much longer, if I haven't already, I'll lose this job I've worked so hard to keep.*

Sincerely yours,

Newcomb Mott

After September 30 he was not questioned again for five days. This was undoubtedly because Androv's superiors in Murmansk and Moscow were taking a long hard look at his reports on the prisoner and reaching a decision. It cannot be said unequivocally that their decision resulted in a new approach at the expense of the original plan, which had been to explore the possibility of changing Newcomb Mott's loyalties, but a new plan was put into operation which certainly indicates that the prisoner's loyalties were no longer so important a consideration.

The same method of treatment, of course, continued because the operating procedure had been fixed and cruelty is an ingrained characteristic of those who fixed it. And there is little doubt that no final evaluation had been made as to the prisoner's usability should the new approach fail. However, on a public level, American citizen Newcomb Mott had become a victim of the Cold War and already U. S. Secretary of State Dean Rusk with Ambassadors Goldberg, Thompson, and Kohler had in a weekend of discussions concerning U.S. and USSR relations with Soviet Foreign Minister Andrei Gromyko, and Ambassadors Fedorenko and Dobrynin urged the young man's release.

When the questioning resumed on October 5, the interrogator was no longer Captain Androv, but a man of much higher rank in the KGB, Lt. Colonel Griposeyevich, probably dispatched from Moscow headquarters. Griposeyevich was short and stocky, a man in his forties. He had a cold, withdrawn approach.

It was a month and a day since Newcomb Mott had been taken into custody and the KGB officer led off with the same old question:

"Did the CIA send you to investigate the border?"

"No."

"Are you a spy?"

"No. Are *you* a spy?"

Griposeyevich ignored the sarcasm and developed the same tissue of lies as had his predecessor. He maintained the Norwegians had stated Newcomb Mott was a spy, and if he wasn't one, why was the U. S. Embassy ignoring him?

The prisoner had no reply.

The questioning continued off and on through October 8. It covered familiar ground, and much of it dealt with the beliefs and the life and times of Newcomb Mott. The assassination of President Kennedy was also touched on. Only twice was espionage mentioned, but throughout it all, Griposeyevich spun his web of doubt. The Embassy was doing nothing. The prisoner's second letter to the official Shinn, which had described prison treatment and interrogation, had been confiscated. No, there had been no letters from home or from anyone else.

Then on the eighth the KGB officer lowered the boom. He informed the accused that he was going to be tried secretly, convicted, and sent to a labor camp. No, there was no possibility of a suspended sentence. His lawyer would be appointed by the court. It would be up to the court to decide whether an Embassy observer would be permitted to attend.

Naturally shaken, Newcomb Mott asked if the Embassy had been notified of the trial—and Griposeyevich, lying, assured him that the Embassy had known of it since September 13. Then the prisoner asked the date of the trial. The KGB officer compounded the blow by saying the date was secret. Finally he brought forth for signing a document which he said was a transcript of the prisoner's statements. The prisoner refused to sign it until he was warned that refusal could be held against him by the judge.

And then it was Nina who came to succor him with a sympathetic suggestion. Why didn't he write again to the Embassy and suggest an exchange be made for some Russian who might be in U.S. hands? She had heard that such exchanges had been arranged before.

Her supposedly spontaneous and kind suggestion was at last a ray of light in a world whose increasing climatic cold and darkness were now equal to what he saw as the cold and darkness of his own future.

In a letter dated October 10, Newcomb Mott, after once again detailing his summer travels from July 19 to September 4, wrote:

MOSCOW A-655

Since I (I say unintentionally-illegally) committed the act, circumstantial evidence suggesting it was not unintentional would not be hard to accumulate. I do not commit illegal acts. I was naïve, but I had no interest in doing something illegal. As you know, good intentions in a situation like mine are rather hard to prove.

On Sept. 13th, you learned there would be a trial. You know what penalty is prescribed by Article 83—1–3 years in a labor camp or a prison. Only occasionally, is a transgressor in the USSR fined (an indefinite amount of money) instead of imprisoned. *The only other alternative, as I understand it, is American Embassy negotiations of my release. It is this that I ask you and the United States government for. I hope, somehow, to be released so that I can go home soon. I know that the U.S. has often in the past successfully negotiated the release of other American tourists, and even of Americans accused of serious crimes, like Barghoorn of Yale. Since, under Russian law, I have committed a crime, I imagine (I don't know) that something tangible would have to be given or promised in return for my release. If the only way I could be released soon was by U.S. exchange of a Russian prisoner of some sort, I hope the United States would do it.* [Italics added.]

At times in some of the following paragraphs I may seem to congratulate myself on my perfection. I am not perfect by a long shot and except for my present situation, I would not mention some of the things at all. Now, obviously, I know I'm not so important to the U.S. as Professor Barghoorn (if I'm considered important at all), whether he was innocent or guilty. I think that when you read my job description (in an earlier letter) as college traveler for D. Van Nostrand Co., of N.J., you will see that my job has a certain measure of importance for the U.S.A. and higher education, and that I bring something worthwhile to the job. Calling on college professors in my territory about textbooks and supplementary paperbacks for course use and manuscripts they may be writing is a job which I like very much. I would like to stay with Van Nostrand and keep the job.

I have never in the past been accused of or arrested for any crime anywhere (except speeding). Never have I spent so much as ¼ hour in a jail or prison. This, in a foreign country, one in which I don't speak the language, is now the 37th day of my (punishment and) imprisonment—and most of it in a prison with all that implies. Many, many more days are possible. I am in danger of losing my liberty, my country, my family, my job, my friends and other relatives and all the comforts of life for an indefinite, but long period. Any time, I begrudge, but I can now do nothing about it. I have never been subversive; I vote in elections; I'm not delinquent on my taxes; I am truthful and honest; while abroad as a tourist (I've been in 21 countries since 1959), in addition to enjoying myself, I try to behave appropriately because people unconsciously rate you as a representative of your country (no matter which one); and I consider it my pleasure, and my duty as an American citizen, to possess and increase my knowledge of world and national affairs.

For substantiation of my general good character, truthfulness, honesty and worth, the following people (mostly friends) could be consulted: Frank W. H. Adams of N.Y.C., former police commissioner of N.Y.C., and now a lawyer, 2. Theodore A. Saros, College Department Director, D. Van Nostrand Co., 120 Alexander St., Princeton, N.J., 3. Malcolm Macdonald, Science Editor for D. V. N., 4. Edward Crane, Jr., President of D. V. N., 5. Richard Qu. Calvelli, Sales Manager at D. V. N., 6. others at D. V. N., 7. my parents and brother (who could be fairly objective), 8. Mr. F. W. Beinecke of N. Y. C., recently retired Chairman-of-the-Board of Sperry and Hutchinson Co., of N. Y. C. ("S & H"), 9. my uncle, John C. Mott, Asst. Vice President of the Irving Trust Co. (N. Y. C.), 10. William Arbogast, head of the A.P. in the House Press Gallery in Washington, D.C. (where I worked in 1960), 11. David Helmstadter, English and Education Editor for Addison-Wesley Publishing Co., Reading, Mass., 12. Fritz Liebert, Rare Book Librarian of the Beinecke Library, Yale University, 13. Roger Williams, my former advisor, professor of history at Antioch College, Yellow Springs, Ohio, 14. Joseph G. E. Hopkins, History Reference Editor (and former professor at Columbia University), Charles Scribner's Sons, Inc., (Publishers in N. Y. C. on 5th Ave.), 15. Warren Bender, Electronics research engineer for Bell Labs., Murray Hill, N.J., 16. Jacob Blanc, bibliographer of the *Bibliography of American Literature,* in residence at the Houghton (rare book) Library, Harvard University, 17. William Little, Assoc. Professor and Chairman of the Department of German at Tufts University (Mass.), 18. Mark Savage, Vice President of McClelland & Stewart Co., Ltd., Toronto, Ontario, Canada (largest book publishing co. in Canada) and my parents could probably think of many more.

I hope that Van Nostrand knows about my imprisonment, is holding my job somehow, and is trying through the American Textbook Publishers Institute, the book publishing industry, or on its own to get me out soon.

You were, I hope, able to inform Frank W. H. Adams and President James Dixon at Antioch College of my story and request for help. I realize that the American Embassy may be chary of passing along information to people who may bring pressure to bear upon the State Department, your parent body, but I hope the American idea of justice and mercy will dismiss that notion. It would do well if some (or all) of the people on my long list were also given my story and request for help.

I hope the Speaker is still interested and is using his influence to get me out. Please thank him for me. Representative McCormack may be interested to know that I worked in the House Press Gallery from January through March, 1960, while on an Antioch College co-op job, as the AP copy boy. Please tell him what you can.

My parents and brother, other relatives and friends, I hope, are not taking it too hard. Is there any news from them or Van Nostrand?

Everyone should keep in mind that everything mailed to prisoners is examined first.

I would like the following men informed of my plight and request for help; Senator Edward Kennedy, Senator Leverett Saltonstall, Representative Silvio Conte, Governor John Volpe (Mass.) and Massachusetts Attorney General Edward Brooke.

I would like the American Embassy present at any trial. Several times I have requested additional visits by you, Mr. Shinn, but at last I've been told that you have to request the visits yourself. Please come! I would be most interested, of course, if you could bring news of my impending release, or, what is being done about it. I appreciate all your efforts, Mr. Shinn.

As of now I can console myself with the notion that it hasn't been a complete loss because I have reduced by about 25 unnecessary pounds with little effort on my part.

Due to my unthinking action, my parents and brother, my other relatives, Van Nostrand and I have all suffered. Problems, I never had any intention of creating, have arisen for the U.S. and USSR governments as well. I am very sorry it happened.

I look at your calling card everyday to renew my hope. If the word "hope" seems to appear frequently, it is because hope and my knowledge that I speak the truth are all I have for comfort.

I am told that the American Embassy can send me food, parcels and money (for buying food here). I need something else to supplement my diet here in prison. However, some extra food is provided for me by the kind asst. director of the prison. I would appreciate having some newspapers.

Sincerely yours,

Newcomb Mott

At the time Newcomb Mott wrote his letter there was only one Russian in the United States whom the Soviets were anxious to bring home. He was Igor A. Ivanov who, until his arrest by the FBI on the night of October 29, 1963, had been employed as a chauffeur for Amtorg, the official Soviet trading firm in the U.S. Amtorg, since its establishment in New York City in 1924, has acted as a cover for a great many "chauffeur"-type employees who were doubling as Soviet spies. Ivanov, a handsome, blond, thirty-three-year-old driver, was simply the latest the FBI had apprehended in extracurricular activities. He was caught with three fellow intelligence officers, all members of the Soviet mission to the United Nations, and John Butenko, a U.S. electronics engineer. Butenko had been passing the quartet information which involved the highly sensitive and secret control system of the Strategic Air Command. Ivanov's fellow agents were quickly sent back to the USSR via the diplomatic immunity *persona non grata* route. Their expulsion on November 1, 1963 raised to thirty the number of UN Soviet and bloc officials and their dependents who had been sent packing for the selfsame reasons. Ivanov, however, did not possess the same immunity, and he and Butenko were indicted and brought to trial in December 1964. They were both found guilty as charged and the penalty could have been death, but Judge Anthony T. Augelli sentenced Butenko to thirty years and Ivanov to twenty. Prior to the trial and sentencing the Soviet agent had been free on $100,000 bail put up by the Kremlin, and after sentence was passed he continued free, pending an appeal of the verdict. At this writing the appeal has not come up for judgment and Igor Ivanov, unlike Butenko, the American, remains out of prison.

The KGB was, and is, anxious to negotiate his return for several known reasons. Any Soviet agent assigned to the U.S., be he KGB or its military subordinate GRU, is a highly trained person and of superior intelligence. His loyalty and dedication to the Communist cause is considered to be exemplary. *Esprit de corps* in the Soviet foreign service is an important morale factor, and one way in which it is stimulated is by the agent's knowledge that if he is caught he will not be abandoned. Everything possible will be done to retrieve him. The putting up of $100,000 bail for Ivanov is a case in point.

Now with an American tourist in hand, who through his own admission had broken a Soviet law, it was only natural that KGB Chairman Vladimir T. Semichastny and his comrades would seek to get Ivanov and the $100,000 bail money back. However, for obvious reasons, they wished the plea for exchange to appear to come as a suggestion from the prisoner and not from the Soviet Government. As a result, there were just *two* reasons why the U. S. Embassy in Moscow was informed on October 13 that a Consular representative would again be permitted to journey to Murmansk to visit Newcomb Mott. The first was so that the letter of October 10 could be delivered, and the second, so that the prisoner could tell the Embassy official that he was facing a secret trial and conviction. The latter, of course, would bring considerable protest, but it also might help to influence strong considerations for the exchange.

1. Soviet tourist compound at Boris Gleb taken from the church tower by Finnish photographer Helge Heinonen shortly after Newcomb Mott's capture. Mott was lost amid the terrain beyond the compound.

2. Boris Gleb tourist compound with old church, looking north. The road curves around the end of the hill in the background, going to the Soviet and Norwegian border control stations beyond the hill. Just to the right of the church but out of sight is the Pasvik River. The bluffs at the far right are partially in Russian and partly in Norwegian territory. (Photo by Rolf Arvola)

3. The main tourist building where Newcomb Mott was first taken after his detention on the morning of September 4, 1965. The vehicle on the far left is the Russian-made Gaz used to transport Mott across the river to the village of Boris Gleb. The other cars are all from Norway; Saturday afternoon tourists come to buy vodka. This photo was taken by Finnish photographer Helge Heinonen on the afternoon of September 4.

4, 5, and 6. Three Soviet Intourist hostesses at Boris Gleb. Vicki Kochimalkin, to whom Newcomb Mott first spoke upon his arrival at the compound, is on the far left. Note that the billboard on the building wall is written in Norwegian and English. Business is brisk at the bar in any language. The male bartender is Alexander, a very popular fellow, believed to double as a KGB agent. His female counterpart sells not only beverages but American-brand cigarettes, which can be seen beside the flowers. (4. Photo by Helge Heinonen. 5. Photo by Rolf Arvola. 6. Photo by Helge Heinonen)

7. Vicki Kochimalkin in tourist compound office with Intourist chief from Murmansk who is also believed to be a key KGB officer in the Boris Gleb area. The man at left is a news editor from Kirkenes. (Photo by Rolf Arvola)

8. Village of Boris Gleb on the east side of the Pasvik River where Newcomb Mott was taken and held for three days in the second story of one of the houses shown. This photograph was actually shot at the time Newcomb Mott was being detained. (Photo by Helge Heinonen)

Newcomb Mott and Bill Shinn met for the second time at three-thirty on the afternoon of October 15. The meeting place was on the second floor of the Murmansk Ministry for Public Protection—which means police headquarters. Prior to the meeting, which included the same dramatis personae as the first—Griposeyevich not attending—Androv handed Newcomb Mott's letter to Shinn. The Vice Consul took the time to read it on the spot but he made no comment. In his previous visit he had come to Murmansk bringing a knowledge of Soviet legal procedure; now he had arrived with a package containing food, candy, books, and magazines, plus twenty roubles. He also requested to see the prison doctor in order to hand over Newcomb Mott's medical record and a supply of penicillin, for despite his size and athletic abilities the prisoner suffered from acute *glomerulonephritis* —a kidney ailment—and at the onset of any strep throat infection, penicillin was to be administered immediately.

Androv refused Shinn's request to see the doctor and was reluctant to accept the drug.

When the two Americans shook hands once again, Shinn immediately noticed that Mott had lost considerable weight. There were also signs of strain showing in his face, and he was very anxious to talk. He was wearing his own clothes this time, and his shoes had been repaired and shined by the prison cobbler. Mention of the package and its contents cheered him immensely.

The meeting lasted until five o'clock. During it Shinn asked if the letter had been Mott's own idea. Because he had been advised by Nina that the swap would have more chance if he did not admit it had been suggested, Mott said yes, and then tried to cover the whole thing further by asking if he had written something he shouldn't have. Nevertheless Shinn saw the truth of the matter.

When he learned of the threatened secret trial and what would follow it, he did not turn on Androv but used his powers of persuasion to try and convince the prisoner that he must not believe such things. If there was going to be a trial, he said, the decision rested with the court and not with *any* interrogator regardless of his rank. Since the preliminary investigation had not been completed, the court had made no ruling. Meanwhile the Embassy was doing everything it could to secure his freedom. If worst did come to worst and there was a trial, the proceedings would be held in public and the Embassy would see that a lawyer worthy of the name would be provided to handle the defense. It was the best Shinn could offer, and it was cold comfort.

They discussed the matter of health. Mott said he was all right but admitted prolonged isolation was making him nervous. The guards had been kind to him, as had Captain Vilkov. He had received no mail, and again Shinn tried to reassure him that this was not because his family had neglected to write or that people in high places weren't working to bring about his release.*

In a brief aside Mott said he had originally been suspected of espionage but that he was no longer. He was unaware that the KGB had never openly accused him of such.

The meeting, while longer than the first, did not leave the prisoner with the same degree of optimism as had the initial contact. If in a month and a half of trying, the U. S. Government had been unable to extract him from a situation whose reality was beyond anything he had ever imagined, small wonder he did not take comfort from Bill Shinn's attempt to be encouraging. The grim words of Lt. Colonel Griposeyevich had the iron ring of inevitability. Before they took him away, Shinn gave him the first word from his parents. They sent him their love and told him that his job with Van Nostrand was waiting.

When they had taken him away, Androv smugly reiterated to Shinn that indeed there would be a trial.

* Actually, the Motts did not write to their son because the State Department told them the Soviets had not given Newcomb an address.

"How can you make that kind of a statement when you don't have the authority to make it!" Shinn snapped back.

And Captain Androv, who knew full well that the KGB could command any action of the court, replied with a shrug.

Although Bill Shinn had not brought good news, he had brought reading material, and just as the extra food helped to sustain Newcomb Mott physically, the books and magazines were a great boost in helping to shield him from the torments of isolation. Among the articles he read was "Running Away" by John Keats in *Holiday* magazine. It was an article he had originally read in June.

Keats wrote: ". . . why I applaud the youthful dramatist, the would-be adventurer, who breaks the pattern, who with mounting excitement writes the farewell note and slips out . . . I believe I know how he feels. More important, I know that he is not running away from something so much as he is running toward something: toward life, toward himself; toward an end that cannot be known. I wish him well. His chances of finding what he seeks are never good, but they are at least better than the chances of those who stay at home, placidly accepting patterns they never made or chose."

These sentences suited Mott's mood perfectly. He had thought of attempting to escape many times, but he recognized such contemplation as a measure of his growing sense of desperation, and he knew his only escape was into the realm of the books and articles Shinn had brought him, and through his own memories of a time when his freedom was complete . . . as it had once been in Mexico.

"Guanajuato has a small town provincial flavor, although it is the capital of the state. The population is 24,000 situated in a long narrow valley. This city was one of the most important in the independence movement against Spain.

"The drinking water and the milk are boiled in our house. They are very careful to see that all the food is well cleaned. Almost every day we are served something new to us. We've had: rice with bananas, tortillas, tacos-fried tortillas with

Mexican baked beans inside, onion-potato-meat dish for breakfast, and a number of others. This week we have had breakfast about 9; next week regular classes begin so we will eat at 7 most mornings. Lunch is between 2 and 3; it is the heaviest meal. . . . All good Mexican girls are off the street by 10, unless there is a special occasion like a late starting dance sponsored by the University. Opposite numbers very obviously look each other over. There is a special place, where it is done en masse. On Tuesday, Thursday, and Sunday nights the young people gather in a particular plaza from 8 until 10. The boys walk clockwise and the girls the other way. There isn't a general signal; at various times a boy will stop and then start walking with a group of girls or a number of boys will; usually two and never more than three. People hardly ever walk in less than 2's. Everyone walks around and around the park. You look each other over. This is called the Serenata. If a girl smiles at you or something of that sort you can, if you want walk around with her and talk and then if you feel it's worth it, ask her group to go and have a coke at one of the many places around the *Jardin*. Public gatherings like this are encouraged because they feel nothing will go wrong in a public place. Unless a couple is almost engaged the boy doesn't go into the girl's house. Frequently, he meets her on a date in the Plaza. We've got a lot to learn in the way of customs. Foster and I had coke with three girls on Thursday night. Foster made a date with the cutest of the three last night. He was 10 minutes late meeting her in the Plaza . . . he couldn't find her! We've had girls stare at us all over the city; frequently they smile. Mexican girls are quite flirtatious. . . ."

That was the way it had been for him in the spring of his twentieth year.

There were no more sessions with the KGB. He did not realize that what came next depended entirely on a judgment to be made in Washington, D.C.

On Saturday, October 23, John C. Guthrie, U. S. Chargé d'Affaires, called on Mikhail N. Smirnovski, Director of the American Section of the Soviet Ministry of Foreign Affairs. Guthrie's call was the seventh contact made to the Ministry in connection with Newcomb Mott.

Guthrie made himself clear. Aside from the whole affair becoming extremely distasteful to the U. S. Government and the American people, just what kind of game was the Soviet Government playing? By what right and under what Soviet law was Newcomb Mott being threatened with a secret trial and conviction before the investigation into his alleged act had been completed? The Government of the United States took an exceedingly dim view of such harassment.

Smirnovski admitted that Captain Androv had been in error to make such a statement. He confessed that some of what Guthrie was saying was news to him.

Guthrie then gave him more news, the answer which the KGB was awaiting. Although it was couched in diplomatic language, it added up to the fact that the United States Government was not about to exchange Soviet spy Igor A. Ivanov for one of its citizens, Newcomb N. Mott. The rejection was as much a reality of the Cold War as were the espionage of Ivanov and the unjust imprisonment of Mott. To have agreed to the exchange would have been to have set a bad precedent. Any time a Soviet spy was apprehended in the U.S. who could not escape through diplomatic immunity, the Kremlin would know that by the simple means of jailing a U.S. citizen on trumped-up charges, it could get its man home free.

Guthrie concluded the interview with the implied threat that should Newcomb Mott be brought to trial, it would have an extremely adverse effect on U.S. tourism to the USSR.

Now with the rejection, the pace of events quickened. Four days later, Deputy Director Oberenko informed Political Affairs Counselor David Boster that the investigation was coming to an end and that Newcomb Mott would be permitted to retain his own attorney if he so chose. This in effect was throwing the Embassy's complaint, as voiced by Guthrie, back in its face. It was in fact a direct admission that the form of Soviet legality had nothing whatever to do with the *substance* of Kremlin decisions. Boster, of course, protested the implication.

Newcomb Mott learned the news in a different manner. Because he had lost so much weight, he was measured for a suit which he believed was for wear in a labor camp. He was given a physical examination. His blood pressure was 155 over 90, which under the circumstances was not overly high. The prison dentist had a look at his teeth and decided to replace an old filling and keep it as a souvenir.

The prisoner began to feel like a lamb being groomed for the slaughter. In the blue-lit solitude of his cell he had to fight to keep his equilibrium. Had he been a religious man, no doubt he would have spent some of his time in prayer. Even though he had visited and worshiped in churches of many different denominations, he had found no single faith to hold him, and he saw himself as an agnostic. Therefore it was only his courage as an individual on which he had to draw for strength, and when on October 28 he was officially informed that he was going to be tried, his courage was as tall as himself.

October 26, 1965

In Washington Ambassador [at Large] Llewellyn Thompson raised Mott case with Ambassador Dobrynin, expressing concern over situation noted by Shinn on second visit. *Dobrynin promised to look into the case.* [Italics added.]

From State Department Chronology of Mott case

Chapter Six

On Thursday, October 28, a mild fall day along the Potomac, Howard and Phyllis Mott and their son Rusty arrived in Washington. Two days before, with the concurrence and advice of State Department officials, they had telephoned the Soviet Embassy from New York City to ask for an appointment with Ambassador Anatoly F. Dobrynin. Outside of internal contacts with the Soviet Ministry of Foreign Affairs, Ambassador Dobrynin had been acquainted with the case for at least a month: officially (as already noted) in talks at the UN and in Washington, and prior to those talks, unofficially, through the following letter:

September 25, 1965

Ambassador Anatoly Dobrynin
1125 16th Street
Soviet Embassy
Washington, D.C.

Your Excellency:

On September 4 our son Newcomb Mott strayed over the northern border of Norway into USSR territory, near Boris Gleb. He was taken in custody by a border guard and has been held at Murmansk for the past three weeks.

He has a spirit of adventure but he has always shown respect for the laws and customs of all countries. He has done a great deal of traveling ever since he was fifteen years old, and has earned his own money to do so. On the Antioch College Program he spent three months at the University of Guanajuato and afterward traveled throughout Mexico and remote sections of Yucatan. Although he visits the large cities, he prefers to go where it is not so heavily populated with tourists; last summer he included Lichtenstein and Andorra in his travels.

We are very disturbed to hear that he is not well and is highly nervous. The latter is understandable—his parents are also feeling the strain of uncertainty. Newcomb has the added worry of knowing that the longer he is away the more his job is being jeopardized.

For the past two and a half years he has worked as a college representative for a textbook publishing firm. As soon as the colleges close and his reports are finished his time is free until fall. He was supposed to have returned to work on September 20. Even under the best of conditions he works under great pressure of time and this delay means that undoubtedly his production will be below that of the past college year.

We know that your time is occupied with many important things and that the problem of a stray American tourist and his family may not be important on your agenda. However, the problem looms very large in our lives; in fact we are concerned with it night and day.

We will be very grateful for any aid or information you will give us.

Sincerely yours,

Phyllis Mott

On October 2 the Motts had received a brief acknowledgment:

EMBASSY OF THE
UNION OF SOVIET SOCIALIST REPUBLICS
WASHINGON 6, D.C.

Mr. & Mrs. Mott
Sheffield, Mass.
01257

October 2, 1965

Dear Mr. & Mrs. Mott:

I would like to acknowledge your letter of September 25, 1965 addressed to Ambassador Anatoly F. Dobrynin.

At the present moment we can only advise you that Newcomb Mott has by-passed the pass control post on the Soviet-Norwegian border and thus violated the existing border regulations. This matter is now under investigation by the appropriate Soviet authorities.

Sincerely,

A. Zinchuk,
Counselor of the Embassy

Since communication had been established with the State Department on September 15, the Motts had been in constant contact with the Office of Soviet Union Affairs and most particularly with Carroll Woods, in charge of Political Affairs. Woods, a dark-haired, quiet-spoken, pipe-smoking career officer had served two tours of duty with the Embassy in Moscow and he spoke Russian. It was he who advised the Motts on the best tack to take in making an appointment with the Soviet Ambassador.

In placing their call on October 26, the same time that Ambassador Thompson was discussing the case with Dobrynin, the Motts were hopeful of getting an appointment as a nicely timed follow-up with the Soviet official the next day.

It was Phyllis Mott who did the telephoning, and when she told the Embassy operator who she was, she could hear her name being repeated and broadcast in the background as though she were being paged. After a short wait Alexander Zinchuk, the Embassy's Minister Counselor and number-two man, came on the phone.

The brief introduction accomplished, Phyllis Mott made her request and was informed that Ambassador Dobrynin was out of town and would not be back. However, if Mr. and Mrs. Mott wished to talk to Counselor Zinchuk, he would receive them.

She agreed and, as instructed, asked for an eleven o'clock appointment on the following day.

Zinchuk replied that ten o'clock Thursday would be much better.

And so at five minutes to ten on Thursday, the three Motts crossed Sixteenth Street and approached the official Soviet residence, which even on a clear day resembles a Charles Addams cartoon of a haunted house. The windows on the ground floor are barred and blocked with drapes, and those on the three floors above facing the street are tightly shuttered. The building's massive cement face, topped by a high slated crown, does nothing to enhance its architectural lack of grace. There is no other embassy in Washington that presents a more closed-in aspect.

The Embassy's outward appearance did nothing to reassure the three visitors, who, in entering into a cavernous interior requiring lights, departed the special autumnal charm of an October day in Washington. An extensive red-carpeted corridor, walled by checkered rows of painted-over glass, debouched into a barnlike foyer, also red-carpeted. At the rear of the room an ornate staircase circled upward. To its left there were a desk and a receptionist.

Phyllis Mott led the way toward the female attendant, who eyed their approach blankly. "Good morning," she said. "We're the Motts. We have an appointment with Mr. Zinchuk."

"You're early," the receptionist replied.

"I know."

"Will you sit down?" She nodded toward some chairs against the far wall.

The elder Motts moved to do so while Rusty, having noted a long black table covered with Soviet English-language magazines, gravitated toward it. Rusty was not so big as his older brother but standing six foot three and weighing nearly two hundred pounds he presented a rather formidable figure. In September he had volunteered for the Navy, and as he had not yet received his orders, he had accompanied his parents to Washington.

While the Motts sat and Rusty perused the reading material, an inconspicuous-looking man of slight build, dressed in gray, hovered about like a moth. He had smiled at the Motts as they had proceeded to sit down, and they had assumed he was a minor Embassy functionary. Now he went over and spoke quietly to the receptionist, and she arose, and the two came toward the visitors.

"Mr. Zinchuk is still busy," she announced, "but you may go upstairs."

They stood, and the little man said in good English, "I am Mr. Mikhailov. I shall take you."

As they all started toward the staircase Phyllis Mott turned and said, "Come on, Rusty."

Both she and her husband noticed the startled look of surprise that momentarily froze on Mikhailov's face. He turned and stared at Rusty and then said, "Oh, there are three of you?"

"Yes, this is our son Rusty."

Mikhailov, who held the title of First Secretary, led the way up the stairs in silence and upon reaching the landing, turned to the left, bringing his guests into an enormous empty room, the windows covered with red drapes. To the right of the entrance there were a love seat and three chairs, and to the left four chairs. This was the only furniture, and in retrospect the Motts believe it was expected that they would sit in the four chairs to the left where no doubt there was a concealed microphone with an attachment to record their conversation. Instead, because Rusty was with them, Phyllis Mott turned away from Mikhailov's lead and proceeded to the love seat.

They all sat down and made small talk, Mikhailov describing the beauty of the Embassy which had once been the manse of George Pullman of railroad fame. Phyllis Mott, never one to hide her opinions under a bushel basket, even if it was Soviet-occupied, said it didn't look too cozy to her.

First Secretary Valerian V. Mikhailov did not have an immediate response and was saved the effort of finding one as Minister Counselor Alexander I. Zinchuk made his entrance.

Zinchuk was a stocky man of better than medium height with slightly bowed shoulders. He had a broad pointed face with puffy brown eyes and a mop of black hair combed straight back. Soberly dressed in a dark brown suit with a matching tie, he took over the interview although to the Motts he appeared more ill at ease than his apparent subordinate.

Prior to the meeting the Motts had been briefed by State Department contacts on what they might expect. They were told to watch Zinchuk's right eye. If it twitched it would mean they had him on the defensive. In the course of the conversation they observed that not only did his right eye twitch but his left eye and mouth as well.

Mikhailov barely opened his mouth, but when Howard Mott offered him a cigarette he took one, which showed that he, too, was nervous, for they had learned also at their briefing that he did not smoke and was in fact disturbed about his son's smoking.

Actually the Motts did most of the talking. They pointed out that so far there had been little publicity about their son's case. This was because Newcomb was an unimportant tourist and everyone was sure he would soon be let go. His crossing the border had been unintentional and he was quite harmless to anyone. But the lack of publicity was also due to their own efforts. Being in the book business they had a great many friends in publishing, and they had prevailed on their friends not to raise a hue and cry. Now, however, if their son wasn't set free, if in fact he was brought to trial, there would be nothing they could do to stop the publicity, which would no doubt have an adverse effect on tourism to the USSR.

The Russians listened, Zinchuk keeping his eyes focused on Rusty.

The Motts then discussed the possibility of a trial. If, in spite of everything that made sense, there was going to be one, they wished to be present and also requested that Newcomb be paroled in their care during the course of it.

Zinchuk then inadvertently disclosed that he knew there would be a trial by suggesting that they could write to him, requesting visas and parole for their son. But in the next breath he stressed that *neither he nor anyone else in the Embassy knew anything about the case. It was all being handled in Russia.*

When the Motts descended the circular staircase they took with them no new information about Newcomb, his status, or whether they would be permitted to go to the Soviet Union should he be brought to trial. All they had was the dubious satisfaction of knowing that their visit had made two Soviet officials nervous, plus the suspicion that the pair believed Rusty was not their son but a CIA agent playing the part. As for agents, there is no doubt that Zinchuk and Mikhailov were the only agents present, not CIA but KGB.

The Motts had another stop to make that morning. They wished to say hello to their friends the McShanes, owners of Lowdermilk's Book Store on Twelfth Street. Howard Mott could never remember the address so when they reached the receptionist's desk again, he asked if he could use the telephone directory. Strangely, the receptionist did not have a directory, and it took a bit of doing before one could be procured from upstairs. When it arrived Mikhailov did the honors, looking up the address of a store of his own choosing where he said books on Russia could be obtained. Howard Mott explained that this was not the idea, Lowdermilk's was the only shop in which they were interested.

On that note they took their leave of Soviet officialdom, but as they drove to the Twelfth Street address they became convinced that they were being followed not by one but by two cars, a Ford station wagon and, close behind it, a black sedan. Both vehicles arrived at Lowdermilk's with them, and as they pulled into a parking lot near the store the cars went on slowly past.

A short time later while visiting with their friends in an office alcove near the rear of the store, they became aware of a customer who appeared to be more interested in overhearing their conversation than in finding a book. When they moved away, his browsing became even more noticeable. A clerk approached him, and the man asked for a book that was not available. Even then he did not depart and the Motts and the McShanes moved to a back office where they could talk in private.

In retrospect, Howard and Phyllis Mott realized, keyed up as they were, that pursuing cars and a swarthy little man in a bookstore might well assume melodramatic connotations in the place of normal explanations. However, as they were to learn later, their suspicions were not at all exaggerated and were in keeping with Soviet practices.

The next morning, having spent the night with friends in McLean, Virginia, the Motts received a call from Carroll Woods. He did not offer good news. The word had come through that there was going to be a trial. He suggested that depositions be obtained attesting to Newcomb's good character; about forty would do.

The Motts bid a hasty farewell to their friends and headed back for Sheffield. On the way they stopped off in New Haven to get advice on the legal procedures to follow from Professor Leon Lipson, Yale's leading authority on Soviet law.

On Monday, November 1, Phyllis Mott wrote to Minister Counselor Zinchuk. In so doing, she purposely refrained from mentioning that she already knew there was going to be a trial.

November 1, 1965

Mr. Alexander Zinchuk
Embassy of the USSR
Washington 6, D.C.

Dear Mr. Zinchuk:

This letter is written to embody the statements put to you orally last Thursday in our talk with you at the Russian Embassy in Washington.

We still hope that the Soviet officials will recognize the fact that Newcomb's crossing the border was unintentional trespassing and quite harmless to anybody.

We understand that Newcomb could be tried on Article 83. We have no idea that we would enjoy any part of it but we are, quite naturally, anxious to attend if a trial should eventuate. If this does happen will you please notify us well in advance so that our applications for visas may be processed quickly?

We also request that Newcomb be paroled on the word of the American Embassy and be permitted to live in a hotel while awaiting trial (if there is a trial). If this courtesy is permitted we should like to go and stay at the same hotel all the time he is there.

We also understand that a representative of the American Embassy will be permitted to attend a trial of any American citizen.

It is rather ironic that on Friday, as members of the Grolier Club of New York City, we received an announcement of a three-week trip to Russia, an 18,000-mile trip, next spring—to visit various museums, libraries and view collections. We knew of the preliminary plans and hoped to be there at that time. We have been part of a group of eighty-one on other trips. However, $3600 for the two of us for three weeks is way beyond our pocketbooks if it is necessary to take a trip to Murmansk. We sincerely hope that it will be possible for us to give this invitation favorable consideration.

Thank you very much for giving your time to us and your consideration of this letter.

Very truly yours,

Phyllis Mott

For the next two weeks the Motts spent between eight and ten hours a day on the telephone, calling friends and explaining the ground rules to all those who had known their son and who they thought would have the ability to write the kind of character reference that would stand up in a Soviet court. It was a long, exhausting, and expensive exercise in futility. In that short space of time their telephone bill exceeded $225, and the combined efforts of all those who wrote in Newcomb's behalf had no bearing whatsoever on what followed.

November 8, 1965

TO WHOM IT MAY CONCERN:

I wish to submit for your consideration a character deposition for Mr. Newcomb Mott of Sheffield, Massachusetts, U.S.A.

Let me first introduce myself. I am Assistant Professor of Clinical Orthopaedic Surgery of the College of Physicians and Surgeons, Columbia University, New York City, and Attending Surgeon at the New York Orthopaedic and Presbyterian Hospitals at the Columbia-Presbyterian Medical Center in New York City. I am a Fellow of the American College of Surgeons and a member of its National Committee on Trauma. I am a Fellow of the American Association for the Surgery of Trauma and Secretary for this Association. My medical specialty is orthopaedic surgery and the surgery of trauma.

I have known Newcomb Mott for nineteen years, since I first operated on his mother in 1946 and became a professional as well as social friend of the family. At that time, Newcomb was approximately eight years of age. I have always been impressed with Newcomb's studiousness, industry and outstanding character.

In 1958, I operated on Mr. Newcomb Mott's knee for the removal of a loose body at the Presbyterian Hospital in New York City. During his hospital stay, he was on a large ward with many other patients and won the respect of the professional staff and his fellow patients for his consideration and thoughtfulness of them. I recall one specific instance which gave me further insight into his character. The patient in the bed next to him had had an operation for cancer. Newcomb Mott was aware of this and was always aware of the patient's grave prognosis. Following discharge from the hospi-

tal, Newcomb Mott returned for numerous visits to cheer up his new friend and, subsequently, corresponded with him after his discharge from the hospital. This act of compassion is indicative of Mr. Newcomb Mott's feeling toward his fellow man.

Mr. Newcomb Mott attended Antioch College which has a curriculum different from most colleges in the United States. The academic year is divided into periods of study and periods of work, the latter generally entailing considerable travel about the United States and to countries abroad.

Mr. Mott has traveled extensively and has maintained a great interest in the mores and culture of the peoples of other countries. This interest serves no purpose other than self-education and is put to no purpose other than the broadening of his personal knowledge of the world.

In summary, I should like to say that in the nineteen years I have known Newcomb Mott, I have been impressed by his forthrightness, self-honesty and the courage of his convictions to explore the opportunities of travel to satisfy his curiosity and enhance his knowledge of his fellow man in the world at large.

Sincerely yours,

Sawnie R. Gaston, M.D.

Chapter Seven

At 11:30 A.M., on Saturday October 30, Newcomb Mott and Bill Shinn met for the third time. Also present were Lt. Colonel Griposeyevich, Captain Androv, and Nina. Before the meeting Androv handed Shinn the prisoner's letter of October 2. Two weeks earlier he had informed the U. S. Vice Consul that this letter had been sent to the Foreign Ministry in Moscow for delivery to the U. S. Embassy. It had been just one more lie in a blizzard of prevarication.

But one thing the Russians had not lied about was their plan to bring the prisoner to trial. For at least a month they had been saying it, first to help stimulate an exchange for Ivanov, and then because they meant it. And for nearly the same period of time U.S. officials in Washington and Moscow had been telling the Russians they had no right to make such statements because they ran counter to Soviet law. However, by the time Newcomb Mott and Bill Shinn sat down together in Murmansk, such protests were recognized, although hardly admitted, as having been so much wind passing through the Kremlin rigging.

With another package of food and reading material but no letters, Shinn brought news that a defense attorney could be hired for about $300, plus expenses, and that the prisoner's parents wanted him to have the best lawyer available, no matter what the cost. Mott agreed and Shinn said he would contact the Embassy and the lawyer would come up to Murmansk as soon as possible; his name was Boris Zolotukhin. Actually the Embassy had tentatively retained Zolotukhin on the same day the Motts had visited the Soviet Embassy in Washington.

There are two bodies of lawyers organized under the Communist State in the Soviet Union. One handles civil cases and the other criminal. It was to the Chairman of this latter group, Samsanov, that the Embassy turned. Samsanov recommended Zolotukhin, a member of the legal consultation office in Moscow. In fact, by the time Samsanov was contacted he had *already* spoken to Zolotukhin about taking the case, and the lawyer had agreed and said he was willing to make the long hard trip to snowbound Murmansk where round-the-clock darkness was frigidly moving in.

Even Androv used the weather as an excuse to try and explain away Newcomb Mott's nervousness. The adverse climate affected people in different ways, he said. But Bill Shinn could see that his big fellow countryman had lost more weight, that he didn't look well, and that fifty-seven days of solitary confinement had a lot more to do with his condition than the grim weather—although no doubt the damp cold of his cell was a factor. Nevertheless, after admitting his growing sense of tension and his desire for some tranquilizers, Newcomb concentrated on other matters. He wished Shinn to thank Ambassador Foy Kohler and the Embassy staff for their efforts on his behalf. He requested that Shinn attend the trial, for in their brief encounters he had come to respect and like him. He also sent his love to his parents and asked how Rusty was, for he knew his brother had been planning to join the Navy.

Shinn broke the news that the prisoner's parents hoped to attend the trial. At first he protested. It would cost too much. There was nothing they could do. But after Shinn pointed out how anxious they were to see him, he understood their feelings and said they could come if they wanted to, but they must realize it would be a waste of time and money.

And now Griposeyevich put his oar into the conversation. He declared that although the preliminary investigation was over, whether or not there would be a trial depended on the decision of the court after the Procurator had made his own investigation, which could not be done until the indictment was handed to him! In view of the KGB's threats of a secret trial and the already noted statements made in Murmansk and Moscow that there was going to be a trial of some sort, this after-the-fact observation by the KGB interrogator was nothing less than weird.

Was it sarcasm? Was he trying to stretch the string of hope tighter? Or was it simply common Soviet gall announcing a return to following the form of law because now it was possible to do so?

There is no telling, and Bill Shinn didn't bother to ask. Instead, seeing the statement as something more subtle than the obvious, he took up the conversation with both KGB men, suggesting the possibility of release on the basis of mitigating circumstances. Now it was he and not Nina who did the translating for the prisoner. It was brought out that admitting you crossed a border does not mean that you intended to cross. Actually, the discussion was all a bag of words and as meaningless as Griposeyevich's earlier statement.

The interview was terminated at 1:30 P.M. Before it was over, Newcomb Mott asked if Shinn could inform him on the state of Van Nostrand's business. He also wanted his thanks sent to Francis Adams for everything he had been able to do. When Shinn asked him just how he felt, he referred to

John Keats's article on running away and said that the piece described his feelings perfectly. Later Embassy officials wondered if he meant he might be planning to try to escape. They decided the prisoner was being literal. Such deliberation hardly seemed necessary, for if they didn't know it, Newcomb Mott knew escape was impossible.

They took him back to the prison in a closed van. He had no watch but he estimated that it was only about a ten-minute journey. He had come to believe his cell was not on a regular floor of the prison. Although he was not allowed to mix with the other inmates, he caught occasional glimpses of them—shaved heads in the exercise yard, women marching by in the corridor at night, carrying mops. In his cell he had a new batch of reading material. He had his folk songs to sing, his memories, extra food. They could help fill the emptiness of time and the vacuum of isolation, but only on the trial he had to face could he attempt to fasten his badly stretched hopes. No longer could he attach them to his government's ability to extricate him. Instead, he must grapple them to the tender mercy of Soviet justice.

Upon receiving word that he had been retained, Boris Zolotukhin hit the trail north, flying directly to Murmansk. He arrived there on Tuesday morning, November 2.

Zolotukhin was a short, dark-complexioned, scholarly-looking man. With his horn-rimmed glasses and quiet manner of speaking, he appeared to be more the academic type than a trial lawyer. He had never defended an American before, and although he could speak some English, he professed not to be able to read it. No matter what his linguistic abilities, there can be no doubt that Nina, who was present as interpreter when attorney and client met, would have been on hand anyway.

It is not known where the meeting took place, possibly in the prison office of Captain Vilkov, possibly in the Procurator's office, but it is known that Newcomb Mott came away from the interview heartened. He had finally met a

Russian who represented the State and was going to work to get him set free. Quick to form an impression, and under the circumstances finely tuned to individual nuances, he was reassured by Zolotukhin's apparent sincerity and competence.

Later that day Bill Shinn, who had remained in Murmansk to meet Zolotukhin, got together with him at the Northern Hotel. Shinn had two suggestions to offer the Moscow lawyer on ways to secure Newcomb Mott's pretrial release. The first was on the personal pledge of the Embassy that the prisoner would be available for the trial when the date was fixed. This method had previously been used in the case of Peter Landerman, a young American who had accidentally killed a Russian while driving a car.

Zolotukhin said he would explore the possibility but this kind of motion was seldom granted in the Soviet Union.

The second suggestion was the oft-repeated one of bail. Then Shinn presented an Embassy innovation of sorts. Under Soviet law it is possible for a prisoner's fellow workers to file a petition with the court stating that the accused is basically a good fellow, and if the court will free him, the signers will take the responsibility for his rehabilitation. In Mott's behalf a petition from his friends in the United States could be submitted on the same basis.

The idea took Zolotukhin by surprise. The presentation of a petition, he said, was only used in a Socialist state. It had never occurred to him that such a legal devise might be attempted by someone from a foreign state. Nevertheless he promised to give the idea some thought.

They then discussed the element of "direct intent" and various Soviet commentaries and legal opinions of the interpretation of Article 83. Under the Article the Procurator had to prove that the accused had desired to cross the border.

Shinn next brought up the possibility of a "conditional sentence" under Article 44 of the RSFSR Criminal Code. Zolotukhin agreed this, too, was a point of consideration, but as he saw the case now he would base his defense on mitigating circumstances. He planned to stay on in Murmansk and review all the material connected with the case. Upon his return to Moscow he would be in touch.

Shinn, who on his October 15 journey to Murmansk had been snowbound for five days, headed back to Moscow to report to his superiors.

Four days later, on November 6, Zolotukhin returned and gave his evaluation of the case. In his opinion there was enough evidence to prove that Newcomb Mott had violated Article 83, as charged, and had knowingly crossed the Soviet frontier. Zolotukhin also believed there was enough evidence to prove direct intent. The court, he reported, had rejected both the suggestion of a conditional release and the posting of bail.

He felt there was still the possibility of a suspended sentence, but as to the handling of the case he did not believe the idea of presenting a petition was a good one since Article 44 was related only to social organizations in the Soviet Union. Instead, the character references that were being obtained would be helpful. These should stress Newcomb Mott's character, work habits, and absence of a previous criminal record. As Zolotukhin had originally decided, he was going to base his defense on mitigating circumstances and ask that the prisoner be released and sent home. No date had been set for the trial but he expected to talk with his client again before it took place. Since Newcomb Mott's term of confinement had been extended to December 4 by order of the Murmansk Procurator's Office, most probably the court would convene sometime within the month.

Whether Boris Zolotukhin was simply going through the motions as a lawyer for the defense under higher orders or whether his efforts were genuinely sincere cannot be stated with certainty. Surface evidence would indicate the latter is true, and that those in higher places who had already determined the outcome of the trial to follow would have wanted Zolotukhin to do his best for the prisoner unencumbered by prior knowledge of the verdict. It would look better in the court, and it would look better to the world. That Zolotukhin did not present telling evidence that was available to support his defense of Newcomb Mott on the plea of mitigating circumstances will be explored in another chapter, but more important than what was to come was what had been accepted by both State Department and U. S. Embassy officials handling the case.

Knowing that a trial was inevitable, they had concentrated their efforts on gaining Newcomb Mott's freedom through bail or a conditional release based on a gaggle of Soviet legal mandates. In this they attained the same degree of success they had obtained in earlier efforts to bring the outright release of the prisoner. Now that these avenues of approach had all been closed one after the other, they remained "optimistic" over the hope for a suspended sentence.

On November 10, the Embassy received word that Howard and Phyllis Mott had applied for visas to come to the Soviet Union. If the applications were granted, they wished to have a two-day consultation with the pertaining Embassy officers.

Three days later Oberenko informed the Embassy that the Motts would be allowed to attend the trial and that an Embassy representative could also be present.

On November 15, Zolotukhin called Shinn and announced that the trial date had been set for November 22.

In his cell Newcomb Mott paced his nine paces, beat his arms against the cold, and believed his ordeal was coming to an end.

Upon reaching Holland on their return from the Soviet Union, Phyllis Mott wrote for her friends an account of the journey she and her husband had taken in order to be present at their son's trial. A portion of her account follows.

Chapter Eight

The usual tourist to Russia is shepherded by an Intourist guide (part of the USSR information line) taken on tours, shown the most attractive sights, generally treated with deference (this because of the desire for American dollars), and goes home thinking this can't be too bad a society. In actuality he has seen nothing at all—only what it is deemed advisable for him to see. Up until now neither one of us could believe that people aren't the same the world over and that the differences were only minor ones. The KGB has such power that it is completely incomprehensible to the people on the other side of the Iron Curtain. The Foreign Ministry gets the play in the papers but that is not where the power lies.

You, of course, know the marvelous treatment we were given by SAS and the N. Y. Police Department—arranged by Boxie and Frank Adams. Two of the detectives accompanied us to our seats on the plane. The plane was nearly full but we were given two seats by ourselves.

In Copenhagen, after a very smooth flight, we were

greeted by an SAS representative—told that a car was at our disposal—a hotel room hired for us—lunch—and a taxi back to the airport. Howie was not in the mood to sleep so took the car to the Boghallen, where he saw our friend Ole Dam. I went to bed and slept for two and a half hours. Ole returned to the hotel and had lunch with us.

At the airport we were again taken in tow by an SAS agent and passports, etc. facilitated. Upon arriving in Transit we were given a taste of what was going to follow. Three reporters had somehow, by showing their passports, managed to get into the Transit Hall and were waiting, with a photographer, for us. We underwent a grueling cross-examination—each one trying to twist our words for an unfavorable report on Newcomb and what the State Department was or had been doing. One of them even tried to involve Van Nostrand by saying that there had been talk of irregularities in their salesmen in Denmark—this, of course, also to discredit Newcomb—Howie insisted on getting his card. After arriving in Moscow we learned that actually the article in the Danish newspaper had been a very nice one.

At four we took Airflote to Moscow. This was quite an experience—the Russian pilots take off, land, and fly in great swoops. The pressure is put on in the cabins all at once and your eardrums feel as though they had 100 pounds pressure.

At 8:30 P.M. Moscow time we were met at the airport by William Shinn—the man in the Consular Section who had been handling New's case from the beginning. Then began the waiting in line, which is a constant thing in Russia. No one else was required to do more than open a bag, but it took us one and a half hours to get through Customs as they insisted on our listing every piece of jewelry—gold, silver, stones, etc., telling us that if we didn't we wouldn't be allowed to leave Russia when the time came. At that point I couldn't find my small jewelry box and every blasted thing in my large suitcase had to be taken out and repacked—even had to look through dresses to make sure I had missed nothing. Poor Mr. Shinn showed great stamina then and as he did throughout—most days he worked at least sixteen hours on our behalf.

An Embassy car was waiting and drove all of us to the Ukraine Hotel. A monster hotel with hundreds of people milling around in the lobby—rather grubby and dirty and with sullen help, which is customary. In the lobby we met John and Eileen Slocum and their daughter Margie. We had had lunch with John in Washington about ten days before, but had not expected he would still be in Moscow when we arrived. They were to go out to dinner but gave this up to come to our room and talk to us and Bill Shinn for about two hours. As you know, John was Deputy Director of USIA. UPI and the CBS man were at the desk when we came in—wanted an interview but we were just too exhausted—Bill ran interference for us as he did through the ten days. In the room there were two more calls from reporters.

Thursday, the eighteenth, Bill called for us at 9:00 A.M.; stood one hour in line for money and Intourist tickets. From ten until two we were at the Embassy. There we had meetings with Mr. Armitage and Mr. Boster, Mr. Anderson and a Mr. Kupiac, who was in Russia on U.S. passport business. Poor man, the Embassy was so taken up with our affairs that he spent much time just waiting. We had lunch at the Embassy. From two until four we had an interview with Newcomb's lawyer, Boris Zolotukhin—Bill, who speaks fluent Russian, doing the interpreting. Zolotukhin understands a little English but is afraid to attempt it very much. We were very impressed with him—an attractive personality and gives the impression of being very capable. We also had the feeling that he would do his very best for Newcomb, and we think he did. He left for Murmansk that night, arriving well before we did as foreigners are not allowed to fly direct but must go to Arkangel first.

At four we were interviewed by twenty members of the American press. This was set up for us as a matter of consideration by the press so we wouldn't have to give individual interviews. After that, pictures were taken in front of the American Embassy seal outside the Embassy. All of this took one hour. The commissary was supposed to be closed but the nice West German boy in charge opened it especially for us so we could select various things to pack in a box for Newcomb. After that the librarian, who was also supposed to be off duty, stayed and helped us select any books, magazines, and papers we wanted for Newcomb. Another hour was spent there selecting and packing materials from the Embassy and what we had brought from home.

Back to the hotel for an hour (at all times we were driven by an Embassy driver or, if by taxi, with Bill along). The Shinns had asked us to their apartment for dinner, which was a great relief to us as the curiosity shown in us was incredible, and everywhere we went in the hotel or street, people even walked backward to look at us. (This all over Russia.) We were fortunate to get a ride after dinner to the hotel from the Embassy with a Mr. Moyens, as taxi drivers will not pick you up if they have filled their quota for the day. In fact, Bill called out to one, and he shouted in Russian, "Go to hell!" No matter how many fares they pick up, the drivers get the same salary. Tipping theoretically is not allowed, but most of them are not above it if no one is watching them, also other help.

On Friday the nineteenth we were up at 6:00 A.M. Bill and taxi were late as the taxi got the wrong address (S.O.P.) and Bill had to walk blocks to find him. Incidentally, the Shinns' apartment, which is in a modern building, about six years old, is kept in the usual disrepair and the halls remind one of slums in N.Y.C. We are told that this building is a paradise compared to some others. We drove to the Embassy to leave two of our bags for storage and pick up the boxes for Newcomb and any mail that might have arrived by pouch. Drove to the airport, which takes about fifty minutes.

We feared that the weather was going to delay us, but although there was frost on the plane we took off nearly on time on the first leg of our flight to Murmansk. The flight to Arkangel took only one and three quarters hours. Flew over the White Sea with one of the most gorgeous sunsets we have ever seen—this just a little after 1:00 P.M.—interminable brilliant orange streaks over a blue-black sea. Our plane was twin engine with seat belts that were made for appearance only.

In Arkangel Airport, which is very similar to that at Goose Bay (just tundra), we were obliged to carry all our bags to the taxi, as the taxi driver refused to drive to the entrance to pick us up. We loaded our own bags as the driver refused to be occupied with such mundane matters. We rode with heavy bags on our laps; only one door could be opened! The driver also stood by while we unloaded at the hotel. To call this place a hotel is one of the overstatements of the year. The desk clerks wear heavy coats, boots, and head scarves all the time. The temperature outside (it was snowing) was bitterly cold.

We arrived at this hotel because when Bill inquired about our tickets to Murmansk he discovered that our tickets had been canceled and there were no seats for us. He spent a good bit of time at the Airflote office, but to no avail, and we were told that we could have a room for the night which would be ready at 5:00 P.M. One room for the three of us—with this kind of intimacy you now know why we call Mr. Shinn "Bill." Under such conditions one quickly reaches an informal basis with even an Embassy official. Actually, it wasn't only that—we became extremely fond of Bill. He has an extraordinarily high IQ, personality, devotion to duty, quiet efficiency, and a charming person to boot. He left absolutely nothing undone and even when seemingly relaxed was watchful of the people and surroundings. Since he has been a student in Russia as well as on a tour of duty in the USSR, he seems to have a terrific insight into the Russian mind, and his fluent Russian is a great asset. We have the greatest confidence in him, and it became obvious that Newcomb does also.

Although there was an Intourist guide at the hotel they refused to take our Intourist coupons. We had hoped to get to Murmansk that night so we could see Newcomb. In the meantime we learned that the Procurator at Murmansk had ruled that Newcomb would be held incommunicado in jail until December 4, and that we would not be allowed to talk with him before the trial—also that the tranquilizers he had asked for were refused him as they wanted him as nervous as possible. Phone calls back and forth to Moscow were going on constantly and I won't go into those except to say that to get through often takes an hour, or more.

After lunch we walked around Arkangel—a dismal city with just a very few houses (log and gingerbread decoration) left over from the Revolution and the German devastation of the city. Went into some of the department stores which look like the worst country emporium you can imagine—long queues waiting for cheap-looking but very expensive merchandise. There are no manners either in the country or the cities and the pushing and shoving is unbelievable. The cruelty of the Russians to each other is also unbelievable—the lame, the old, the drunks, all get the same inconsiderate treatment.

The latter are often given rabbit punches and knocked to the ground. There is so much drunkenness that it would be hard for you to visualize. These people have nothing much to live for, and they drown their sorrows in vodka and beer and Cognac. However, it is never a gay drunkenness—it is a drunkenness to forget—very somber and drinking to stupefaction. The hotels have brute bouncers and often one meets two or three drunks falling down stairs in a stupor. The police pick them up and they are thrown into jail . . . what their treatment there is can only be imagined. One sees this less in Moscow, as Americans go only to a few hotels, but we were in areas that normally are not open to tourists. We understand that any place fifty miles or more from Moscow all of this is true (or from other tourist cities).

After this short walk—necessarily short because of the biting cold, we spent three hours in an upstairs lounge. Bill was busy with Embassy affairs and airline tickets trying to insure our flight for the next day. We both slept. It was here that we had our first experience of kindness. Howie slept before I did, and although my eyes were closed I was not asleep—when I suddenly realized that all noise had stopped (this is very unusual, as most people seem to talk at the top of their lungs). The little old woman at the desk was shushing everyone who came by—just so we could sleep. By this time, of course, our being there had been broadcast to everyone—and the reason. At lunch, Bill finally had to explain to the Intourist guide exactly why it was essential that we get on the plane to Murmansk. Unfortunately, I awakened crying and when the Intourist guide took us to our room she was very insistent about my sadness.

We knew that Bill had told her the circumstances so I asked, "Didn't Mr. Shinn tell you?" Whereupon she lied and said no. She wanted to see if our stories matched. Tried to trap me into saying New was either a Navy or Army officer. The techniques are sometimes so obvious and sometimes so damned subtle. She wasn't a particularly smart operator, but the one in Murmansk was a dilly.

The story the airline office gave Bill was that they had had two wires—one reserving three seats and one canceling; the latter purportedly from the Embassy—another lie. Bill was absolutely furious—the only time we ever saw him tearing mad. The rest of the time he was under perfect control even though seething underneath.

Our room turned out to be two connecting rooms—no door, the bath in our bedroom, and a small cot for Bill who is almost as tall as Newcomb.

Fortunately we were able to keep busy that night as a Ukrainian chorus was in town. Aside from singing some damned Party song at the beginning, they were excellent. Even sang *Ave Maria,* which surprised us. As usual, our taxi didn't show up—walked and finally took a streetcar. Most of the hotels have a very loud orchestra of sorts in the evening. We went in to listen and have a beer. A Russian Naval officer sat at our table, bought us beer, and gave us a toast in English: "May there be peace between all nations." This was the extent of his English. The whole place filled with sailors and officers. It soon became evident that Bill wanted us out of there so we all left.

On Saturday our tickets came through for Murmansk—and news of the important forthcoming wire from Mr. Guthrie transmitting the information from the Norwegian officials giving dates and names of other violators of the border at Boris Gleb.

At 3:00 P.M. we finally got on the plane to Murmansk (the twin-engine plane and sunset I mentioned earlier were here—not from Moscow). This was a two-and-a-half-hour flight. It was, of course, dark when we arrived, as here the sun never really shines at this time of year—headlights are on until 11:00 A.M. and at 2:30 P.M. it is dark again. Snows every day and it is bitter cold.

At the airport an Intourist guide, Ludmilla, met us with a taxi and went with us on the forty-minute drive into the city of Murmansk, a city of about 250,000. The trees were covered with frost and it looked like fairyland. This is the only attractive thing about the whole place.

We were given a two-room suite with a bath, Bill a single room, and his bath was on the next floor above. Shortly after dinner Henry Bradsher, head of the AP Bureau in Moscow, and Aline Mosby from UPI arrived. Through the usual foul-up they had been given a room together. Bill and Henry moved in together, and Aline took Bill's room. Our bath was used as a community bath. Our hotel had no dining room so we had to walk to another hotel, about five minutes away, for meals. Sailors, bouncers, loud music, and poor service. We discovered that Zolotukhin was already there, as he was allowed to take the direct airline, and that he had seen Newcomb for a short time. He visited us and said that he had told Newcomb we were there, which he felt gave New a good bit of encouragement. Bill tried again for us to see Newcomb but no luck.

When we returned to our hotel, we found a Tass reporter and Novosti photographer wanting to take our pictures. We refused. Only two American reporters were allowed at the trial and no photographers except Novosti—a Russian outfit who sells their photos to all services and *Life*—this to provide dollars to the USSR.

All of us were exhausted and nervous and went to bed early, trying to prepare ourselves for the next day—this after UPI and AP had obtained statements from us. We have a great deal of respect for both of them and feel that Newcomb and we were very fortunate to have them there. At one point word had been given that only one American reporter would be allowed. They rode the thirty-one-hour train in order to be there.

The twenty-second—the first day of the trial, if it can be dignified by the word "trial," the court opened at 10:00 A.M. At five minutes of ten the five of us walked in, having been put in a special room beforehand. After the judge and the two People's Assessors walked in and sat in the three high-backed chairs in the front, Newcomb was led in and taken to the prisoner's box by three prison guards. He gave a quick look around and saw us two benches away. He smiled but could say nothing—neither could we. That boy stood with courage and dignity in that box for five and a half hours that first day.

Mr. William Shinn
American Consul
Severnaya Hotel
Murmansk

I understand from your telephone conversation with the Embassy tonight that a statement has been made to the court in the trial of Newcomb Mott that there have not been any previous cases of illegal border crossing at Borisoglebsk by foreigners. Please advise Mr. Zolotukhin, Mr. Mott's attorney, and request that he inform the court that this statement is not in accord with information received by the United States' Department of State from Norwegian authorities that on July 29, 1964, Otto Wolfgang Wiegandt, a German national, was arrested in the Borisoglebsk area by Soviet authorities for illegal border crossing and on August 12, 1964 was released to the Norwegian authorities; and that in 1947 Louis Tarleton, a United States citizen, was arrested in Borisoglebsk by the Soviet authorities for illegal border crossing, was imprisoned for four weeks in Murmansk, and then was released to the Norwegian authorities. In addition, the Department of State understands from Norwegian authorities that in 1947 three French and one Swiss citizen crossed the border at Pasvik, were held five days by the Soviet authorities, and then released to Norway; and in 1962 a Finnish citizen crossed the border at Pasvik, was held four weeks by the Soviet authorities, and then released to Norway where he was fined 400 kroner.

John C. Guthrie
Chargé d'Affairs ad Interim
American Embassy

Chapter Nine

The courtroom's décor was a chill off-white, its furnishings hard functional benches, chairs, and tables. The overhead lights remained on throughout the proceedings. Two large windows made up most of the right-hand wall. One, its drapes pulled back, looked out on a walled play yard, for ironically enough, the basement of the yellow two-story court housed a kindergarten. During the day the voices of children sifted up from below and at recess time their laughter and shouts from the playground supplied faint but shrill dissonance to the deliberations of their ridiculous elders.

Because the conclusion of the trial was already known to those who had staged it, its development was in the nature of a scenario to Phyllis and Howard Mott, who, although they did not realize it at the time, were important stage props. Their presence was needed to indicate the authenticity and humaneness of Soviet justice. Other stage props, to supplement the effect and provide proof of public interest, were approximately fifteen old men and women who sat stolidly on the back benches. By the second day their number had dwindled somewhat. In front of them were several Russian newsmen, two from Moscow and one a local reporter. With the Motts and Bill Shinn were Aline Mosby and Henry Bradsher.

As to the principals, the judge, G. I. Klementev, president of the Criminal Collegium of Murmansk Oblast, sat stage center, hunched and introspective in his high-backed chair. He was flanked on his right by a heavy-set woman who spoke no word and gave no sign of being present throughout the three acts. To the judge's left was ensconced a tall man with a shaven head. The woman was a schoolteacher, the man an engineer. They are listed in the cast as "two People's Assessors," nameless.

The Procurator, Stepan Lebedyuk, squat with thick horn-rimmed glasses, wore a kind of priestly garb of the Soviet order. He had lost his right arm at the siege of Leningrad, and in both appearance and manner he complemented the oppressive cold of the setting. He sat center stage, left, facing the dock where they had placed the prisoner, and at his side, down stage, were two more women, designated as court stenographers.

The remainder of the cast, aside from three prison guards who took turns making sure the defendant would not escape, were Boris Zolotukhin, Nina Kulikova, and a Moscow interpreter, one Vladimir Alekseyev. The three were seated in a line, stage right, Zolotukhin with his back to the dock. He and Nina have already been described, but Alekseyev, who was placed down stage closest to the judge's bench, deserves comment. He was dark, about thirty, wore glasses, and was dressed in an English-cut suit with shoes not made in Russia. He spoke English like an American, because he had gone to college in the U.S.A. What college and when are not known. He had been dispatched by an unnamed Soviet agency to participate in the drama as an interpreter for the judge, the assessors, and the Procurator, while Nina, placed to his right, had been selected to act as interpreter between the prisoner and his attorney.

The prisoner, of course, was the principal character. Newcomb Mott stood tall and pale in the dock. To his parents, he seemed thin. Since they had seen him last he had lost forty or so pounds. The suit he wore had been made in the prison, his shirt of Red Chinese manufacture—both gifts of the KGB for which the Motts would later be billed. Phyllis Mott had greeted her son with a smile and a finger signal for good luck. He had smiled his greeting in return, and when possible he looked toward his parents, reassuring and reassured.

As the curtain rose only Phyllis Mott wore an overcoat against the chill. This, too, could be appraised as an example of Soviet graciousness, for it is a custom and a rule in Soviet public buildings for everyone to check his or her coat in a cloakroom because of a continuing problem with lice.

Actually it was not Judge G. I. Klementev who had the opening line, but a clerk who had preceded him and his two helpers into the room and had shouted at the assembled to "Stand up!"

The order obeyed, the clerk went swiftly off stage and there remained until the first recess, whereupon he reappeared and spoke the same words with the same feeling. From there on, those in the court waited for him as they would the striking of a gong to announce the entrances and exits of Authority.

The court convened and the judge addressed the defendant, asking him to verify that he had received a copy of the indictment against him, and being so assured, he proceeded to the reading of the charge.

Although the meat of it was simple enough—American citizen Newcomb Mott was accused of having violated Article 83 of the Criminal Code of the RSFSR—there was an additional point that demanded clarification and none was ever forthcoming. Reference was made to it in an earlier chapter and it was included in the body of the indictment. Newcomb Mott was said to have entered the Soviet Union at the 212th border marker, first having broken a wire fence and then crossing an eight-meter strip of cleared land. He then *had supposedly intruded two thirds of a mile into Soviet territory*. Since he reached the Norwegian reindeer fence at no later than 8:30 A.M. and it was not until two hours later that he had come out of the brush at Boris Gleb, where was he in the long interim? With the border so poorly defined there is no telling, but Newcomb Mott certainly covered a great deal more than two thirds of a mile in two hours of wandering. Emphasis on this point would have helped to show just how "hot and tired and lost" he really was. But the point was ignored.

One part of the indictment, however, did raise a strong objection. Included in the charges was a purported letter sent to the Murmansk Procurator under the signature of Kirkenese Border Commissioner Keilland Rygg. The letter had supposedly been written by Deputy Border Commissioner Lt. Colonel Odd Stube Aune to Colonel Gravrilko, the Soviet Border Commissioner. It was dated September 7, 1965, and its most damning statement was that "He [Newcomb Mott] was fully aware that he could not cross over on the usual passport because his attention had been drawn to this fact by Norwegian officials."

The Norwegian Government and press took exception to the statement for the very good reason that it wasn't true. The Norwegian Parliament asked the Norwegian Foreign Ministry to clarify the matter and this was done by explaining that Lt. Colonel Aune's letter had been mistranslated by the Soviets. None of it made any difference, however. Norway was a third party to the matter and its findings were not noted until the play was over.

The judge concluded the reading of the indictment which made three points: (1) Newcomb Mott had intended from the beginning of his visit to Kirkenes to visit Boris Gleb.

(2) He knew he could not do so legally. (3) Therefore he attempted to do so illegally and by doing so intentionally violated Article 83 of the RSFSR Criminal Code.

When the reading had been completed and translated, the prisoner was asked to comment. Unlike the rest of the cast, he was required to stand when he spoke.

Mott: "I did not use force to climb through the reindeer fence, and—"

Judge (interrupting): "You may reserve your comments for later testimony. Do you admit crossing the border?"

Mott: "Of course, this is true. But I did not intend to violate Soviet law."

This response concluded the first scene, and while the court stood in recess for fifteen minutes the Soviet correspondents were able to file stories that Newcomb Mott had pleaded guilty to the charge.

The production resumed with the judge instructing the prisoner in his rights. Klementev intoned a comfortable liturgy, telling Newcomb Mott that he could object to the participation of any of those assembled at the trial, he could submit an explanation of his actions to the court, he could cross-examine witnesses, submit petitions in his own behalf, make a final statement, and appeal the verdict.

The prisoner in return had two requests, that he be allowed to use notes and tell his story right through without interruption. The requests were granted and Phyllis Mott observed: "The judge gave him permission to use notes and confer with Zolotukhin and his interpreter when necessary. This encouraged all of us as this is not usually done in a Russian court. We, of course, later learned that this was just trimming in order to give the appearance of a fair trial."

One could say it was not so much the "suiting of the action to the word" as it was the suiting of the word to an unalterable conclusion.

One additional observation was made by the judge. Boris Gleb Border Guard Ivan D. Rubenenko was unable to be present due to an appendectomy. Were there any objections to the trial continuing without him? There was none.

Little detail or emphasis was given in the American press to the manner and quality of Newcomb Mott's defense. This was no play, no charade for him. What he said came from the heart and mind of himself. No one had informed him that the reality of his role was based on an illusion. Later much was written to give the impression that by nature he was a nervous, high-strung person. It was never so, and it was not so even after eleven weeks of solitary confinement, mental torture, and Soviet conditioning.

To have exhibited no symptoms of strain would have made him something less than human, but little of it came through as he carefully told the story of his life and the events of the fateful few days that had led him to the prisoner's dock. Correspondent Mosby in her description of the trial made note that Newcomb Mott chuckled occasionally. Neither she nor anyone else in the courtroom besides his parents understood that this was a symptom of the pressure under which he delivered his defense. Once his mother laughed at a statement he made. The judge, not at all amused, gaveled for silence. It was her error, the judge's misinterpretation. She only wished to indicate her support of a son fighting for his freedom.

In recounting the events of his life, he told of his interests in history and how he had majored in the subject at Antioch College. In doing so he pointed out that he had read a great deal about Russia and its creative people. He mentioned composers Prokofiev and Shostakovich, told how he had hoped to go to Leningrad and was particularly interested in seeing its famous museum, the Hermitage. On the political level he was familiar with the writings of Marx and Lenin.

He described his background with meticulous care and explained Antioch's on-the-job training program in which he had participated. Under the program he had worked as a handy man at a resort, the inn on Cabbage Key in Florida;

spent a summer assisting a forest ranger in the Berkshires; served as a copy boy on the Toledo *Blade;* traveled in Mexico; aided his father in the rare-book business; learned U. S. Government firsthand as a copy boy in the press gallery of the House of Representatives; taught elementary school. In all of these endeavors he had been given top rating by his employers, some of whom wanted him to return on a permanent basis. After graduation he had taught a year of private school and then gone into the business of selling college textbooks, first for Macmillan and then D. Van Nostrand. His ambition at age twenty-seven was to become an editor.

He turned next to the explanation of how he had come to Boris Gleb. It was an explanation he had given many times. But when he said that one of his reasons for seeking out the border control point was to get his passport stamped, Zolotukhin interrupted and introduced the passport as evidence, reading off the visa stamps of twenty-one countries visited.

Judge Klementev then asked if Americans were allowed to keep their passports. And in assuring him that they were, Newcomb Mott also stressed that he had had no idea there was a penalty for crossing a border where none appeared to exist. In declaring once again that he had no idea that he had violated Soviet law, he recounted the events leading up to the act in clear, chronological detail.

When he reached the portion of his story that dealt with events occurring after his arrest, he made mention of the KGB. The translation of his words caused the Russian portion of the cast to gulp. There was a moment of uncomfortable silence, and the prisoner asked, "Oh, is that something I'm not supposed to say?"

He was told to continue, and twice more he brought up the KGB, the second time to state that he had been asked by the investigator to send a clipping of the case from the New York *Times* once he got home. Here Judge Klementev snapped that it was not necessary to make such references.

At times the defendant spoke very rapidly, and once he stopped himself and said to Alekseyev, "Did you get that?" and Alekseyev replied curtly, "I got that," and Newcomb Mott chuckled.

Aside from the story of his life, his travels, his job, and the details of his capture, there were some things he said with a simple eloquence that added their own warmth to a very cold scene.

Mott (explaining how prison life had taught him something about himself, quoting from John Keats's article on escaping): "No matter how much we share with all mankind, each of us is totally alone . . . and the ultimate destination of every traveler is always himself."

He concluded his defense by once again repeating his apology to the Soviet Government and his own for having caused so much trouble.

Mott: "Everyone at the prison wished me good luck in court, even the chief investigator. . . . They hope I'd be set free, and this is what I hope also."

As the court recessed and the prisoner was led out by his three guards, Bill Shinn managed to say, "Good work."

And now Judge Klementev began his cross-examination of a defense which had taken two and a half hours to deliver. It was as though Newcomb Mott had never spoken, had never told his story. All the questions centered on points for which he had already supplied detailed answers.

Judge: "You have admitted that officials in Kirkenes told you you could not visit Boris Gleb without a visa. Why with this information did you try to go to the border?"

Mott: "I did not think that the desk clerks spoke officially, and others had told me I could go."

Judge: "Why didn't you stop and ask for directions?"

Mott: "The only place I saw had a 'Forbidden' sign in front of it."

Judge: "How did you know this?"

Mott: "I knew this because the word was the same as it is in Swedish."

Judge: "Why did you want to visit Russia?"

Mott: "To get a stamp on my passport, to buy souvenirs, presents for my parents. I wanted to have a look behind the Iron Curtain."

Judge (in an aside to the engineer assessor): "Some Iron Curtain, a reindeer fence!"

The engineer, having been brought into the act, took this as his cue and dispatched a query on his own: "Why did you not ask Norwegian officials before you started for Borisoglebsk?"

Mott: "The thought never occurred to me. I expected to ask my questions at the Customs point."

Now Procurator Lebedyuk sallied forth with opening lines full of negatives. "I do not accept Mr. Mott's explanation that the hotel clerks had not convinced him that he was not permitted to cross the border without a visa. Hotel clerks are responsible for advising tourists."

Mott: "At the time I didn't know how good their advice was."

The engineer continued the cross-examination, and like the judge's, his questions had already been answered by the defendant.

Following the cross-examination and an hour's intermission, three witnesses were called, making their entrances and exits one at a time.

Border Guard Andrei Rogov led off. A small, dark, unobtrusive soldier with quick-darting eyes, he recounted his meeting with the prisoner on the morning of September 4. He told only one lie.

Judge: "Did you request the defendant's documents before they were presented?"

Rogov: "Yes, I did."

The statement went unchallenged.

Victoria Kochimalkin took the stand next. She was ill at

ease, displeased with her role. She could not bring herself to look at Newcomb Mott, but she testified in his behalf as best she could.

Judge: "Did he seem pleased to see you?"

Vicki: "Yes, he seemed pleased to see people."

Judge: "Did he show you his documents or did you ask for them?"

Vicki: "He had his passport in his hand, and he gave it to me."

Judge: "Did he seem tired or hot to you?"

Vicki: "Yes, he did. I noticed his feet were wet. He was walking toward us when the guard signaled for him to come."

Her testimony was brief and tense, and she was relieved to make her exit. Later the Motts heard from Shinn that Ludmilla had informed him that Vicki had come to their hotel and left a message saying she was sorry about Newcomb, but when Howard Mott questioned Ludmilla about it, she refused to answer.

Border Guard Viktor Ribekin had close-cropped blond hair, square chin, strong hands, and a bad case of jitters. The Motts thought of him as the dogman not because of his looks but because of his part in the affair. His testimony got off to a ragged start.

Judge (to Ribekin): "Do you know the prisoner?"

Ribekin: "Yes."

Judge (to Mott): "Do you know this man?"

Mott: "I never saw him before in my life."

The judge's expression was one of consternation. Ribekin managed to backwater fast, retracting his original assertion, explaining he had been given a piece of paper from Newcomb Mott's notebook, and with this and his tracking dogs he claimed to have retraced the intruder's footsteps to the border. Ribekin's legs began to shake and they did not stop, the trembling setting up a steady ripple in the legs of his uniform pants. When his hands also began to shake, he put them behind his back and kept them tightly clasped. It was on the basis of his findings that it was determined when, where, how far, and how long Newcomb Mott had violated the Soviet border.

Ribekin: "I began my investigation at ten-thirty. Two hours later I checked the reindeer fence and found a break near the 212th marker. I saw a couple on the Norwegian side picking berries."

Engineer: "Was the break in the fence new?"

Ribekin: "I couldn't tell, it was on the Norwegian side."

Mott: "Could the break in the fence have been an old one?"

Ribekin: "Yes, it could."

Engineer: "Could you see Borisoglebsk from the 212th marker?"

Ribekin: "Yes."

It was a damning statement. The credibility of the witness was further illustrated in a more sensitive area.

Judge: "Were there any previous violations of the border?"

Ribekin: "No. The tourist compound was just opened in the past year."

Judge: "Could anyone cross the border and get back unseen?"

Ribekin (his voice shaking like his pants legs): "The border is carefully guarded. There is no illegal crossing. It is well marked. There is a cleared strip, and a sign in Norwegian. . . . It is not possible to cross accidentally."

Engineer: "If the border is so well guarded, how did Mr. Mott get across without being seen?"

Ribekin: "The . . . the border is scanned every five to eight minutes. He . . . he just slipped through."

Engineer: "How long have you been working in the Borisoglebsk area?"

Ribekin: "Since 1959."

Engineer: "Were there any violations before the tourist compound was open?"

Ribekin: "No, none. There have been no previous violations."

On that false note the court stood adjourned, and the first act was ended. It was 6:30 P.M. Phyllis and Howard Mott were not too disheartened. The engineer assessor appeared to be objective and straight, the judge not overly hostile. They considered that their son had done an excellent job in his own defense. As they left the court they caught a glimpse of him being led away by his guards. He wore a handsome Russian coat with a beaver collar and a fur hat. Leaving the building, he turned and called back, "Good night, Mother."

That evening marked the end of the Motts' first five days in the USSR. In that short span of time they had observed Soviet life as few American tourists have seen it.

Their two-room suite in Murmansk's best hotel boasted the only private bathroom on the entire floor. They shared it with Bill Shinn and the two correspondents. They also shared the accommodations with a horde of black bugs and cockroaches. The hotel was only five years old, but the restaurant portion of it had collapsed, and this made it necessary to eat at the Articia Hotel.

The Dollar Store, though a center of attraction for window-shopping Russians, offered poorly displayed cheap goods that could be bought with American dollars or British pounds.

In the morning they awoke to the sound of scraping shovels, and from their second-floor window they could see women of Murmansk removing the ice from the street while trucks driven by men came behind plucking up the fruits of their labor.

They saw a great deal of drunkenness, and once when they were starting up to their rooms two sodden sailors came rolling down the long curving staircase, nearly sweeping them along in the wreckage.

There was no service to speak of. The waitress in the restaurant refused to bring a second cup of so-called coffee because she had already made out the bill. Except for one instance the hotel people were rude and hostile. Only the woman who acted as the second-floor concierge was kind. She sewed a button on Howard Mott's coat and refused to accept any kind of gratuity.

The Motts' Intourist guide, Ludmilla, was a raven-eyed escort whose seeming interest in her charges and their son's case was as thin as the Murmansk sunshine. On one occasion Bill Shinn could not join the Motts for lunch, and he specifically asked Ludmilla to be present to do the ordering. She failed to show up until long after the meal was over, pleading the press of business when her only business was the Motts.

Through it all, the bitter cold, the long hours of darkness which ended about 10 A.M. and began again at 2:30 P.M., the sullen aura of the people who stared, who mocked, who grunted negatively at polite requests, Phyllis Mott had maintained her composure. In court she had not cried; in court she would not cry; but that night after the first day of the trial, as she put it, "I blew my top!"

Actually, it was Aline Mosby who unwittingly triggered the outburst. In trying to say something helpful she remarked fatuously that tragedy had a way of enriching one's experience. In her outburst which took place as she sat trying to play solitaire in the hotel room, Phyllis Mott bitterly damned the lying of the border guards, particularly Ribekin. Later she and her husband and Bill Shinn came to believe her outcry had a significant bearing on a change that took place in act two of the trial and also proved that their suite was bugged not only by insects.

When the court convened at ten the next morning for the second act, Alexander Mironichev, chief of the border patrol, took the stand. To the Motts their son looked rested and calm—he had slept twelve hours that night—and Mironichev, dark, square-set, solid, gave the impression of competence.

Another point of hope was the fact that Bill Shinn had arrived in the court out of breath. They knew he had an important piece of evidence to be introduced.

As the session got under way Mironichev testified how he had heard of Newcomb Mott's arrival in Boris Gleb, and the steps he took following it. Then it was the engineer who pressed the questioning.

Engineer: "Do people come to the tourist base by any other route than the control point?"

Mironichev: "No. The official time of admission is 11 A.M. to 11 P.M."

Engineer: "Have any other non-Scandinavians tried to cross the border?"

Mironichev: "Yes. An Englishman tried, but he turned back when identified."

And now the prisoner asked a question, and the answer put an icicle through the Motts' hopes.

Mott: "Do you remember telling me that I could have entered Boris Gleb legally without a visa if I had gone through the regular custom's point?"

Mironichev: "No, I deny saying anything like that."

The engineer brought the focus back to the place that Newcomb Mott was said to have entered the Soviet Union. And here Mironichev flatly contradicted his subordinate, Ribekin. The tourist compound, he said, could *not* be seen from the 212th border marker, nor could the flagpoles at the Norwegian and Soviet control points. He further admitted to the prisoner's query that the spot in contention was not on high ground but in a depression.

The judge recalled Ribekin, and in his second performance the guard's trembling was more pronounced than in his first.

But this time Ribekin had his ducks lined up properly. In his previous testimony he had not meant to say that it was possible to see the flagpoles or the tourist compound from the 212th marker, but only the village of Borisoglebsk on the east side of the Pasvik River.

Procurator Lebedyuk helped to smooth out the rough spots by establishing that once one got about six hundred meters into Soviet territory, one could see the tourist compound, and since the road ran straight on the Norwegian side to the reindeer fence, it was not possible to get lost.

The prisoner stated that Procurator Lebedyuk was in error, and was called to the judge's bench to prove his point on a map. On it he indicated that indeed the track he had followed did not run straight. But the whole purpose in recalling Border Guard Ribekin was not a matter of roads or meters, but to get his testimony in line with Mironichev's and the facts. His recall was totally unexpected and must have been arranged before the session began. This gives credence to the Motts' belief that everything they said and did in their suite was overheard or taped.

After all, the air of judiciousness had to be preserved if the drama was to gain public acceptance.

The witnesses heard and dismissed, Judge Klementev announced he would introduce some of the more important documents in the case. He led off with Lt. Colonel Odd Stude Aune's letter of September 7, already referred to in the indictment, and then asked the prisoner for his opinion of how his illegal entry had come to the attention of the Norwegian officials.

Newcomb Mott assumed correctly that someone at the hotel must have informed them when he did not return.

The judge referred next to an article in the Kirkenese newspaper *Finnmarken* of September 9, 1965. It reported that the American tourist had been seen around the border in the vicinity of the Elvenes bridge.

Judge: "This is not evidence, but I'd like to hear your comments."

Mott: "The article is not accurate. I was only at the border once on September 4."

Judge: "Was your action something frivolous in your character or is this kind of action common in your native country?"

The prisoner paused before he replied and then said quietly: "I consider my act a frivolous one."

Judge: "Do you respect laws of other countries?"

Mott: "I respect all law."

The judge continued to quote from documents of evidence. There was Mironichev's official report of the case; there was a letter addressed to Lt. Colonel Griposeyevich from Colonel Gravrilko of the border station explaining how Scandinavians entered the tourist compound. There were a weather report for September 4 and the prisoner's medical record. And finally the judge asked Boris Zolotukhin if he had any documents to submit.

The defense attorney did have documents to submit, and he had been given one by Bill Shinn that previously he had known nothing about. Following the close of court on the day before, Shinn had called Moscow and asked that it be sent up at once. Because of the slowness of Soviet communication and transport, and the quality of both its telephone and telegraph service, Shinn had not received the document until the morning of the twenty-third, and then just in time.

Zolotukhin announced he had a copy of a telegram sent by the U. S. Embassy under the signature of John C. Guthrie, Chargé d'Affairs, to Mr. William Shinn. He then supplied the gist of its contents which gave the lie to Border Guard Ribekin's testimony. The telegram stated the names of seven foreign nationals who since 1947 had mistakenly crossed the border at Borisoglebsk and been returned to Norway. The information had been supplied by the Norwegian Government.

Zolotukhin did not read the telegram, nor did he attempt to. Instead, he presented it to Judge Klementev to see if it could be admitted as evidence.

Klementev in turn passed it on to Lebedyuk, who had jumped up and hurried to the bench. The judge asked the Procurator if it could be admitted in evidence, and the reply was a swift *"Neyt!"* Instead he moved that the telegram not be included in the case materials because it was irrelevant to the cause of guilt. It would be enough if the judge and his two helpers read and acquainted themselves with its contents.

The information in the telegram, of course, was critical evidence in the defense of the prisoner. In any court of law that was not a stage play, it would have been so recognized. The defendant's attorney could have pointed out that since testimony had been introduced to prove that no one could cross the border accidently, the seven who had done so previously had committed the same crime as Newcomb Mott, and since they were all freed without trial, he should also be freed.

Instead, Boris Zolotukhin made no objection, said nothing, and submitted instead about thirty of the depositions that Newcomb Mott's parents had worked so hard to get. Originally they had been advised by the State Department's Office of Soviet Union Affairs that it was not necessary to have the documents notarized by the writers. However, Francis W. H. Adams and several others had taken it upon themselves to do so, and these were the few that the judge and his assessors looked at and read with any degree of care. The character reference from the chief of police of Sheffield was given short shrift because it lacked letterhead, state stamps or ribbons. However, excerpts were read aloud from some of the more official-appearing submissions. It is a well-known fact that any document which lacks official seals of approval is given little attention in the Soviet Union.

But official or unofficial, it had all been an exercise in futility. Procurator Lebedyuk proved it as he took center stage and delivered his summation, following the noon recess.

He was harsh and grim and to the point. The Soviet border was sacred territory. Newcomb Mott had consciously and illegally crossed it. Evidence had been introduced to show that Norwegian officials and others had warned him he couldn't cross without a visa, yet he had done so. He was well educated and had traveled enough to know how to ask authorities for advice. That he hadn't done so could only be explained by the fact he knew he was going to do something illegal. The course he had followed proved it, and when he saw the three people at the tourist compound he had no choice but to pretend he had done nothing illegal. Ignorance of the law was no excuse. All factors indicate he knew just what he was doing from start to finish.

Procurator Lebedyuk, expressionless, peering through thick lenses, finishing his summation and made his recommendation: "I ask that the accused Newcomb Mott be sentenced to two and a half years in correctional labor camp."

Boris Zolotukhin, seated with his back to his client, sucked in his breath and muttered in Russian, "This is serious!"

Newcomb Mott, not understanding the words but catching the meaning, leaned over and put his hand on the attorney's shoulder to comfort him.

The drama was certainly real enough, and it continued. Boris Zolotukhin's defense speech—according to Bill Shinn, a lawyer himself—was a masterpiece of court procedure. Even in translation the Motts found it a tremendous uplift after the sickening shock of absorbing Lebedyuk's request.

Zolotukhin did not deny the guilt of his client, but he illustrated with care and detail how it was an unintentional guilt, a spontaneous, spur-of-the-moment thing. He agreed that his client's ignorance of the penalties of border crossing did not eliminate his guilt, but it made possible for the court to understand his actions, and in this, there were mitigating circumstances. He listed them: no premeditation, tourism the purpose the border was crossed, violation of the border around a tourist base less serious than other areas, Mott's genuine fatigue when captured because of two knee operations which had exempted him from military service. Newcomb Mott was sincerely sorry for his illegal act.

In summation, Zolotukhin said that the prisoner's personality, good behavior, and cooperation should be taken into account by the court. Eleven weeks in jail were punishment enough. He requested that the prisoner be given a conditional sentence and permitted to go home.

Thus the second act ended. Phyllis Mott wrote of it: "Zolotukhin came in to see us that night for a short time, obviously agitated. We were all in the same boat—Newcomb's face looked very strained as he left the courthouse that night—that day's session lasted until six-thirty. As he was leaving we were able to tell him we were proud of him—all of us told him. That night none of us slept very well, and New said he had no sleep."

The third act consisted of two brief scenes and an agonizing two-and-a-half-hour wait in between.

It began with the prisoner asked to give "his last words." He gave them in little more than a minute. He thanked the court, expressed his repentance—which is a must in any Soviet tribunal, and concluded quietly: "My parents have come a very long way, and I would like to be set free to go home with them."

The court stood in recess. Phyllis and Howard Mott, Bill Shinn, and the press in one room, and across the hall with his three guards, Newcomb Mott. The time of waiting, while the judge and his helpers deliberated, passed one slow minute after the other. The correspondents of Tass and Novosti asked if they could take pictures of the waiting couple. They were informed they could not. The prisoner waited with his thoughts and hopes.

It was a dreadful intermission, and its only purpose was an attempt to lend an added air of authenticity to a bad play.

The last scene took fifteen minutes. All the lines were spoken by Judge Klementev. All in the court stood, and there was no movement, and no sound but the judge's voice and the smooth, academic voice of the interpreter, Alekseyev. In the reading of the charges and the summing up, Klementev made no mention of mitigating circumstances, thus taking no account of the prisoner's defense. When he got to the verdict and the sentencing he reduced the punishment to a year and a half in a routine correctional labor camp, this because of the prisoner's good behavior in prison and in court.

Newcomb Mott looked stunned, ashen faced; Phyllis and Howard Mott, crushed; Bill Shinn, grim and angry; and Zolotukhin stood with his head bowed, his gaze averted. This was as one would expect, but it was Nina, the KGB interpreter, who revealed the underlying truth and torment of the entire charade. She stood with fists and jaws clenched, anguish and pain freezing her features, her silent reaction more articulate and evocative than all the words that had been spoken since the curtain had gone up.

A thing of the State, Nina Kulikova was nevertheless a warmhearted human being. She did her job as instructed, at what cost there is no telling, but in that last moment of the trial she showed that the alien prisoner Newcomb Mott had broken through the humanless stamp of the State and touched her heart. Hers was the only manifestation of hope in the entire wretched affair.

Much praise was given to Moscow lawyer Boris Zolotukhin for his defense of the prisoner. But although it was apparent before the end that no defense could have freed Newcomb Mott, there was still information and evidence Zolotukhin could have introduced which would have made it more difficult for the Soviets to have given a quality of credibility to the trial.

When the Motts had first met Boris Zolotukhin they had presented him an extract which had been sent to them by Professor Leon Lipson of Yale. It had been taken from the *Commentary on the Criminal Code of the Russian Soviet Federated Socialist Republic of 1960,* and published by Leningrad University in 1962. On Article 83, under which Newcomb Mott was convicted, it stated:

> 8. Departure from or entry into the USSR or crossing of the border of the State entails criminal liability only where intentional guilt is present. A negligent infringement of the State border of the USSR does not constitute an element of a criminal act. For ex-

ample, one who has lost his way in the woods or lost his bearings at sea and negligently violates the State border of the USSR is not subject to criminal prosecution. . . .

10. The motives and purposes of illegal departure from the USSR, entry into the USSR, or crossing of the border of the State may be diverse: meeting with one's relatives, tourism, and the like. Actions the purpose of which is the commission of especially dangerous State crimes must entail liability under corresponding articles of the Criminal Code that envisage liability for those crimes.

Zolotukhin did not attempt to introduce the extract as evidence, possibly because he accepted that his client had intentionally and not negligently crossed the border. Still, it might have been a debatable point, even in a Soviet court of law.

A more significant oversight was the failure of the prisoner to recall why Birger Kvammen, the Sydvaranger engineer, had told him he needed no visa to go to Boris Gleb. One could argue that a thorough lawyer would have drawn this information from his client in pretrial questioning.

Kvammen, it will be recalled, had based his information on a Murmansk broadcast. Others in Kirkenes had heard similar broadcasts. It is ironic to think that evidence could have been submitted, to go with Guthrie's telegram, that would have placed a large measure of blame for creating confusion over border requirements at Boris Gleb on the government of the Murmansk Oblast.

In this realm of confusion there was yet another piece of peripheral evidence that State Department investigation at the time should also have been able to uncover.

Finnair is the government-operated Finnish airline. Its manager in North America during the period in question was Jukka Syrjänen. Syrjänen was close to Soviet Intourist officials in New York. They gave him some information, which was issued as a news release from the Finnair offices in New York and California on May 11, 1965.

FINNAIR NEWS

FINNAIR ACTIVE IN VISA-FREE VISITS TO RUSSIA

Finnair will process hotel reservations for passengers bound for *the only Russian city which requires no visas from Americans*—Borisoglebsk. [Finnair's italics.]

Borisoglebsk or Boris Gleb is directly opposite Kirkenes on the Russo-Norwegian border and Finnair provides the only through service from a major city—Helsinki. It has just recently been announced that U.S. visitors will be allowed to visit the Russian border town, located about seventy-five miles west of Murmansk, without visas and that the Soviet Union plans to develop Borisoglebsk into a major tourist center with tax-free shopping.

Jukka Syrjänen, manager for North America, Finnair, said he expects considerable interest in this development as Americans visiting Scandinavia may well wish to do some shopping for Russian articles as well as have a peek into Russia.

The Finnish airline will increase its seat capacity to Kirkenes by 66 percent next summer. There are plenty of taxis available at Finnair City Terminal, from where it takes only ten minutes to ride to Borisoglebsk.

Prior to the Russo-Finnish War, Borisoglebsk was a very popular Finnish resort, attracting skiers in the winter and swimmers and anglers in the warmer months. It was formerly known as Koltta-kongas, Koltta being the name of a Lapp tribe and "kongas" meaning rapids or falls in Lapp. The town is presently the site of a large power plant which was built for Russia by Norwegians. Mr. Syrjänen noted that there are also other very interesting excursions to be made along the Russo-Norwegian border, starting in Kirkenes.

Hotel accommodations in Kirkenes can be arranged through Finnair offices at:

10 East 40th Street, New York, New York
1318 West Mossberg Avenue, West Covina, Calif.

Whether the news release was issued with or without the knowledge of the Finnish Government is not known. Later, when inquiries were made about it and similar releases, Mr. Syrjänen had been recalled to Finland, and still has not returned.

Since the information in all the Finnair releases came from Soviet sources, it illustrates the kind of contradictory and inaccurate information on Boris Gleb that was being issued through official Soviet channels.

None of it, of course, could have set Newcomb Mott free, for as *Dagbladet,* Norway's largest afternoon paper, commented on November 26: "This is a brutal sentence. . . . There are obvious reasons to believe that the judges have, beside judicial deliberations, also played a foreign policy game. . . . The American was jailed for one and a half years. This is no compliment for Soviet administration of justice. It is a sign that Soviet courts to a deplorable extent still are looking to politicians in the Kremlin."

Each man walks alone.

Newcomb Mott

Chapter Ten

Dazed and exhausted, Phyllis and Howard Mott were taken to a room across the corridor from the court. After the sentencing they had seen their son led out by his three guards. Bill Shinn had vanished, and they suspected he was trying to arrange for a meeting with Newcomb. It was close to noon. When Bill Shinn returned he admitted that most likely the KGB had phoned the judge to give him instructions on sentencing.

Sometime later, possibly an hour, the Novosti correspondent stepped into the room. He was a stocky, youngish man with a pleasant manner. He spoke English well and he brought news that a family reunion was to be permitted. He asked if he could take a photograph of them waiting, and then one of the meeting. They refused, and with Bill Shinn they carried four packages and an airline bag down the corridor to a small room next to the court. There their son stood waiting for them.

Phyllis Mott went quickly to him, grabbed the fur collar of his coat, and laid her head on his chest.

He put his arms around her and said, "Mother, please don't cry."

She said, "I'll try not to."

Howard Mott clasped his son's hand, kissed his cheek, and then returned quickly to the door to block the entry of correspondents, American and Russian. The guard on the door announced they would have an hour to visit.

Phyllis Mott swung around and adamantly shook her head, holding up five fingers.

The guard shrugged and disappeared, seeking instruction. He returned a moment later and held up two fingers with a smile.

Once again he left the room as Phyllis Mott refused to compromise. It was settled at three, but actually became a four-hour meeting.

It began after Howard Mott angrily ordered that the door be shut so they could have some privacy. It was, and they were finally alone except for the guard.

Newcomb Mott was upset, furious. He shot accusingly at Bill Shinn: "It's completely unjustified! Brutal! Senseless!" He began to pace the small room.

The furnishings consisted of a broken-spring love seat, a desk, and two wooden chairs. Phyllis Mott took the love seat, her husband and Bill Shinn the chairs.

At the outset Phyllis Mott had indicated by sign language that she thought the room was probably taped. Bill Shinn, who believed his Moscow apartment was similarly wired, had little doubt that this was true. He said, "We'll just have to accept it."

The convicted man didn't think so, but he had other things on his mind. He wanted to know what came next, what could be done about an appeal. Bill Shinn offered some comfort by saying that according to Soviet law with the sentence of a year and a half, he would be due for parole about June of 1967.

"But what about an appeal!"

Bill Shinn carefully explained the method of appeal; he described three types and explained what Newcomb must do to assist.

In retrospect Phyllis and Howard Mott remember the four hours by way of the subjects discussed and some of the things said.

"Kennedy got Barghoorn out of here. Can't someone get me out in the same way?"

"No," Shinn shook his head, "the circumstances are quite different."

"Then how about an exchange?"

"It's out of the question. All we've got is a guy named Ivanov, a spy out on $100,000 bail in New Jersey. The U.S. isn't going to swap a known spy for an American tourist," Shinn explained. "They could grab anyone they wanted under those conditions and demand an exchange."

"Isn't there some other way?"

"Not that I know of."

"I've heard that prisoners can be purchased, that $10,000 would be a fair price."

Bill Shinn said, "I'm afraid not."

Newcomb Mott was frustrated and downcast. "I not only have a year and a half here, but I'm told I face arrest in Norway when they send me back."

The three shook their heads.

"No? They told me I was."

"No. Forget it," Bill Shinn said.

After a time he stopped his pacing and calmed down. "I'm talking about myself too much."

"No, you go on and get things straightened out with Bill," his mother said. He came and sat down next to her, and when she took his hand in hers she found it was wet with perspiration.

The heat had been turned off in the room, and it had grown very cold, and the dim light of arctic day was fading.

Phyllis Mott told her son about the packages they had brought to him. They contained clothing, food, books. The librarian in the U. S. Embassy had been very helpful in supplying the last. On her own time she had aided the Motts in their selection. Within the contents of one box there were several packages of Wilkinson razor blades, a Gillette razor, and an ample supply of shoelaces. The items were to be of later significance.

"We've brought lots of books and magazines, New," Howard Mott said.

"I probably won't get them for a while."

"Why not?"

"Because every book or magazine or newspaper is gone over page by page to look for secret messages."

"We've also brought a letter from Rusty," his mother said.

"How is Rusty? How is he taking this?"

In a letter which Phyllis Mott had written to her son in October, she had said that Rusty would be going away for three years and might meet Ray Little on his tour. As Ray Little was in the Navy, it was her way of telling Newcomb that Rusty was also going in the Navy. He never received the letter and yet he asked if Rusty had met Ray Little. At the time and under the circumstances it made little impression on the Motts. But later they realized that no doubt when his interrogator had asked him about Ray Little he got the meaning of the questioning. Whether the KGB learned that Newcomb Mott had a brother in the U. S. Navy is not known. The State Department and the Motts took every precaution to keep the information out of the press for fear that the Soviets might try to get to Rusty and attempt to blackmail him on the basis of information in exchange for his brother's safety. Had any such overture been made to Rusty Mott it is safe to say that the reply would have two hundred and twenty pounds of fist in the teeth.

There were two reasons why Newcomb didn't read the letter from his brother right then and there. It would have taken precious time, and it was not permitted. His mother found it out by trying to give him a piece of butterscotch candy. He refused and said, "Mother, I can't take anything, not even a piece of paper, unless a guard gives it to me."

"Bill," Phyllis Mott said angrily, "ask that guard if he can have a piece of candy!"

Shinn did so. The guard smiled and nodded agreement and refused the offer of candy for himself.

And as for Rusty, about to leave for Navy boot camp, his brother said to Bill Shinn, "You know, Rusty is my best friend."

Time sped quickly by, and during much of it the convicted prisoner gave careful and meticulous details to Bill Shinn on the techniques the KGB had used on him since September 4. He described the methods of mental torture. Nothing had been done to him physically, and yet he was concerned about the possibility.

"What about torture?"

"They don't do that sort of thing any more."

"Are you sure, Bill?"

"Yes. Times have changed."

The Motts had never seen fear on their son's face. He never talked about death. He was more concerned about the welfare of other people. But Phyllis Mott saw fear in his eyes at that moment, and both she and her husband also realized he was very worried about their welfare.

"Are you both all right? . . . Are you sure you'll be all right?" He kept saying that, and they kept reassuring him, and finally Phyllis Mott asked, "New, why are you so worried about us?"

He leaned over and whispered in her ear, "Fire!"

They saw that their own safety had been thrown at him, a threat given. What kind of threat? Why?

"I'm beginning to feel I'm a paranoiac," he said.

They told him no matter what anyone told him, that they were sick, or hurt, or anything, not to believe any of it unless he got a letter from Bill Shinn or from Newcomb's Uncle John in his own handwriting telling him so.

Before their trip to the Soviet Union they had been advised by Professor Lipson and others that their son would need to be reassured over and over again, and that even after he was set free, this kind of therapy would have to continue. When one is under the hand of the KGB, nothing is the same. At the U. S. Embassy in Moscow they had been further informed, and they came to see how this was true. His own lack of guile made it more so.

Although he knew that the guards lied as a matter of routine and would never tell him anything, he believed that Androv, outside the interrogation room and visiting in his cell, as he did once or twice a week, was not a bad sort, quite sympathetic, almost as much as Nina.

Here Bill Shinn joined in talking hard and fast, explaining that there was no difference in any of them. He must watch out for indoctrination, blackmail, and intimidation. Newcomb couldn't believe it. Shinn insisted and his parents told him how they had been lied to by Ludmilla and other Russians.

He said candidly, "I've tried to tell the truth about everything, but if they'd asked me one question, I would have lied."

His open admission shocked them because of the possibility that it was being taped. They quickly changed the subject to sports events at home and as a result never learned what the question was. Shinn came back to his warning. Indoctrination was a standard practice, so were bribes and threats. "Don't be so nice!"

Bill Shinn's arguments got through and, nodding thoughtfully, the prisoner saw that it was so. In filling Shinn and his parents in on his eleven weeks in prison, he took from his pocket a badly frayed business card.

"You know," he said holding it up, "they had told me no

one knew where I was or cared. Then you came, and this card you left was my one hope. . . . You were my hope. The American Government knew I was held. I looked at this so many times, I can't tell you."

And Shinn replied, "You know, Newcomb, at the time I hadn't any idea why I gave you my card."

Sometime in the course of the meeting Phyllis Mott, sitting on the uncomfortable love seat, thought, Why can't we continue this conversation tomorrow? And then she realized sickeningly there was no tomorrow.

In a closed police van when he was brought to the court, Newcomb had no idea where the prison was, nor did he have a watch. But as best he could, he related to Shinn the turns taken and the time—between seven and ten minutes—that it took from one point to the other. He refused to describe his cell to his mother.

"What do you wear?"

"Prison clothes."

"How cold is it?"

"I have a jacket."

"We brought some cheese that you'll like."

"I'm afraid it won't keep, Mother."

"It's in aluminum paper."

"It still won't keep."

"But, New, it's in a tin box."

"Then I guess it'll be okay."

Thinking over the exchange, Phyllis Mott believed her son did not want to tell her there were rats in his cell.

While describing his prison treatment, Newcomb Mott made a far more direct statement which now has connotations ugly and unexplainable. "Mother, I can't understand it. They let me have a safety razor and allow me to shave in my cell, but at the same time, they won't let me have glass jars of food or anything that could be considered dangerous."

In the packages they had brought him there were a

styptic pencil and Band-Aids. They knew he had deep abhorrence of cutting himself or of being cut.

Twice he spoke of the reason he was being treated in such a fashion by the Soviets. "Why do they want me? Why!"

They couldn't answer, and later he gave a reply to his own question. "I could be Joe Doaks or anyone. It would make no difference as long as I was an American." And again he leaned over and whispered in his mother's ear, "Viet Nam."

In all of it there was only one moment of humor. They asked him if while in Finland he'd seen the Finnish girl he had met in 1962 and with whom he'd carried on a correspondence.

"Yes, I saw her twice. But," he added dryly, "we didn't get along so well because she'd learned to speak English better."

He wanted to know about the American reporters, and they told him the pair had been chosen by their fellow correspondents in Moscow to attend the trial. As Bill Shinn put it, "They wanted one emotional and one analytical type." Still, Newcomb Mott was pleased they were on the scene. He was also extremely appreciative of the depositions that had been written and the efforts of lawmakers in Washington. His parents explained to him why he had received only one letter in all the time he had been held, and this he understood. Over and over they repeated that no matter what anyone told him, they would each write to him once a week.

When the discussion got around to what lay ahead should the appeals fail, Newcomb said he had read about Russian prison camps, and he thought he'd be sent to Siberia. Bill Shinn softened the expectation by telling him that he would undoubtedly be put in a camp where there were other foreigners. He brought up the case of Peter Landerman, who had been sent to a correctional labor camp as a result of having accidentally run down and killed a Russian pedestrian. Newcomb was not familiar with the case, and Shinn pointed out that Landerman had been freed long before his sentence had been completed. He admitted that Landerman had had a tough time for the first two weeks working at a job packing ice. But then he revealed that U-2 pilot Gary Powers had actually been employed in a factory making envelopes. He pointed out that in a fourth-class labor camp Newcomb would be getting exercise, freed from solitary confinement. He went on to say that since Newcomb was 4-F, he could consider his time spent in prison and a labor camp as time spent in the Army.

"Yes, I'd thought of that."

"Another thing, you can write about your experiences when you get out. You can write a book."

"No . . . I wouldn't be able to do that."

"At least you can keep notes," his mother said. "We'll send you a notebook."

"Victor says when you come home, no other college traveler will have a chance; you'll be the most sought-after one on every campus."

There are some, considered experts in the field of Soviet affairs, who maintain this exchange was a dangerous one, while there are others, including a former Russian official, who say the suggestion of book writing couldn't have mattered less to the KGB. At any rate, the Motts sent the notebook.

In relating his experiences in prison, Newcomb told how interested the twenty-year-old doctor and other members of the prison staff were in America and American customs. The automobile was a particular subject of conversation, and they couldn't believe that almost every American working man owned one.

As to the manner of his treatment, which he had described step by step, he made outside reference as well. "You remember I talked to you about a professor I met at Binghamton College in New York. He's a Czech and teaches political science. He was once a judge. If you talk to him, you'll know more about my treatment."

But by then they knew enough about his treatment.

"New, we put vitamins in one of the packages."

He shook his head. "They probably won't allow me to have them, Mother. All they'll give me is six Russian aspirin at a time . . . and I have to take them in front of them."

When the Motts had departed for Russia, their close friend Barbara Walden had given Phyllis a good-luck charm, a four-leaf clover in a little glass case. Now she offered it to her son.

"I don't think so, Mother," he said. "I don't know what I'd do with it. I suppose they'll take away this coat and suit they gave me. It's a gift of the KGB."

They agreed this last was probably so, not realizing at the time that it was also a gift they would be billed for.

And now the time was gone, the meeting between parents and son at an end. Outside it was black, inside it was bitter cold.

And Shinn, wishing he didn't have to but knowing he must, lowered the boom.

"Newcomb, when you're sent to the camp, no one is going to know where you are for at least five months. You probably won't have any mail or packages."

"No one!" He stood stricken.

"No one."

In those last seconds, through the grip of their hands, the strength in their eyes, their lips, his mother and father bestowed upon him their benediction of love.

His mother kissed him, "I love you, Newcomb."

His father gripped his son's hand. "Newcomb!"

"I love you both."

He went toward the guard, and the fear was gone from his face. He turned at the door, filling it. "Each man walks alone," he said in farewell, and was gone.

The two American correspondents had waited the four hours in the hope of interviewing him. Aline Mosby got the closest. She saw the guards escorting him to the van.

"Your parents brought you a package," she said.

"That's not exactly what I was hoping for," he replied.

"Good luck," she called.

In the darkness he turned and called back, "Thanks, I'll need it!"

That night Phyllis and Howard Mott and their three fellow Americans took the train south. They departed hurriedly on short notice, special permission having been granted allowing them to travel by train to Moscow.

The last word they had of their son that empty day came from Boris Zolotukhin, who stopped by the hotel as they were in the midst of packing. He reported he had been to the prison and, in reply to their query, said that Newcomb was very upset. Then, knowing there was nothing more that he could say, he had left.

The thirty-one-hour ride on the "Blue Arrow" was one more difficult experience to add to their state of mental and physical exhaustion. Their first-class compartment was an eight-by-six unheated cubicle which they shared with the two correspondents.

Bill Shinn was packed into a nearby compartment with two alcoholic sailors and a damsel in distress. He got little sleep in his top bunk because below him one of the sailors and the damsel, who had just bid her husband a sorrowful adieu, noisily copulated their way southward.

Phyllis Mott could not sleep that night either. She slipped out of the compartment and stood in the dark, frigid corridor, looking out with unseeing eyes at the white wasteland of the wind-blasted tundra passing by . . . passing by . . . passing by. She began to weep and she could not stop. The woman car attendant, a heavily clothed peasant type, awoke Howard Mott and, dressed only in thin pajamas, he went out to his wife and stood for a time trying to comfort her.

Aline Mosby also awoke, and when the woman attendant asked her in Russian what was troubling the lady, she replied, not wanting to explain, "Her son just died."

The next day was Thanksgiving. To reach the dining salon,

it was necessary for them to walk through nine cars and seventy-two doors and then stand and wait for over an hour to be served. They ate goulash and chocolate candies and drank Armenian wine. Aline Mosby and Bill Shinn made a bet of a bottle of champagne over whether the Moscow papers would report the trial. Shinn lost: there were three lines in *Izvestia.*

The "Blue Arrow" is considered a crack Soviet express, but the travelers found the facilities somewhat primitive. In the washroom there was only ice-cold water, no towels, no paper, no soap. At 5 A.M. on Friday morning Phyllis Mott awoke with an inch of virgin snow on her head and pillow. The train radio blasted forth a continuous stream of strident music and propaganda. All were captive to it until journey's end in Moscow at 6 A.M.

In the two days that followed, the Motts made what preparations they could to ease their son's life in prison and continued their efforts for his release.

They saw Boris Zolotukhin twice, and the second time he asked contritely, "Do you still want me as a lawyer after I failed for you?" They assured him they did.

At the Embassy they deposited money to pay Zolotukhin's modest legal fees, and also set up a $600 drawing account for Newcomb. It was then that they learned that all extras the Soviets had so kindly provided their son were to be paid by his parents, and this, of course, included the court fees in Murmansk.

While at the Embassy they wrote their petition of appeal.

Moscow, USSR
November 27, 1965

PETITION TO THE SUPREME SOVIET OF THE RUSSIAN SOVIET FEDERATIVE SOCIALIST REPUBLIC

Our son, Newcomb Mott, a United States citizen, resident of Sheffield, Massachusetts, has been in the USSR for several months, but we have known him, loved him, and had faith in him for over twenty-seven years. A practical demonstration of this was our attendance throughout his trial in Murmansk.

Newcomb has proved to his family, his friends, his fellow workers, and his employers that he is a useful and productive citizen. This was shown by the many letters written by them to the Murmansk court, in which they expressed their high regard for his abilities and his character.

Prior to September 4, 1965, Newcomb had never been involved in any wrongdoing. We, his parents, know that he is honestly repentant for his incautious act and for the difficulties that he has caused the Soviet Government.

We hope that you will agree with us that Newcomb has already been sufficiently punished for his actions and that further time spent in a labor camp would serve only to delay his return to his work, to his family, and to his friends. He is a good young man and a good worker, and we are confident that he will continue to make a positive contribution to society and to the cause of international friendship after he is released.

We therefore respectfully and earnestly urge you to consider our appeal for clemency for our son.

Phyllis N. Mott

Howard S. Mott

They were also instructed at the Embassy: "If you write something down you wish to get rid of, don't just flush it. Here we burn first, and then flush."

At the Intourist office, where they went to get authorization to leave the country, they were cheated out of nearly $200 worth of Soviet coupons. That night, unable to get served, they went to bed without dinner, but now they were so exhausted and worn down it made little difference.

Finally on Sunday morning, all their efforts completed, all their interviews over, they went with Bill Shinn to the airport. There they said farewell to a young man whom they had come to know and like and respect.

When the Motts boarded the KLM flight for Amsterdam,

they were accompanied unobtrusively by two Embassy military officers who they realized had been assigned to see them safely to the West.

During a forty-minute layover in Warsaw, Phyllis Mott had a bizarre encounter in the airline terminal. While her husband and the two officers were momentarily engaged in making a purchase, she moved away to window-shop. She paused before a lighted glass showcase featuring colorful Polish dolls, and suddenly she was not alone. A thin, gray-suited, gray-haired, gray-faced man had come to stand beside her.

"I once had a doll," he said in accented but good English.

"Oh?" Momentarily she was off balance.

"Yes, but I lost it in Germany." He continued staring at the case.

"Well, here's your opportunity to buy another one." Her response was pure reflex.

"I think I'll wait till I get to Holland."

"But you won't get a Polish doll in Holland." She had no idea why she was talking to him, and all at once the two military officers were behind her, and the gray man scuttled away. She joined the officers and her husband, bewildered by the exchange.

Later that day the Motts checked into a small, little-known Amsterdam hotel. In the registry they saw that another guest had just checked in from Warsaw. Phyllis Mott asked who he was, and the clerk replied that he had something to do with toys. Still later they heard the voice of a man talking in the room above, and she was sure it was the same man who had spoken to her in the air terminal. She never saw him again, and at that time she and her husband were so weary, so emotionally sick at heart, so suspicious of strangers that anything could have seemed possible.

Of their journey Phyllis Mott wrote: "Our twelve days in Russia have changed us a lot—what it will do to New is difficult to guess. One learns quickly to be suspicious of everything, and the feeling of being on guard must never leave you. A seeming kindness can be very dangerous because it is always calculated. This is not just us—we talked with many Americans who have lived there for some time and all walk as though on a precipice. At one point Howie made the remark that perhaps in a hundred years these people might become something besides animals. A serious answer was that he was too optimistic. For example, someone wanted to buy the high boots that I bought for Rusty—fortunately, I didn't sell them—I could have been jailed and also the buyer. It is a reign of terror, and no matter how much we prate about getting along with them, it is not going to work because common decency is considered a weakness and brutality is the norm."

They spent the next few days in Holland, trying to recover their strength and a measure of their peace of mind. They did not succeed. Phyllis Mott became progressively less well, and her husband could not shake headaches and stomach cramps. They had a warm and gratifying meeting with the U. S. Ambassador to Holland, William R. Tyler. [Ambassador Tyler later rejected an invitation to dine with the Soviet Ambassador, giving as his reason for refusal the treatment of Newcomb Mott.] But it was at this time that their feelings toward the State Department, and particularly the Office of Soviet Union Affairs, began to go sour. The corner had actually been turned in Russia, but when William Morgan in a transatlantic telephone conversation from Washington told them they must hold a press conference in London, and then instructed them in exactly what they must and must not say, their annoyance and lack of confidence took firm root. For example, they could say Newcomb's sentence was "harsh" but not "brutal"; "unprecedented" but not "unjust."

The press conference was held in London on December 8. The Motts followed State Department instructions, which were also economically costly to them. When after the conference UPI misquoted Howard Mott as stating that no one had ever crossed the border at Boris Gleb by mistake, he demanded retraction through the U. S. Embassy. An Embassy press officer passed it off and said nothing could be done about it. Howard Mott lost his temper, pointing out that he had a tape recording of the conference and so did UPI, and something had better be done about the error damned fast. The officer thought better of doing nothing, and he went to the London UPI office. As a result, UPI sent out a correction.

Little more than a month later the conclusion of their trip to Murmansk was written by Phyllis Mott in a letter to Bill Shinn. "At the moment Howie and I are each patients in the Sharon Hospital in Sharon, Connecticut. Howie with lobar pneumonia and me with bacillary dysentery. We arrived home on the evening of January 2, whereupon I was rushed to the hospital for intravenous feedings to help replace some of the twenty pounds I had lost while being ill in London. Today I am much better and expect to be home very shortly now. Howie came into the hospital with a temperature of nearly 105. Thanks to all the needles he has been getting and the pills, his temperature is down a little, and we feel slightly better. We are in adjoining rooms and can telephone each other and commiserate. 1966 is off to a great start!"

I therefore am emboldened to suggest to the Soviet Government that it make a signal and effective contribution to the cause of peace and brotherhood by suspending the sentence of Newcomb Mott and sending this youth back to his family in the United States.

From a letter written by
Senator Edward W. Brooke, then Attorney General,
to the Supreme Soviet RSFSR
on December 7, 1965

Chapter Eleven

Between September 8, 1965, the date the U. S. Embassy in Moscow learned through an AP newspaper correspondent that the Soviets were holding Newcomb Mott, and the commencement of his trial on November 22, Embassy officials and State Department officers had held nineteen different meetings with their Soviet opposite numbers to try and bring the young traveler's release. Aside from these official contacts, there had also been a great many unofficial overtures made by U.S. diplomatic personnel, serving in countries where they were in touch with Soviets. As already noted, some of the official efforts involved diplomats of the very highest rank, such as Secretary of State Dean Rusk and Soviet Foreign Minister Andrei Gromyko. Their meeting of September 29–October 1, took place at the UN and included two dinners and a cocktail party, which they attended with their ambassadorial aides.

There is some contradiction as to whether Newcomb Mott was indeed a subject of discussion during these social get-togethers, for Howard and Phyllis Mott were informed by State after the UN affair that time had not been found to discuss their son's case. Later this statement was denied and assurances were given that his plight had been included in the talks. If we accept this as so, it should be noted that Andrei Gromyko was at the time a full member of the all-powerful Soviet Central Committee and his position as Foreign Minister placed him on the same diplomatic level as Secretary of State Dean Rusk. That Gromyko was attended by Ambassadors Dobrynin and Fedorenko is also significant in considering the level of approach. Nor did it stop there, for a month after Newcomb's trial, U. S. Ambassador Foy Kohler had a meeting in Moscow with the Soviet's number-three man Nikolai V. Podgorny, in which he appealed to the Soviet Chief of State to have Newcomb Mott released. Added to these State Department pleas were those advanced by Governor John Volpe of Massachusetts, Speaker of the House John McCormack, Senators Leverett Saltonstall and Edward Kennedy, Attorney General of Massachusetts Edward Brooke, and Congressman Silvio Conte. Other lawmakers such as Senator Peter H. Dominick of Colorado spoke out on the floor of the Senate in Mott's behalf. Thus in total it can be said that these high-governmental bridge-building efforts to the Soviets were sustained and consistent. They lacked only direct White House action, and yet all of these contacts, meetings, letters, discussions, and diplomatic powwows could not engineer the release of one American citizen whose only crime was that he had gotten lost and crossed a poorly-defined border.

At the outset the White House and the State Department had decided that the President would not take a hand in the affair by using one of his most dependable tools, the telephone. No doubt this was because it was believed the State Department could handle the problem and extract Mott from the Soviet gluepot. Yet the State Department must have known by the end of October that the entire case was motivated by Soviet political decisions and Mott's freedom could be obtained only by a political counterdecision. Instead, officials in Washington and Moscow who were calling the shots continued to conduct their efforts as though they were dealing primarily with the intricacies of Soviet legality, confident that even if the Murmansk court did find the prisoner guilty, it would let him go. And if on the other hand the Soviets failed to let him go and sent him to a labor camp, it wouldn't be for long. After all the record showed that in most cases foreign prisoners of the Soviets did not serve out their terms. The realpolitik of the matter was that Newcomb Mott simply wasn't an important enough figure or factor over which to get tough. The array of diplomats who spoke to the Soviets is impressive enough, but the crux of such panoply lay not in rank or numbers but in what was said.

Because diplomatic exchanges are kept confidential, unless there is some reason to "leak" them, it is not known specifically in most of these contacts who said what to whom. It is known that a decrease in tourism by Americans to the USSR was offered as a probable result stemming from harsh Soviet treatment of Newcomb Mott. It is known that various officials "protested," "strongly objected to," and "seriously questioned" the prisoner's prolonged detention and incarceration. It is known that previous leniency by the Soviets toward American citizens held on more serious charges was discussed as a good reason for setting Mott free. Undoubtedly U.S. public antagonism was also raised as an ultimate result, thus souring the era of "peaceful coexistence" and impeding President Johnson's drive for "convergence." But from available evidence that is as far as it ever went.

It was roving Ambassador Averell Harriman who perhaps best summed up State Department thinking toward the Soviet Union in the fall of 1965. Upon his return from a trip to the USSR and talks with the Kremlin chiefs he found them "embarrassed" by the war in Viet Nam. From this and the record one can conclude that it was decided it was not in the best interests of the United States Government to "embarrass" the Soviets over Newcomb Mott.

Since the Soviets had offered to exchange Mott for Ivanov and the offer had rightly been rejected, the question naturally arises what other avenues of bargaining were left open?

In the meeting with his parents, following the trial, the prisoner had suggested that his freedom might be bought outright from the Communists. This was not bail, and the attempt was never made to carry out such a transaction; clemency appeals were pursued instead. The other side of the coin was to take a hard stand and threaten the Soviets with a counteraction which would not warrant their holding the prisoner.

What counteractions?

The threat to discontinue the cultural exchange. In November 1965 the entire program appeared in danger of being terminated, reportedly because of the Viet Nam situation. But as one authority on the matter, a Russian himself, put it, "the economic advantages alone, to be reaped by say the Bolshoi Ballet or the Moscow Symphony touring the U.S., made the Soviet threats to discontinue so much eyewash. And don't think we didn't know it."

Accordingly, in Washington, D.C., between March 2 and 12, 1966, a new two-year agreement was negotiated and signed. The agreement continued the policy originally launched in 1958, and was completed just in time to organize the bringing of the Bolshoi Theater Ballet for a New York opening. The Moscow Philharmonic Chamber Orchestra also toured the U.S. in 1966 and the Soviet Festival of the Arts was scheduled for 1967. Altogether not a bad chunk of foreign exchange for the Kremlin, whose policy during the summer of 1965 was one of harassment of U.S. exhibits and an abrupt cancellation of the musical comedy *Hello, Dolly!* On the Soviets' part this was the same old business of pretending to act tough so that when they appear to act reasonably, it can be taken as one more proof that they are moderating.

That the cultural exchange reaps its own benefits to the U.S., which has nothing to do with money, is true enough. But the issue of a new agreement was not raised as the price of extracting Newcomb Mott in the fall of 1965, and then a few months later a new agreement was signed.

One might argue—could we afford to jeopardize the entire cultural exchange program for the sake of one American captive of the Soviets? The answer might just be found in a past incident. In 1963 Professor Frederick C. Barghoorn of Yale was in the Soviet Union as a part of the cultural exchange program. He was arrested in Moscow by the KGB, framed, and accused of espionage. President Kennedy took direct action and the professor was sent home quickly enough. Quite naturally, the continuance of the cultural exchange program hung on the Soviet response to President Kennedy's demand.

When Secretary of State Dean Rusk spoke to Foreign Minister Andrei Gromyko he could have told him that *the United States Government was seriously considering revoking Amtorg's trading license.*

Amtorg has been operating in the U.S. since 1924, and aside from acting as a cover for spies such as Ivanov, it has served as the official Soviet purchasing agency in America. Secretary Rusk could have added correctly that public opinion over the Mott case would support such an action.

At a later date when Ambassador Llewellyn Thompson had his talk with Soviet Ambassador Anatoly Dobrynin he could have pointed out that *due to the Mott case the U. S. Government was seriously considering putting travel to the USSR off limits to all American citizens.* The determination to do so would depend on how soon Newcomb Mott was sent home.

These are but three suggestions for counteraction. They would have brought no threats of war, no breaking of diplomatic relations, but all would have been economic reprisals of great enough magnitude to make the Soviets realize that holding Newcomb Mott wasn't going to be worth the results. Instead, the Soviets saw they had nothing to lose by making an example of Newcomb Mott; nothing to lose by showing to the world what they could do to an innocent American citizen; nothing to lose by furthering their image of toughness; and nothing to lose by literally throwing the rejection of compassion into the faces of a host of our top officials.

Nowhere is this degree of Soviet arrogance more lucidly illustrated than in an examination of the labors and thinking of Senator Edward M. Kennedy in his approach to the case. Prior to a trip to the Far East in October, he had on Newcomb Mott's behalf contacted Douglas MacArthur, II, Assistant Secretary of Congressional Relations at the State Department. He was informed that State felt there would be no trial and it would be better if the Senator did nothing for fear of rocking the diplomatic boat. Upon his return to Washington, Senator Kennedy learned that State's appraisal had been in error, and on November 11, he received a letter from Phyllis Mott asking for his assistance.

She wrote in part: "As Senator from Newcomb's home state would you consider it unethical to make a statement or to write a letter to the court in Murmansk? This, of course, after you have acquainted yourself with the facts of the case and studied Newcomb's letters. This letter would be read in the court along with other letters from friends, relatives, and employers. We have no expectation that any one letter will bring forth a verdict of 'innocent.' However, there is the possibility that a letter from you might help to mitigate his sentence. . . ."

The Senator, working in concert with those at State handling the case, complied. The letter he wrote did not reach the court in time to be used in Newcomb Mott's defense.

When the word came through on November 24 that Newcomb Mott had been convicted, Senator Kennedy learned of the sentencing before it was publicly known. He was in New Bedford, Massachusetts, lecturing before high school and college students on his findings in Viet Nam. In one of these lectures he spoke about the case and that evening his office released the following statement:

November 24, 1965

Senator Edward M. Kennedy, D-Mass., today speaking in New Bedford, expressed his great concern over the 1½ year sentence given to Newcomb Mott, a young American from Sheffield, Massachusetts, by a Murmansk court.

Senator Kennedy said, "From all we can learn and from the reported testimony at the trial, young Mott's sentence is extremely harsh and inconsistent with the minor nature of his violation of the Soviet border. It appears that Mott's straying into Soviet Union territory was inadvertent and that the sentence was far in excess of the normal punishment for such mistakes. I certainly hope that the appeal, which I understand has been taken by Mott's defense counsel, will be successful. I would further urge that this situation is one which would warrant the appropriate Soviet authorities arranging for this boy's release. I have been in touch with the State Department and asked that my feelings on this matter regarding one of my constituents be conveyed to the appropriate Soviet Government authorities.

Upon his return to the capital the Senator learned that an attitude of optimism continued to prevail at the State Department; the expectation being that what followed would only be a matter of form before the prisoner was finally set free. However, it was agreed that Senator Kennedy could contribute ammunition to the appeal by writing another letter on Newcomb's behalf. After consultation with Professor Harold Berman, an authority on Soviet law at Harvard, the proper document was carefully drafted.

November 30, 1965

Chairman N. G. Ignatov
The Supreme Soviet
Russian Soviet Federated Socialist Republic
Moscow, USSR

Dear Mr. Chairman:

I am writing this letter to you on behalf of a constituent of mine, Mr. Newcomb Mott, a young American from Sheffield, Massachusetts. On November 24, 1965, I was informed of the one and a half year sentence given Mr. Mott by a Murmansk court for a violation of the Soviet border.

I have personally investigated this matter in an attempt to determine the circumstances surrounding Mr. Mott's actions. On the basis of all of the information I can learn, and from the reported testimony at the trial, I feel that Mr. Mott's straying into Soviet Union territory was inadvertent; moreover, I am convinced that his violation was of a relatively minor nature and that he is truthfully and sincerely remorseful for his error.

There is presently pending an appeal taken by Mr. Mott from the sentence of the Murmansk court. I would sincerely urge that great consideration be given to the merits of Mr. Mott's appeal, to his remorse, and to his desire to return to his home state of Massachusetts.

It strikes me that this young man is in no sense a criminal, a villain, or a person who need be taught a permanent lesson through an extended jail term. I therefore respectfully request that Mr. Mott's appeal receive favorable treatment and that he be allowed to come home to his family.

Sincerely,

Edward M. Kennedy

In a follow-up letter to the Motts on December 6, Senator Kennedy outlined the steps he had taken in their son's interest.

In this letter he said: "The State Department has taken a strong position on the sentence, and I have tried to make my feelings on the matter clear without implying undue criticism of Soviet justice."

On December 1, Boris Zolotukhin filed a judicial appeal against the verdict with the Supreme Soviet of the RSFSR. On the fourteenth the Senator's letter to Chairman Ignatov was submitted to the Soviet Ministry of Foreign Affairs to be transmitted to the Supreme Soviet. The next day Speaker of the House John McCormack's letter was added.

On December 16 the judicial appeal was rejected. A new appeal on grounds of clemency was then instituted by Zolotukhin.

State Department thinking had considered the turndown a foregone conclusion, for had the Supreme Soviet overruled the verdict, this would have been an admission that the Murmansk court had been in error. Thus it was the appeal for clemency on which officialdom hung its hopes. In further abetting such hopes the Senator considered several courses of action. He could go have a man-to-man talk with Ambassador Dobrynin. He could put in a telephone call to Premier Aleksei Kosygin, or he could go directly to Moscow and ask for an audience with both the Premier and his partner in rule, Party Chairman Leonid Brezhnev. Late in December he decided the first course was the best. It was reasoned that to make a telephone call might be confusing because an interpreter would be necessary, whereas going to Moscow would be described by some as a political propaganda play and would not only put undue pressure on the Soviets but might "embarrass" them as well.

In determining to approach Ambassador Dobrynin, it was decided that after the meeting the Senator would send the Ambassador a follow-up letter and then give further consideration to a telephone call to Kosygin to be set up by Dobrynin.

The meeting took place at the Soviet Embassy on January 11, 1966. It included lunch and lasted over two hours. During it the Senator expressed his appreciation for such diplomatic hospitality and regretted the unfortunate circumstances which had made the meeting necessary. He described his deep interest in the case and his sincere hope that the Soviet Government would realize that the penalty was too severe for the crime. He asked Dobrynin's help and offered his deep thanks.

The following day the Senator wrote to the Motts and related that "the Ambassador was courteous, listened intently, and promised to forward a complete summary report of our meeting to appropriate Soviet authorities. . . ."

And the result? The appropriate Soviet authorities made no response.

Just three weeks after his long lunch with the Soviet Ambassador to the United States, Senator Edward M. Kennedy would rise on the floor of the Senate and there sadly supply chorus and epilogue to all his polite efforts in the case.

In that same December–January time period, others of note spoke out for Newcomb Mott. But it was all done in a minor key. No one demanded, all abhorred; no one threatened reprisals, everyone hoped the Soviets would reconsider. The State Department called the tune. The White House was silent. No newspaper launched a campaign to free the prisoner, and no patriotic organization rallied to his cause in order to arouse public opinion. No bearded pickets marched. When internal and external permissiveness has become a way of life, people are slow to anger.

Of all the letters of appeal written to aid Newcomb Mott, none is more eloquent or revealing than that submitted by then Attorney General and now Senator from Massachusetts, Edward W. Brooke. In writing, he reached out and touched the metal of Soviet behavior, and then drew back in horror as though scalded by his own thoughts.

9. The courtroom cast from the left: the prisoner, Newcomb Mott; his defense attorney from Moscow, Boris Zolotukhin; KGB interpreter, Nina Kulikova; Moscow-sent interpreter Vladimir Alekseyev; female assessor, unnamed; Judge G. I. Klementev; male assessor, unnamed; two court stenographers; the prosecutor, Stepan Lebedyuk. (Photo: Tass from Sovfoto)

10. Newcomb Mott, center, discusses his defense with attorney Boris Zolotukhin, left, and KGB interpreter Nina Kulikova on first day of trial. (Photo: Tass from Sovfoto)

11. Stepan Lebedyuk, the one-armed Murmansk Procurator—prosecuting attorney—who led the attack against Newcomb Mott and asked the court to give the prisoner the maximum sentence. (Photo: Tass from Sovfoto)

12. Judge G. I. Klementev flanked by his helpers. (Photo: Tass from Sovfoto)

13, 14. These two photos were taken as the verdict and sentence were being read by Judge Klementev and translated by Alekseyev. The shock of the moment is reflected not only in the faces of Howard and Phyllis Mott and U.S. Embassy Counselor Bill Shinn, at right, but also most revealingly by the clenched fists and jaw of KGB interpreter Nina Kulikova, below. (Photos: Tass from Sovfoto)

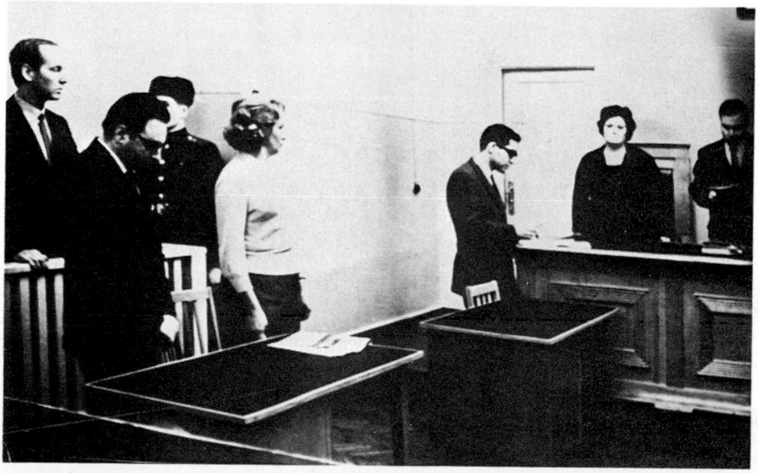

15. Main street of Murmansk on typical day in October. This is the city where Newcomb Mott was imprisoned. It gets about sixteen clear days out of 365, and is in arctic darkness from November to the end of January. (Photo by Helge Heinonen)

December 7, 1965

Supreme Soviet RSFSR
c/o United States Department of State
Office of Soviet Union Affairs
Washington, D.C.

Gentlemen:

On November 24, 1965, Newcomb Mott, a citizen of the United States and of the Commonwealth of Massachusetts, was sentenced to eighteen months at a labor camp by the regional court at Murmansk, USSR. The charge on which he was convicted was for illegally crossing the USSR border at Boris Gleb.

My purpose in addressing you is not to question the propriety or legality of Mr. Mott's trial and conviction; such matters will undoubtedly be handled in a competent manner by the counsel for the defendant. What does disturb me is the severity of the sentence which was imposed.

As one who is charged with enforcement of the law, I have devoted much thought and attention to the subject of fitting and effective punishment of the crime. The purposes of most sentences can be summarized as follows:

A. *Punitive*—Although society has come a long way from the Mosaic code of "an eye for an eye—a tooth for a tooth," it is a fact that some crimes are so revolting in their nature that many governments feel that some form of atonement or retribution is necessary to expiate the offense. I think that we can agree that the crime for which Mr. Mott was convicted does not call for such a response by the state.

B. *Rehabilitative*—As society has grown more enlightened, it has recognized the need to sentence criminal offenders to institutions which can supplement the punishment for the crime by measures designed to educate and train the prisoner to resume his place as a useful member of society. To the extent that such a goal is applicable in this case, I submit that Mr. Mott's rehabilitative education will not be furthered by imprisonment at hard labor for a year and a half, thousands of miles from his family.

It would appear, then, that the imposition of such a severe sentence upon Mr. Mott was not so much to serve the usual ends of justice, such sentences for border trespassing normally consisting of a token imprisonment or expulsion from the country, but to serve some other purpose of the state not directly related to the crime.

If the latter assumption is correct, then I have serious concern about the long range and deep seated implication of this harsh sentence on the good relationships between the peoples of our two great nations. [Italics added.] For it is my firm conviction that, despite the occasional clouds which darken areas of international understanding, this is a time of the greatest hope for eventual mutual solutions of the age old problem of war—a solution which is directly related to the increasing understanding and affection between the average citizens of our countries.

Such understanding has increased tremendously in the past decade as our American people have grown to know your people more intimately. We have thrilled to the Bolshoi Ballet, the Moscow Circus has enchanted both young and old, the incomparable Valery Brumel has become a legendary sports hero, and Americans who have communicated with your people on a personal basis attest to the common interest and sharing with us in the ideals of peace and brotherhood.

But growth of such understanding is threatened by actions such as the Mott sentence; our people just do not understand it. The theory of punishment of one individual to help effectuate an unrelated policy or goal of the state is foreign to our way of thinking.

I therefore am emboldened to suggest to the Soviet Government that it make a signal and effective contribution to the cause of peace and brotherhood by suspending the sentence of Newcomb Mott and sending this youth back to his family in the United States.

By taking such action, the Soviet Government would be displaying not weakness, but strength. As was said of the quality of mercy by William Shakespeare, whose works share universal acclaim with the great Russian writers and poets, "'Tis mightiest in the mighty."

I have discussed this matter at great length and have based my appeal upon merciful understanding, rather than upon legalistic considerations, because I believe that this case is of such grave significance, even though it involves only one young man apprehended in a non-violent act in which he engaged through error or misunderstanding. We all recognize, I am sure, that great events in history are more often directly related to the success or failure of small events in the day to day relationships of ordinary citizens than to the efforts of rulers or diplomats.

Hopefully, therefore, I suggest that magnanimous and understanding action by the Soviet Government in releasing Newcomb Mott will prove to be another great forward step in the march toward greater understanding and brotherhood between the citizens of the Soviet Union and the United States of America.

Respectfully yours,

Edward W. Brooke

Events were to prove that Attorney General Brooke's hopes were at best illusory.

From the time of Newcomb Mott's detention to the time his conviction reached its final appeal, all the collective and individual endeavors put forth to secure his freedom were carried forward with little publicity, the theory being that quiet diplomacy would make the Soviets more amenable to acting human, whereas a full-fledged disclosure of behind-the-scenes maneuvers, plus stated demands, would only anger the Kremlin. If one accepts State Department ground rules for handling the case, there can be little argument with this approach. After all, Newcomb Mott was in Soviet hands, and since publicity was not to be used as a weapon to arouse public demand for a hard line, little purpose was to be served by disclosing details of no less than forty official requests.

This same theory appears to have prevailed in the strange case of Gregory Sarapushkin.

According to State Department records, on November 22, the day Newcomb Mott went on trial, Russian defector Gregory Sarapushkin came to Washington and telephoned the Soviet Embassy. He said he wanted to go home. He had been in the United States since Saturday, August 7, 1965, when he and fellow smelter worker Peter Kalitenko had come ashore near Wales, Alaska, in their whale-skin outboard motorboat. Two days previously, on the fifth, the pair claimed to have departed their home village of Lavrentiya on the Siberian coast. Supposedly on a mushroom-hunting expedition, they had stocked their seventeen-foot skin boat with food, gas, a single-barrel shotgun, and a box of shells. Planning to cross a ten-mile-wide bay, they had become lost in fog and foul weather and after two days of floundering in the Bering Strait, they had made it to the Alaskan shore.

Clarence Ongtowarsuk, a resident of Wales, was one of three fishermen who discovered the Russians. He said later, "Some of us feel those motors must be slow gas eaters because they had plenty of gas left to go a long way. They had much food left, and their skin boat didn't look too wet to us."

Nevertheless the most directly interested agencies of the U. S. Government determined that the Russians were exactly what they claimed to be and were telling the truth. Furthermore, twenty-nine-year-old Sarapushkin said he was married, the father of a five-year-old daughter, and was anxious to return home. Kalitenko, thirty-five, was reported to be both married and a bachelor, but he, too, professed a desire to get back to Lavrentiya.

There is the obvious parallel to be drawn between the Russians' inadvertent arrival in the U.S. and Newcomb Mott's arrival in the USSR. In the Russians' case, U.S. officials in Alaska immediately notified the Soviet Embassy in Washington and were given permission to transport the two men to Big Diomede Island, nearest Russian territory and just twenty-seven miles off the Alaskan coast.

The Coast Guard cutter *Balsam,* skippered by Lt. Commander Daniel S. Bishop, was given the assignment to take the two men back to their home country, and on Monday, August 9, it set out to do so. But all of a sudden Sarapushkin and Kalitenko changed their minds. Speaking enough English to make their intentions clear, they informed the skipper of the *Balsam* that they didn't want to return home after all but wished to begin life anew in the U.S. The *Balsam* reversed course and put in at Point Clearance, seventy miles south of Wales.

After this turnabout there followed a week of dickering in which U. S. Immigration, State Department, and CIA representatives questioned the pair on their unexpected change of heart. The difficulties of adjusting to a new life in the U.S. were stressed. Kalitenko was now sure in his mind that he wished to defect, and although Sarapushkin was not quite so adamant, he, too, resisted the blandishments of Vitautas M. Zenkevichus, Soviet Embassy Second Secretary. Zenkevichus had flown to Anchorage to try and convince the two that they'd best go back home to Lavrentiya. The State Department later said one reason the two had refused the offer was that they feared they would be persecuted if they returned. Thus they sought permission to remain in the U.S. and accordingly made application to do so.

Little more than three months later Sarapushkin made his contact with the Soviet Embassy in Washington, and on November 24, the very day Newcomb Mott was found guilty of doing exactly what the Russian pair had done in reaching the U.S., the Soviet Embassy informed the State Department that Sarapushkin had been in touch and wished to return to the Soviet Union posthaste.

Three days later on the twenty-seventh, Tass, the official Soviet news agency, accused the U. S. Government of holding Sarapushkin against his will, and the Kremlin lodged a protest through its Washington Embassy with the State Department. This action on the twenty-seventh can be viewed from two parallel points. Either between the twenty-fourth and twenty-seventh State Department and other officials were debating the advisability of holding Sarapushkin with the thought of trying to swap him for Mott and the Soviets sought to block the attempt, or the Soviets, knowing the State Department would not hold Sarapushkin, sought, by accusing the U.S. of doing so, to show how the Soviet Union was able to bring its own home while the U.S. was unable to do the same for Mott.

Whatever reasoning motivated this strategy, the result was the same. On November 30, after another meeting between Sarapushkin and U.S. and Soviet representatives, the Russian was flown home immediately. In its December 1 news story on the prodigal's return, the Associated Press failed to draw attention to any similarity between Newcomb Mott and Gregory Sarapushkin. As for Sarapushkin, on December 12, *Izvestia* printed a long interview with him in which he claimed U.S. agents had tried to brainwash him, and that Kalitenko was being held "under the influence of blackmail and deceit."

Howard and Phyllis Mott first heard about Sarapushkin on November 27 while at the U. S. Embassy in Moscow. As Howard Mott put it: "Mr. Shinn was elated over the news and spent well over an hour trying to get more information in the hope of an exchange, or at least a reduction in Newcomb's sentence. . . . Had Washington seen fit to notify Mr. Shinn of Sarapushkin's sudden desire to go home, I feel confident that he would have urged a period of questioning in order to arrange for either an exchange or a sharp lessening in Newcomb's sentence. . . ."

Following their return from the Soviet Union, the Motts, some of their friends, and Senator Edward M. Kennedy raised the question with the State Department as to why an exchange was not at least attempted.

The official answer was written to Howard Mott by Douglas MacArthur, II. After chronologically relating the saga of the two Russians, MacArthur wrote:

> (a.) In stating that the cases were not parallel, I meant to point out the completely different situations of your son and the two Soviet escapees. Newcomb was being held against his will by the Soviets on charges—however unfair—that he violated Soviet law. Kalitenko and, initially, Sarapushkin wished to escape the Soviet system and sought the protection of the United States. This Government could not have legally turned them over to the Soviet authorities against their will, nor would such an act have been possible in view of the American tradition in these matters. Thousands of refugees and escapees from Communist countries have sought to build new lives in this country. To seize any of them and attempt to barter him for an American held by a Communist country would not be in our moral tradition.
>
> Some may argue that Sarapushkin should have been charged with illegal entry and detained against his will for use in a trade after we learned that he wished to return to the USSR. However, given the minor and technical nature of any charges which could have been brought against him, it is highly unlikely that our courts would have permitted detention for long. The courts would have probably also been reluctant to entertain any charges brought against Sarapushkin three months after he entered the U.S., for the political motivation of such a move would be obvious.
>
> Finally, aside from legal and moral considerations we must take into account the prospective Soviet response to any such action on our part. Every time a Soviet citizen

> defected—which is not infrequent—the USSR would be encouraged to obtain his return by trumping up charges against an American tourist in order to use him for barter.

The Motts did not accept the explanation, and in reply Howard Mott took bitter issue with MacArthur's official position.

> The crux of the whole matter is Section (a) page 2 of your letter. You speak of "a trade," as a general matter. Newcomb was the only American prisoner in Russia at the time and the only one whose case of "trespass" could be called comparable. You add ". . . it is highly unlikely that our courts would have permitted detention for long." (How long is "long"—this is an admission that detention for a period would have been permitted and your statement a supposition.)
>
> You go on to say ". . . The courts would have probably also been reluctant to entertain any charges brought against Sarapushkin three months after he entered the U.S., for the political motivation would have been obvious. . . ." I assume the last part of this sentence is an opinion on your part. My opinion is that the humanitarian motive would have also been obvious. It becomes increasingly apparent that the Soviets take better care of their distressed citizens in another country than does the U.S. The Soviet "demands" and fights and we "request." It would have shown more intelligence to have found out by investigating the possibilities than guessing. Again what you have said is purely supposition.
>
> The paragraph on page 3 beginning "Finally" makes no sense at all because nobody expected, until Sarapushkin recanted, that he would be detained for a trade. Much has been made in the State Department releases about the impossibility of exchanging Newcomb, a tourist, for Igor Ivanov the convicted Soviet spy—because of the inequality of the charges against them. As you point out Sara-

pushkin was not *convicted* of any crime. However, legally he could have been held for questioning according to Title 8, U.S. Code, Section 1325.

From the point of view of historical accuracy, the State Department's arguments based on morality and legality simply do not stand up. There are innumerable cases, individual and collective, that can be cited over the span of the past twenty years to illustrate how neither morality nor legality motivated State Department policy vis-à-vis the Soviet Union. For example, one can start in 1945 with "Operation Bootstrap" when literally hundreds of thousands of Russians captured in the allied zone of Germany—soldiers, prisoners, and escapees—begged for asylum in the West and instead, because policy dictated, were turned over to the mercies of the Soviet NKVD. Thousands escaped the fate of their comrades by committing suicide.

A more recent and much better-known case was the exchange of Soviet espionage expert Colonel Rudolph Abel and downed U-2 pilot Gary Powers. Where did morality or legality play any part in this swap?

The records shows that practicality and expediency are the norms set to bring exchange and sanctuary, and the rest is specious platitudes. There is no doubt had the Soviet Union chosen to release Newcomb Mott it would have been because the United States Government faced it with a choice that had nothing to do with moral or legal considerations.

Morality and legality aside, there was an answer the State Department could have given the Motts which they might have found more acceptable. It was that to have held Sarapushkin against his will would have been to completely jeopardize the appeal efforts on behalf of Newcomb Mott. That is unless State had decided a much harder approach was now in order.

Sarapushkin could have been *legally* detained to give answers to a number of unexplained questions: If he and his comrade Kalitenko had been lost at sea for forty-eight hours, how was it that both of them came ashore clean-shaven? If indeed their skin boat was inoperative, how had they managed to bring it in against a strong current? And if both or even one of their motors was still operative, why hadn't they headed for home, since the weather in the area on August 7 was perfectly clear?

As one of the fishermen who discovered the pair said, "They don't have too many gasoline cans, and they don't finish the gasoline even with two motors. When we buck against the current we always have more than twenty gallons. If they come from where they point on map, they would never come across the strait in little boat that cannot be seaworthy."

If Gregory Sarapushkin had been asked these questions before, he and Kalitenko could have been taken into custody to be asked them again and again, for the fishermen who found them have always believed that they came ashore from a ship or a submarine.

Your coming here to Murmansk to be with me, I appreciate more than words can express. I know it was very hard on you. Your presence had a salutary effect, I know, on my ability to perform under pressure. You helped provide that positive hope which was a psychological necessity for me under the conditions of those days. . . .

From a letter written by Newcomb Mott to his parents,
December 8, 1965

Chapter Twelve

And so it was that while the diplomatic choreography continued under the baton of the State Department, the prisoner in Murmansk made adjustments toward his uncertain future. In the beginning he had hoped for swift release; then after a period, if not swift release, release soon. This dream dissolved in turn to hope for an open trial, followed by the hope of release at the trial's conclusion. And then finally in the full dark of arctic December he focused his hope of release upon appeal. From September to December he had seen each and every hope cruelly splintered, but he had not lost the capacity to hope or the will to believe that in the end everything would come out all right.

There were to be no more visits from Bill Shinn. The Soviets would not permit it. His slender contact with the world outside his cell lay in letters. Between the time of his sentencing and January 2, 1966, four were received from him: one to his parents and Bill Shinn dated December 8,

1965, and then two more to Bill Shinn written on the twelfth, and the final one bearing the double date December 28 and January 2. There is no doubt that he wrote other letters to his parents and brother as agreed upon. After Christmas, when he received a number of letters and cards from friends and relatives, it is also reasonable to believe he replied to at least some of them. In the same time period his parents and brother also sent four letters. Only one (from his father) was delivered to him.

It is known from Soviet records that he had a temperature the day after the trial, and it is not surprising under the circumstances. That he did not write until two weeks after the trial was due to the conditions of so-called Soviet legality. But his letters are the only directly tangible insight into how he was bearing up under the continued strain and the prospect of a labor camp. Because much of what he related to his parents on December 8 he also wrote to Bill Shinn, extracts from the two letters are combined.

Murmansk, USSR
December 8, 1965

Dear Dad and Mother,

No doubt you understand that there is not much I can write about. I'll try to be as interesting as possible though. Please excuse the physical appearance of this letter, but I think you understand ballpoint pen, etc. So far the treatment (I mentioned Nov. 24) is the same as before.

On Nov. 27 I wrote my personal appeal to the Supreme Court of the Russian Republic. It, the KGB file on my investigation, and the Murmansk Regional Court's trial minutes were sent to the republic's supreme court on Dec. 3. Dec. 7, Mr. Zolotukhin's (didn't know there was a "k" in his name so you must be right on the pronunciation, Mother) 4-page appeal was sent from Murmansk to that court in Moscow. He will also appeal in person some time this month.

In the most important and last part of my personal appeal I wrote, "The Supreme Court of the RSFSR will be presented with a great deal of material by my defense counsel, Mr. Zolotukhin, which, I believe, proves that: I had legal intentions from start to finish; accidentally I arrived at the border at an improper location; the act of border trespassing was *not* premeditated; my aims were harmless, *not* hostile; the area entered is, indeed, for tourists, not a forbidden place; I made *no* attempt to hide, thus demonstrating that I did *not* realize I broke a law. I am an honest, law-abiding person. I request that the Supreme Court of the Russian Republic reverse this lower court decision, thereby releasing me and allowing me to return to my *own* country, the United States, where I can again return to my *own* work. I apologize for taking up the court's time. Newcomb Mott." With the writing of that appeal I have done all I can to help myself. It is now up to Mr. Zolotukhin, one of the ablest defense lawyers and nicest of men it has been my privilege to know. He did a masterful job in court here.

It occurred to me last night while looking through L.B.J.'s biography that my trial was on the same date (2 years later) as President Kennedy's assassination—an odd coincidence (Nov. 22nd). Ironically, the court's written verdict was given to me Nov. 25th, Thanksgiving, and if the appeal fails, I'll be journeying to a labor camp just before Christmas.

However, it hasn't been a total loss, and I don't suppose a labor camp would be either. I'm no "Pollyanna," but I have learned a good deal about the USSR and about myself. I've met some very nice Russians, and I've lost weight. I still have hope that the most important thing, my personal liberty, will be obtained in the near future. Mr. Zolotukhin would like me to go out with him in Moscow just before this Christmas; I would like to keep the date.

Dec. 8, 1965
Murmansk

Mr. William T. Shinn
Consul of the United States of America
American Embassy
Moscow, USSR

Dear Bill,

I hope I adequately expressed my appreciation when you and my parents were here Nov. 22–24. You have been a bellwether in a storm. I know that your concern for me is greater than simple duty. Really, my thanks are not adequate, but, given present circumstances they are all that I can write.

On Dec. 4 I received a positive answer to my request that I be allowed to send and receive letters from anyone, and receive parcels—from the regional court. Thus comes this letter.

Today (Dec. 7) I received a tiny post card, which I find somewhat mysterious. The only thing that occurs to me is that this person collects letters and autographs of people in the news. Oh, there is another possibility: She (?) may be a crackpot. It was mailed Nov. 24 to me "℅ The Regional Court, Murmansk, USSR." The message: "The days must be much shorter since Sept. 4, and colder than when you crossed to Boris Gleb." The signature of this (unknown by me) person looks like ——. The remainder of the card gives her (?) address: "Chestnut Lodge, Rockville, Maryland 20850," and the notation "November 24, 1965 and November 23, 1965." I think it's kind of amusing. This sort of thing helps to brighten up my otherwise rather dreary days. I don't think I need such a pen-pal however.

The regional court gave me a box number for Murmansk to receive my letters (Box N/X U3—50/1), but as you and the embassy prefer that all my letters come through the embassy (and/or the State Dept.) and be handed on to the Soviet Foreign Ministry for me, I will stick to your program. My parents said they'd write me once weekly.

I thought that my parents withstood the pressure very well.

I was proud of them for it, and especially for their being here to give me the shelter only one's parents or other loved ones can provide. Their presence had a salutary effect on me. (Please excuse the physical condition of this letter.)

The letters were very kind. It should humble me to think that so many people I respect think such of me. I would like to be able to read them, but perhaps my humility could not stand the pressure.

I judge that the State Dept. has informed Van Nostrand of my possibilities, my court appeal and my release date under the regional court's sentence. With Van Nostrand geographical territory is very important to me so that I greatly hope I can return to the upper N.Y. State area and Western Pennsylvania. I have a stake in those areas. I have spent a great deal of time over 2 years trying to get to know the colleges, the departments, curriculums and the professors. I have friends among many of the professors and good-will built up. I have friends off the campuses as well. I also like very many of the cities and towns in that area. When you travel constantly, as is necessary as a college traveler, the geographical area and the colleges it contains are very important to one's equanimity (sp.?). I would hate to think that much of that effort and learning would to a great extent just pass on to another college traveler, and I would have to start over elsewhere. There is little enough security in the job (as well) as it is. I'll include this hope in a letter to DVN.

The prison has informed me that my roubles are running out. I think I have around 10 or so left. Would you please forward from my account some more. I don't know, given the circumstances, how much I should have. I have read all the newspapers and magazines and some of the books—an interesting selection of the latter. I judge that as usual the books with the possible exception of 3 (from home) were all provided by the embassy. Captain Vilkov wanted the Warren Report as a souvenir. Perhaps, you could send me another copy of it for myself and a copy of Witnesses before the Warren Commission, also a Bantam paperback. Would you send some more newspapers and magazines *like: Sport, Sports Illus., Time, Life, Post, Saturday Review, New Republic,*

Reporter, Holiday, The Sporting News (primarily a baseball newspaper), and *Publishers Weekly*. In the U.S. I have a subscription to the last named, but it shouldn't be transferred here unless the appeal(s) fail.

Sincerely,
Newcomb Mott

Four days later on December 12, Newcomb Mott again wrote to Bill Shinn. In both this letter and the ones of the eighth, it will be noted that his mood did not appear to be despondent. In some measure his very matter-of-fact tone was employed to insure delivery of what he wrote, but it is also a guide to his equilibrium. It has been said by those who know that anyone who endures an arctic winter, no matter the circumstances, cannot avoid some adverse effect. And as one traveler to Murmansk put it, "At least the Russians have their vodka to make them forget." Also it will be recalled that Androv, the KGB interpreter, admitted Murmansk weather could be upsetting. Yet none of this is reflected in these several letters Newcomb wrote. Later the press was to make much of his reported nervousness. Yet, amid a winter's cold that was dead and black, he concealed whatever fears may have beset him with a kind of calm that makes it appear as though he were writing from college instead of the empty, frigid, blue-lit confines of his cell:

Murmansk
Dec. 12, 1965

Mr. William T. Shinn
Consul of the United States of America
American Embassy
Moscow, USSR

Dear Bill,

I thought of some additional things I wanted to say now that will supplement the Dec. 8th letter.

The reason the roubles are fast running out (now 5.00 remaining) is that since Nov. 13th, when I was handed the indictment and told I was the property of the court and no longer the prison's, *all* extra food, beyond the usual prison diet, has to be paid for by myself, not the prison. Prior to that time the prison paid for such things as: butter, white bread, soft drinks, cheese and milk. Now I pay for them and for anything fancier that I want, like jam and canned peaches. Therefore, I need enough roubles to pay for these things. You know what the prison food is like. Butter, for example, costs 1.85 roubles per ½ kilo.

Please send any letters air mail. The one I received from you recently took 5 days to get here—by the post mark in Murmansk and the one in Moscow.

If it comes to using Edward M., I suggest that in addition to the others, Silvio Conte join. It might do him & me some good. I know the former has a different association from the others, but it wouldn't hurt him to be seen in their company (in the U.S.A.).

In any parcel would you include 2 large aerosal spray deodorant like Bac for men (from Finland), Gillette's Right Guard or one of several others. I'd also like: 10 Wilkinson or Gillette stainless steel razor blades, a tube (large) of *brushless* shaving cream, 2 large Dental Floss, a small (not too small though) mirror to use for shaving, 2 27″ brown shoe laces, a face cloth. In the way of food, the Fizer (Finnish) chocolate bars are good, but if you can, I prefer their *milk* chocolate with whole hazelnut variety. I meant (Dec. 8) crunchy peanut butter in jars, not crunchy jars. Please don't send any fish, or any more hard candies now. French or Scandinavian mild cheese is good. You may not have the time or opportunity to send these things, I realize. Do you think it advisable to send me American books on the USSR? If you do, I'll request some if I have to stay in USSR much longer. Van Nostrand could send me some of ours.

I thought that Mr. Zolotukhin did a superb job in court here, as I said Nov. 24th. I've thought about it often since then. I don't see how he could have been better.

Mr. Zolotukhin, I forgot to mention, wants me to go out with him just before this Christmas in Moscow. I hope to keep the date. I have some hope that the Supreme Court of the RSFSR will grant our appeal.
(Please tell the 2 reporters (UPI & AP) that I am sorry I did not (on 24th) think of them until too late.)

I have received another epistle from a stranger, but the contents (this time a letter) are at least fairly sensible. I don't know how he got this address though—"Murmansk #27, P. Ya. IZ—50/1." Perhaps the newspapers have released this court address of mine. The writer sent his picture and describes himself as an 18-year-old, high school senior, who plans to major in political science at Clark or Amherst. He said, quite seriously, that he was "grateful that your sentence was relatively light." I wonder what that's relative to? He kindly points out that I could become "quite lonely and even despondent during the *next 18 months,* which shows he didn't read the newspapers carefully, "and so I thought I could write to you weekly, and you could write whenever the authorities allow you to." He goes on to encourage me about time quickly slipping by, adds that I have the prayers (I'm an agnostic, but that doesn't hurt) of himself, his friends and his family. "Keep up that good American spirit and I hope that you will be able to write soon." It's this last past of last sentence which makes me perhaps unduly, suspicious that he has what I suspect —— had in mind. Otherwise it's a genuinely charming and considerate idea and letter. His name is ——. I expect that I may receive similar letters from others, but perhaps not quite so thoughtful. Do you think it a good idea for me to answer this fellow (I think he may be all right) or any others I receive? Until I got these two it hadn't occurred to me that strangers would want to write me, nor that they would do so. Perhaps, despite reading the newspapers, they think I don't have any friends anywhere. This all may sound ungracious—and perhaps it is—but my experiences, as you know, have made me more suspicious than I used to be of other peoples' attitude and intentions. I used to be more willing to take people at face-value, unless they proved otherwise (immediately or at a later time). I'll write some friends though.

Although I had a physical of sorts at a clinic on Oct. 27 I have still not seen any prescriptions I requested at that time—as you knew. The prison Drs. are helpful.

I wrote my parents on Dec. 8th too. I'm happy that you or they included 2 song books (folk songs) because I was getting tired of always singing the same ones over to myself in the cell.

Do you think it a good idea, generally, to write letters of thanks now to the people who took the time to write letters about me? Perhaps I should wait and thank them personally, when I see them. I don't know; I may write them.

Sincerely,

Newcomb Mott

There are two significant points about this letter: one is proof that the prison was robbing the Motts, charging their son double for extra food, and the other is an item of mystery which remains unanswered.

The young man from Maryland who wrote the prisoner was a member of a high school current events club, and it was through the club that the idea of establishing a correspondence with Mott was discussed. The club faculty advisor called the State Department to get the prisoner's address. The address given was the wrong address; it did not come from the State Department, and yet the letter was delivered. It is possible that the address came from the Soviet Embassy, but wherever it came from, it was enough so that strangers could make contact with Newcomb Mott while his parents could not.

In Moscow on December 16 the Supreme Court of the RSFSR rejected the judicial appeal of Newcomb Mott. The court did so in a half-hour perfunctory session. Boris Zolotukhin presented the case for the defendant in what Bill Shinn described as his usual fine presentation. The rebuttal was delivered in a "hackneyed" manner by a female representative of the RSFSR procuracy. There were three judges, and the only other people in the court outside of the attorneys and Bill Shinn were correspondents from AP, UPI, and Tass.

Following the decision, the appeal for clemency was immediately instituted. In seeking clemency two courts could be approached, the Supreme Soviet of the RSFSR and the Supreme Court of the USSR. Legal considerations determined that the appeal should be directed to the former body first. At the same time, a side avenue of appeal was explored.

In explaining this course of action to the Motts, Bill Shinn wrote: "It is to write letters to the Chairman of the Supreme Court of the FSFSR, the Procurator of the RSFSR, and the Procurator General of the USSR, asking them to re-examine the case by way of supervision. This is a time-consuming process, and frankly the chances are slim, but if you approve, we'll get started on it."

Despite the additional cost, the consumption of time, and slimness of success, the Motts approved of the exploration. However, Bill Shinn was correct, and this long shot was rejected while the clemency appeal was still waiting judgment. The latter plea remained as the one narrow avenue still open through which Newcomb Mott could walk to freedom. It required, of course, that the prisoner submit his own personal appeal to the court. This he had been told to make ready in a letter written to him by Bill Shinn on December 6. The idea was that when and if the judicial appeal was turned down the prisoner would be prepared for the next step. However, on the sixteenth, Mott's jailors made no effort to inform him of the turndown, so that while the Embassy in Moscow transmitted to the Soviet Foreign Ministry letters from his parents, and those already noted from Senator Edward M. Kennedy, House Speaker McCormack, Attorney General Brooke, and others, nothing was forthcoming from the prisoner. It was just another nasty bit of Soviet poker played at his expense.

On December 22, U. S. Ambassador Foy Kohler had a meeting with Soviet Foreign Minister Andrei Gromyko. Of it a State Department release said: "Ambassador Kohler expressed the United States Government's disappointment to Gromyko that Mr. Mott had not been treated like others who had violated the border at Boris Gleb and who were simply expelled from the USSR. Ambassador Kohler requested favorable consideration of Mr. Mott's appeal for clemency."

On the following day in Washington, Ambassador-at-Large Llewellyn E. Thompson met with Soviet Ambassador Anatoly F. Dobrynin. The subject of discussion was the release of Newcomb Mott. It should be noted that this conference took place nearly three weeks in advance of the luncheon meeting between the Senator from Massachusetts and Ambassador Dobrynin, and it was the second such meeting between Thompson and Dobrynin.

Ambassador Kohler held still another meeting on the case, this one with the Soviet number-three man, Nikolai Podgorny. The Ambassador's purpose was to seek executive clemency for Newcomb Mott which could only be granted by Kosygin or Brezhnev. Podgorny, in his position, analogous to that of Chief of State, agreed to deliver the request.

Throughout this period and following it, Bill Shinn kept in daily touch with the Soviet Ministry of Foreign Affairs to find out if the clemency appeal had been heard by the court and if there had been any change in the prisoner's address.

The last letter received from Newcomb Mott was dated December 28, 1965 and January 2, 1966. It is reprinted in its entirety.

Murmansk
December 28, 1965
and January 2, 1966

Mr. William T. Shinn, Jr.
Consul of the United States of America
American Embassy
Ulitsa Chaykovskogo 19/21
Moscow, USSR

Dear Bill:

Today, Dec. 28th, when I received your letter of Dec. 23rd, was the first notice I had that the RSFSR Supreme Court had rejected the appeal. You don't say when this short hearing was held so I don't even know that. Consequently, although I wrote my personal clemency appeal on Dec. 22nd, I didn't give it to the prison official before today (I had left it undated), as I understood your previous letter to mean that I should submit one only when and if it became necessary. Yesterday, Dec. 27th, I asked that same prison official if he knew when the hearing of the Supreme Court would be held, and he said he didn't know.

A few minutes ago the prison captain returned to my cell with the appeal rejection by the Supreme Court. Nina Kulikova, who translated it, dated it at the end of the English translation version, December 27th. I see that the hearing was held Dec. 16th. The prison captain says I'll be staying here in Murmansk until the decision of the Supreme Soviet is made. He won't say why, and neither would another person on the prison staff. However, it makes me happy to a degree; I do prefer this prison to a labor camp. My treatment here is, more or less, the same as it was.

Since it's after the Supreme Court, I asked him to return my possessions with the exception of my money and passport. The prison captain replied that such things are not allowed in the possession of Murmansk Prison prisoners or convicts. I don't quite understand this since the Regional Court's verdict didn't specify where, only when, I was to regain my belongings. However, it's not of great importance at the moment.

You mention in your letter that Mr. Zolotukhin again did an excellent job in court. I was thoroughly convinced that he would.

On Dec. 31st, I received the four boxes that you sent me containing: 28 books, 38 magazines, 20 newspapers, a good deal of food, Canadian gloves, photographs of my father, mother and brother, an Andrew Wyeth print, soap, after-shave lotion, and two decks of playing cards. Cards are not normally allowed for prisoners, so there is considerable doubt I'll get them (or the ones my parents brought me) before I am released. The gloves fit very well, and are very nice. I presume they are your contribution. In the unwrapping in the presence of prison officials, I lost track of which present Miss Aline Mosby gave me. I think it was the cards or lotion. In any case, please thank her for me. It was thoughtful of her. It was very kind of various embassy employees to contribute to my welfare. Please thank them. Naturally, it is obvious to me that the greatest amount of thought and work was contributed by you. I greatly appreciate it.

Whenever you next send me a package, I have a few requests. Please include in it, if you can: cough drops, Mennen aerosol deodorant, Scripto pencil erasers or a large eraser, sliced dried beef, Coca-Cola, more of that instant lemonade mix (several), prunes or better yet, figs, "fine" Parker T-ball jotter, ballpoint refill or other ballpoint pen, 2 hams (canned), French, Dutch or Scandinavian *mild* cheese (like Bonbel, Gouda, Munster, etc.), "Isoptofrin" or other ophthalmic solution, Fazer milk chocolate, bouillon cubes, Tang, and/or anything else you can think of. Bergen Evans would approve (greatly) of that preposition. I now have enough dental floss to last a while. You mention (Dec. 23rd) a money order for twenty roubles. I received (the prison did) a money order for thirty roubles (a good amount) on Dec. 20th. Is that what you are referring to? That thirty roubles is now down to about ten roubles. Please send thirty more after you receive this epistle. Food is often twice as expensive in this country.

I have discovered that my parents were right. There is

little difference in some. Change that figure I gave you, when you were here, to the number three. You said you would remember.

You state that Oslo is holding my 2 bags "for the time being." What does that mean? My money, you say, the embassy has here. Please don't change the foreign currency into anything else; I collect coins and some are for my collection. Before I leave the USSR, I'd like 2 or 3 coins of each of the Russian coins through one rouble for my collection (all in good condition); I'd also like the one rouble paper currency. The KGB showed them to me in October. There is a commemorative one rouble coin, too (of East German monument); I'd like three of those. I hope the Russians would permit me to take them home.

Please don't give my two bags to my parents (I want them afterwards) because, as no doubt Oslo has informed you what they contain, there are some things, including presents, that I would rather they did not see. You mention having my air tickets, plural. I presume then that you have my Finnair tickets from Kirkenes to Tampere. I wonder if Finnair would give a refund on that return trip fare?—if not from Kirkenes on Sept. 4th, maybe from Ivalo on Sept. 5th or from Oulu Sept. 6th. I hope, of course, from Kirkenes. Whenever I'm sprung by the Soviet authorities, I would probably prefer to go to Helsinki first after Moscow. You could remind Finnair that I *could* buy a ticket on their airline from Moscow. If the Supreme Soviet frees me in the near future, I would want to spend a couple of days in Helsinki before going home. If they don't, and I were to be paroled late in May, I would probably, since I'm already in Europe, want to spend a couple of months in Europe resting up. In addition, *if* it were at all possible, I'd like to do a little sightseeing in Moscow before I left this country—no matter when I'm freed.

I understood your letter to mean that my representative's and the Governor's letters in Washington were also about me and would be forwarded to Moscow. Is that right? If it were possible, I would like to have copies for myself of the letters they, the 2 Senators, the Speaker of the House and the Attorney General of Massachusetts wrote about me. Perhaps you could give me copies in Moscow. Either in Moscow or here, if you thought the latter wise, I would like copies of the letters used in court too.

In a review of the movie, *Ship of Fools,* the reviewer stated that only someone with some sort of infirmity laying them up would have the gumption to plow all the way through the book. You included the novel in the Nov. 24th box; I've read it now. Except for part of the *Devil's Dictionary,* I've read all of the Ambrose Bierce anthology. His pessimism made me somewhat optimistic. I liked it on the whole, although some of it was pretty gruesome for me. In his *Wolves and Dogs,* one of the Fantastic Fables, he wrote, "Why should there be strife between us?" said the wolves to the sheep. "It is all owing to those meddlesome dogs. Dismiss them, and we shall have peace." "You seem," replied the sheep, "to think it an easy thing to dismiss dogs." A contemporary parable?

The prison officials have yet to check through the books, newspapers, and magazines for secret messages, so I haven't read them yet. However, I glanced at the book titles, an excellent selection and I'm sure I'll enjoy most of them, but someone must be convinced I'm quite intellectually-minded.

I've read all but 5 of the books you brought Nov. 24th, and some of them (the 5) are ones I probably won't read since I have this new batch of interesting books. I've read sections of the Warren Commission Report. Introducing it is James Reston's column of Sept. 27, 1964; it shows that he had little time to read and digest the report. He says that we get only "glimpses" of some intriguing things. I think the answers are quite adequate. They are: 1. The Commission offers several possible motives, of which all or one could be the motivation for Oswald; 2. The neighbor who got the job (for Oswald) in the Texas Schoolbook Depository is on P. 657—Mrs. Linnie Randle mentioned the possibility of an opening and Marina asked Mrs. Ruth Paine to telephone to verify it and the next day Oswald was interviewed and given a temporary job there; 3. Oswald's attempted suicide is on P. 616–17; 4. Who sent Oswald to Minsk? on P. 621—the MVD; 5. How did Oswald meet his wife is on P. 625—

at a dance; 6. Why was he allowed to return to the U.S. with a State Dept. loan is on P. 634—loans to Americans otherwise stranded abroad are not uncommon, I know. I have discovered that some Russians, on the other hand, are still convinced it was the work of a conspiracy (right-wing), although of all the attempted and actual Presidential assassinations (including an ex-President and a President-elect—making 8), only one attempt was by more than one assassin (Truman) and only one assassin had undercover accomplices (Lincoln); so there is no tradition of conspiracy in this act in the United States, as there is of conspiracy in other countries. It certainly is a problem—how to make the democratically-elected President accessible to the public without endangering his safety. I see that Miss Aline Mosby was the 1st American reporter to interview Oswald in Moscow. On P. 451 you can read Frank Adams' background.

Outside of this letter and the two you received, I've written only one other letter—that to my parents on December 8th. I thought it was a better idea to wait a while. I'll write some more now. My father says in his December 8th letter that, "many people tell us they have or will write to you." I presume these people have written to me directly, rather than through the embassy. My father goes on to say that, "We hope their letters get through." Besides the card and letter I wrote to you about before, I have not seen any letters sent to me directly.

I hope you have received the package from Van Nostrand by now and can send it up. . . . It was thoughtful of Ted and the others to send me that Christmas card.

I've been trying, unsuccessfully, to figure out the fahrenheit-centigrade equation and how to use it. Today, Jan. 2nd, it is —20 Centigrade and on Dec. 15, it was —22 C. Can you tell me?

When I am again a free man, I am going to eat, as soon as possible, some thick, loin lamb chops, steak, scrambled eggs, cheese omelette, and (Danish style) bacon (not all at once). I daydream about them, particularly. You can see I'm not primarily a vegetarian. But since Prison fare, outside of soup, includes only the vegetable, potato, I imagine I'll also be enthusiastic about them. The prison meat and fish are not thrilling.

I'll soon write Ted Saros of DVN. When I do, I'll request some DVN paperback books and a few hardbacks too—about twenty books all together. Most of them are about 200 pages or between 135–150 pages (i.e. the ones I'll request). I've thought rather carefully which ones I'd like and which ones I'd like—but might better eliminate. They are all harmless in every way.

Do you know by any chance who Boris Gleb was to have a site named after him?

Here are some perceptive comments about human beings as uttered by characters in Porter's *Ship of Fools*. "Each one carried signed, stamped papers as proof that he had been born in a certain time and place . . ." (Alfred Hitchcock once did a TV script in which a character in the plot was dead certain that he could completely change his identity and existence by a change of papers of identification; he believed we only exist through official recognition of that existence as symbolized by our papers—driver's license, etc. Unfortunately for him, he had a very large birth-mark on the side of his face.) "Had a name of his own, a foothold of some kind in this world, a journey in view for good and sufficient reasons, and possessions worth looking into at international frontiers." "They never win; they don't even know they are just fighting for a change of masters." "That near candor" (speaking of strangers traveling on the same transportation) "which comes of the possibility of future indifference." "You mean you'd think he'd make an exception for you?" (This is about a Jew's hate of gentiles, but Richard Wright in *Native Son* makes the same point about Negroes' hate of whites.) "He just couldn't help seeing how sincere you are? Well, he might hate you worse for that very thing!" About 50% of Antioch's students were Jews, and I knew several Negroes too: this point-of-view I never witnessed. "She had not expected anything better of them; she was only tired of the unkindness of people to each other." "What nonsense to say anyone was doomed until his last breath!" "The bride repented of her uncharitable feelings, and being honest, she knew they were caused by her horror of age and ugliness and sickness and her fear of them, and her greater fear of death, which was the only alternative, the one possible escape from them." Anyway, I think those comments and others are perceptive, which, of course, also shows something about me. But then I've never been a pariah before simply because of my nationality.

Sincerely yours,

Newcomb Mott

A man's character can be said to be prismatic in nature. Held up for examination in the clear light of noonday, it reflects colors which are the measure of its content. In the letters of a brief lifetime; in the associations made at home and over much of the earth; in the loves and friendships knitting family and friends; in the relationships and contacts with teachers, employers, and clients; and finally throughout the long ordeal of a nightmare, Newcomb Mott's character can be so examined. But those who knew him knew the kind of person he was, and those who didn't can judge from what has been recounted here, and ordinarily that would be enough. But there remains another reason for examination, and it concerns his final letter. There are those who have studied it, Howard and Phyllis Mott included, who believe that he was trying desperately to send a message to Bill Shinn saying that he feared for his life. Neither Shinn nor officials in the Embassy or the State Department saw anything unusual in the letter's contents. To them the letter was simply Newcomb Mott, detailed, accurate, and completely without guile.

That he was a kindly young man of considerable courage, no one would question, not even his jailors. But officialdom in dealing with him, in trying to secure his freedom, could not help feeling he had been less than bright in stumbling into such a mess. That he admitted the same did little to correct the original impression. And furthermore, officialdom did not know him; only Bill Shinn knew him and then only after the act that brought imprisonment. But Newcomb Mott had lived on either side of the act, freely for twenty-seven years and then in a cell for four months. The latter period did not change his essential character, although judgment of it was based in part on how he had become captive and on his behavior during the period itself. However, by the time he wrote his final letter there were certain colorings of his nature that were as obvious to officialdom as they were to his friends. He was extremely literal; he possessed an equally high degree of integrity; he was not overly imaginative. He sought out the facts of a matter, not the hues that surrounded and illuminated them. In all the letters he wrote through December 12 he is concerned only with those things that centered on or around his case, plus his mental and physical needs. He craves books, magazines, newspapers to occupy his thoughts and keep his mind off his predicament. He wants extra food to satisfy his hunger and keep his big body strong. In none of his letters to Shinn, and the one received by his parents, does he depart from those things which are important to matters at hand. In fact, in all the many letters he wrote home over the years he followed much the same pattern. What he sees he describes in literal terms; he is extremely observant and has a good eye for detail, but he is not subtle. He is intelligent and interested and reasonable, but he is not conspiratorial or particularly inventive . . . that is, until his last letter. No one is ever going to know with certainty whether at this juncture he found it necessary to become inventive and clever out of desperation, that he was using the only weapon he had with which to fight—his brain—in a vain call for help. The hypothesis that follows is advanced on such an assumption.

Newcomb Mott's call for help is contained in reference to and quotes from Katherine Anne Porter's novel *Ship of Fools* and the key to it is in the question that precedes the quotes: "Do you know by any chance who Boris Gleb was to have a site named after him?"

All the rest, the cryptic statements about his parents being right, changing the number to three, the answers to James Reston found in the Warren Commission Report, are straight and explainable. They were included because Newcomb Mott knew his captors would question him about them. He made a point of referring to the Warren Commission Report because, as it will be recalled, he had already given Captain Vilkov his original copy of it. A KGB check of his long discourse to Shinn on the Report would be found to be accurate. In other words, he was doing his best to convince his censors that his letter was a long exercise in penmanship and literal exposition and this particularly applies to his quotes from *Ship of Fools.* It can be reasoned he would not have gone to such lengths to write about matters that had absolutely nothing to do with his case, and which could be of no interest to Bill Shinn or anyone else in the Embassy, unless he hoped they would recognize the same incongruity.

For nearly three handwritten pages his letter follows a normal pattern and then suddenly he interrupts himself and comments: "In a review of the movie, *Ship of Fools,* the reviewer stated that only someone with some sort of infirmity laying them up would have the gumption to plow all the way through the book. You included the novel in the November 24th box; I've read it now."

In the original letter he wrote the words *courage* and *gumption* and crossed them both out and then settled for the word *gumption.* This statement could have been his way of saying that he was sick. "Some sort of infirmity laying them up. . . . I've read it now."

The fact that he returns to the *Ship of Fools* in the final long paragraph of his letter points up the hypothesis. The supposition takes on much firmer credence, however, after one evaluates his question about Boris Gleb, preceding the quotes.

Newcomb Mott knew the answer to his own question, knew

that Boris and Gleb were two princes, and prefaced what followed because Boris Gleb was the *international frontier* where his ordeal had started.

"Here are some perceptive comments about human beings as uttered by characters in Porter's *Ship of Fools."*

The key word is *perceptive.* He wants Shinn to be perceptive.

"Each one carried signed, stamped papers as proof that he had been born in a certain time and place, had a name of his own, a foothold of some kind in this world, a journey in view for good and sufficient reasons, and possessions worth looking into at international frontiers."

This quote comes from page 9 of the book and Mott picked it up in the middle of a sentence which begins: "Imperfectly washed, untidy and dusty, vaguely not-present in eyes dark-circled by fatigue and anxiety—each one," etc.

In this passage he is describing himself. All the extraneous material about Alfred Hitchcock is to divert the Soviets, as are the other comment passages.

"They never win; they don't know they are just fighting for a change of masters."

This quote is taken from page 8 of the book, which is further indication that the prisoner was selectively trying to put his message together, otherwise his quotes would have been in sequence. Furthermore, he leaves out of the quote, "They're such cattle . . ." He is referring to his captors as the character in the book was referring to *the proletariat.*

"That near candor (speaking of strangers traveling on the same transportation) which comes of the possibility of future indifference." From page 89.

The significant word in this quote is *indifference.* An individual who lived for ten years in the Soviet Union and during World War II was imprisoned by the Gestapo maintains that "Totalitarian powers have an indifference toward the individual which is utterly terrifying to the uninitiated who suddenly realizes he could be eliminated like a fly and with as little concern."

Newcomb Mott may be saying that he has been told that his clemency appeal means nothing and that he is going to be shipped somewhere where things are going to get rough and his interrogators couldn't care less.

"You mean you think he'd make an exception for you?"

"He just couldn't help seeing how sincere you are? Well, he might hate you worse for that very thing!" From page 339.

He's saying they certainly aren't going to change their decision because he's innocent of any wrongdoing and sincerely wants to be friendly. In fact, his sincerity makes them dislike him all the more.

There is an ugly allegory between the above quotes. In his parenthetical remark, Newcomb refers to Richard Wright's *Native Son*. The hero of Wright's novel was a Negro named "Bigger." Newcomb stood six foot five. Bigger through no desire of his own committed a crime and was put in jail. In jail he did not hate his jailors so much as he feared them. He thought they would kill him, and they finally did.

"She had not expected anything better of them; she was only tired of the unkindness of people to each other."

This is from page 342, and it is more of the same. He purposely used the female sex to make his quotes appear to be nothing more than observations.

"What nonsense to say that anyone was doomed until his last breath!"

This significant statement from page 374 is preceded by the sentence: "A warm surge of human grief for that creature who was doomed maybe beyond his or any human help filled him like a tide body and mind, bringing its own healing."

And then finally from page 439: "The bride repented of her uncharitable feelings, and being honest, she knew they were caused by her horror of age, ugliness and sickness and her fear of them, and her greater fear of death, which was the only alternative, the one possible escape from them."

He fears they mean to kill him, and he knows it is the only way he can really escape them.

Unless!

"Anyway I think those comments and others are perceptive, which, of course, also shows something about me. But then I've never been a pariah before simply because of my nationality."

He hopes that Shinn will be perceptive, too, and read between the lines. His only crime is that he's an American, but it's enough to get him killed.

In further support of this hypothesis, it can be stated that the quotes chosen are not all that perceptive as against many others in this 497-page book unless they were chosen for the afore-declared reason.

In the five-day interim between the beginning of the letter on December 28 and the major portion of it written on January 2, there is no telling what happened to Newcomb Mott or what he was told about his future. It will be recalled that earlier for their own reasons KGB officers threatened him with a secret trial and conviction. Now they may have threatened him with something worse, and unable to contact Shinn directly, he tried to do his best by being clever. As to whether the Soviets were more perceptive than the U. S. Embassy officials who read the letter, there is the possibility they wanted him to call for help, knew that he would call for help, on the theory that if his message was understood, U.S. officials would weaken and agree to let Ivanov go for the safe return of Newcomb Mott.

Newcomb Mott's best friend (next to his brother) was given this final letter without preamble and asked to read it carefully. After he had done so, he remarked, "It's Newcomb all right, but the last part about *Ship of Fools* is certainly out of character."

No one is ever likely to know whether in being out of character Newcomb Mott was trying to send a message. Only one thing about the letter is known with certainty. The date, January 2, preceded Newcomb Mott's murder by eighteen days.

The results of this investigation into the circumstances of Newcomb Mott's suicide will be made known to the U. S. Embassy in Moscow, which will then be able to inform the American authorities. However, it is surprising that some highly placed Americans, who are not familiar with the circumstances of the case and who are obviously pursuing political aims, are raising an unjustified clamor over Mott's suicide.

From a commentary by
Aleksander Serbin, Tass international service,
February 4, 1966

Chapter Thirteen

Three days before Christmas an official of the Soviet Foreign Ministry personally informed Bill Shinn that Newcomb Mott was still in Murmansk. Also on that day Shinn received the prisoner's letter of December 12, in which, among other things, he requested a supply of Wilkinson safety razor blades. In the parcels his parents had left him on November 24, there had been six five-blade packs of Wilkinsons and a traveling-kit Gillette razor. Since the prisoner was requesting more razor blades just eighteen days after his parents had supplied him with thirty of them, it is reasonable to conclude that at best he was doled out one at a time, or possibly had never received any of them, having to use a Russian-made blade for his shaving.

On the strength of the Foreign Ministry's assurance that the prisoner was still in Murmansk, Shinn prepared and sent out that same day a Christmas package to Newcomb Mott. In it he included some of the items requested in the letter of the twelfth.

The next and final communication from Murmansk prison was received by Bill Shinn on January 11, 1966; Newcomb's dual letter dated December 28 and January 2. The Embassy personnel who read and evaluated it considered the most important item in it the statement that the prisoner had been told he would not be moved until his clemency appeal was heard. As a result, Shinn dispatched reading glasses, forwarded from Mott's belongings earlier sent from Kirkenes to the U. S. Embassy in Oslo, and then on the fourteenth, another food package. Over a month later this package would be returned undelivered, its contents so badly damaged they had to be destroyed. Thus the package sent on December 22, which the prisoner received on the last day of the year, was the final one to reach him, *and it contained no razor blades of any kind.*

On Thursday, January 21, 1966, Bill Shinn wrote a letter to the Motts summarizing a talk he had had that day with Boris Zolotukhin, concerning various other appeal approaches that were being explored.

At 3:00 P.M. David Boster, Embassy Political Affairs Counselor, went to the Soviet Foreign Ministry, where he was informed that Newcomb Mott was still in Murmansk and there were "no new developments."

Three hours later John C. Guthrie, the Embassy's second in command, received a telephone call asking him to come to the Soviet Foreign Ministry. There he met with Georgy M. Korniyenk, who informed him that American citizen Newcomb Mott on the night of January 20 while en route to the place where his prison sentence was to be served had committed suicide by cutting his throat. No particular sympathy for the tragedy was expressed by the Soviet official.

Shaken and sick at heart, Guthrie brought the news back to the Embassy, where it hit everyone with stunning force. All had taken a keen interest in Newcomb Mott's welfare. Some had been more closely involved with his case than others, but all, from Ambassador Foy Kohler on down, had been directly affected by the terrible treatment suffered by their fellow American.

The Ambassador issued an immediate statement. "I am profoundly shocked by the news of the death of Newcomb Mott and deplore the handling of this matter which has now come to this unhappy end."

Bill Shinn was hit hardest by the ghastly news. It was brought to him at the theater where he and his wife had gone to see a play. The word came at intermission time, and he returned at once to the Embassy.

The shock wave was transmitted to the State Department via top-priority cable.

It was Carroll Woods who called Howard Mott in the forenoon of January 21, just two days after the Motts had been released from the hospital.*

Afterward, Howard Mott went up the long flight of colonial stairs in his home, calling out in anguish to his wife. "There's something I have to tell you, but I can't tell you! I can't tell you!"

And she, sensing the awfulness of his news, cried out, "Tell me!"

And he told her.

The word came to Rusty Mott at Great Lakes Naval Training Center. It was brought to his barracks by an officer, and when his eighty-one bunkmates learned of it, each got up and went out of the barracks so that Newcomb's brother and best friend could have some privacy.

On that same morning Russian time, and so eight hours earlier than in Sheffield, Massachusetts, Ambassador Kohler, having asked for a meeting with Soviet Foreign Minister Andrei Gromyko, went to the Soviet Foreign Ministry. Instead, he confronted First Deputy Vasiliy V. Kuznetzov. Gromyko did not choose to face the diplomat.

In a prepared statement Kohler requested an investigation

* The time difference between Moscow and Washington is eight hours.

into the circumstances of the death and said, "News of the pitiful death of a young American Newcomb Mott in a place far removed from his home and under circumstances not yet fully clear has naturally caused deep sorrow and shock to the public in the United States and elsewhere."

He then went on to declare that Newcomb Mott's death could have been avoided if the Soviets had but listened to the appeals on his behalf and that neither the U. S. Government nor the public could understand why the Soviet had acted so harshly over such a minor infraction of their laws.

The statement had been drafted in Washington, and the wording sounded as though it had been fashioned out of vanilla pudding. The only note of anger was in the Ambassador's voice.

Kuznetzov, pale and shaken nonetheless, made no direct reply to the request for an investigation, saying only that a medical examination would take place. He regretted the incident, reiterated that the Soviet Government had handled the case following the strict letter of the law, and hoped that American-Soviet relations would improve.

Prior to this formal meeting, Bill Shinn and Political Counselor Dexter Anderson had gone to the airport in an attempt to get a ride on the mail plane to Kirov, where the Soviets said the body had been taken. The previous night they had learned of the flight. The Soviets had informed them they would not be able to take it, but they went to the airport anyway. So far the details of Newcomb Mott's death were not clear. He was said to have cut his throat in the washroom of a trans-Siberian train taking him to an undisclosed labor camp. Kirov was five hundred miles east of Moscow and the mail plane was the quickest way to get there, but the two Americans were prevented from boarding it.

The next-best transportation was the train, which left Moscow around noon and arrived in Kirov at 1 A.M. The two Americans returned to the Embassy, planning to take the train. There they were informed the trip would not be necessary since Kuznetzov had sent word the body was being shipped west and would arrive in Moscow the following day.

Had Washington advised that the body remain just where the Soviets said it was until Embassy representatives had a chance to arrive on the scene and identify it, the answer would have undoubtedly have been *"Nyet!"* Still, was it not time to make a few infuriated demands in the place of velvet-lined diplomatic requests?

It is the Soviets who have said that Newcomb Mott died in the prison car of a train bound from Leningrad to Sverdlovsk, and there is absolutely not one scintilla of evidence beyond the statement itself that he died en route to anywhere. Conversely, evidence will be brought forth to show that he met his death under circumstances hard to duplicate in a prison car. A trip to Kirov by Shinn and Anderson would have at least established that the victim was east of Moscow when he died. Not only did the Soviets prevent this journey with U.S. acquiescence, but it appears they also delayed the return of the body by a full day.

However, the idea of death on the train was bought by the Embassy, the State Department, and the press. The place of death, later identified by the Soviets, was said to be station Shar'ya, 150 miles west of Kirov.

Howard and Phyllis Mott made two significant telephone calls that dreadful day. The first, in the newness of their black grief, was to the Soviet Embassy in Washington. Their plan was to have their son's body sent home. They spoke to First Secretary Valerian Mikhailov, the diplomat who had greeted them at the Embassy during their visit there in November. At first Mikhailov pretended not to know who they were, never to have met them or have heard of them.

And then Howard Mott, his voice shrill with fury, shouted, "Look, goddamn it, you've got a son of your own! How do you think you'd feel if it was your son!"

First Secretary Mikhailov backed off and said he'd see what could be done.

At two that afternoon Phyllis Mott spoke directly to Bill Shinn in Moscow. "Bill, it's murder and you know it."

"I know how you feel." The words came wearily back across the miles.

The overseas operator broke in. "Look, honey, be careful what you say," she warned. "You'll be cut off."

"Bill, we want him back."

"Yes, Phyl. I'll do the best I can."

That same afternoon a representative of SAS called the Motts from Boston. "I hate to intrude," he said, "but we want you to know any place you want to go that we can fly you, you'll go as our guests."

Exactly when Newcomb Mott's body arrived in Moscow or from where is known only by the KGB authorities handling the case. The Soviet Foreign Ministry had agreed that a U. S. Embassy representative could be present when an autopsy was performed by a team of Soviet pathologists. The Embassy was not informed when the body arrived, and notified of the autopsy only a half hour before it actually took place. Bill Shinn and Captain James W. Bizzell, Assistant Air Attaché and Embassy doctor, were directed to go to Moscow City Morgue No. 2. They were directed to a dimly lit white-walled room where there were four Soviet doctors, plus L. N. Sedov, State Counselor of Justice and General Prosecutor of the USSR, an assistant from the Prosecutor's Department, a representative from the Soviet Ministry of Foreign Affairs, and a number of armed guards.

The autopsy began at two-thirty on the afternoon of January 24. It ended at five forty-five. For Bill Shinn it was a ghastly and agonizing experience. When the wooden coffin bound with heavy cord, bearing in three places the seal of the Kirov Procuracy, was opened, he made the identification.

Over Newcomb Mott's body lay a sheet stamped "Railroad Hospital Kirov I.65." Folded under his head was the overcoat in which Shinn had last seen him dressed. He wore a flannel gray-green checked shirt and light brown pants, and under them a cotton T shirt and shorts, and under them a suit of thermal underwear which had been in the package his parents brought to the trial. On his feet were two pairs of socks, wool and cotton, and to one side black boots. He was not clean-shaven; there were several days of beard growth on his face. Since he normally had a light, slow-growing beard, there was no telling how long it had been since he had shaved. A pair of white mesh shorts and a T shirt had been wrapped around his lacerated neck. The death wound was a deep five-inch slash across the throat which had cut through the windpipe and esophagus. The carotid arteries and jugular vein had not been damaged and the victim had died from the "aspiration of blood into his lungs"—or to put it bluntly, he had drowned in his own blood, which had also saturated his clothing.

There were, however, other wounds on the body of Newcomb Mott.

On either side of his neck, starting beneath his ears, there were sixteen incised cuts: ten on the right, six on the left.

On his throat, over the trachea, just beneath the death wound, there was a large two-inch purplish bruise.

On the inner portion of his right wrist there were approximately sixteen closely spaced slashes. In the same location on his left wrist there were the same number of cuts.

There were bruises on the back of his left wrist and hand.

There were a number of horizontal slash marks crisscrossing his right arm at the front of the elbow.

In the same area of the left arm there was an inch-long slash.

On the middle knuckle of the right hand there were a bruise and some evidence of a confining or restraining agent having held the wrist.

There were a total of six cuts and unidentifiable abrasions on both elbows.

On two fingers of his right hand there were vertical incisions.

Across his stomach on the left side there were three slashes, one of them two and a half inches long, yet his flannel shirt and two pair of undershirts were not damaged.

In the area around his groin there were bruises.

There were also bruises on his feet and shins and instep and on the back of his right leg.

Thus, aside from the death wound, there were more than sixty-five slashes on the body of Newcomb Mott, plus numerous bruises and abrasions.

During the course of the autopsy Dr. Bizzell took photographs. At its conclusion he was told by the Soviet officials to hand the film over. He did so and despite Embassy protests, the film was never returned.

That night, with no official version of what weapon Newcomb Mott had used to carve himself up, a story was circulated by "informed Soviet sources." The scene of death was shifted from a train lavatory to a barred compartment of a passenger car. There, as the train was approaching station Shar'ya, a guard walking along the corridor discovered Mott throwing jars of marmalade at the bars of the compartment. When the guard tried to enter, the prisoner took a razor blade from a gift package and cut his throat.

This unofficial version soon became the accepted version with various modifications.

The U. S. Embassy did not "accept or reject" the unofficial Soviet account, refusing to make a judgment until the investigation into the death was completed.

Two days after the autopsy the Soviets issued a death certificate, giving no cause of death. This was unusual, for it is normal procedure for the Soviets to make a point of listing the cause in order to keep the record straight.

Plans to bring the body home had been purposely delayed following the autopsy. The Soviets stalled on filling out the necessary forms and said the death certificate must come from Kirov. Yet when it came, it was signed by an official in the Moscow Registrar of Civilian Statistics and dated January 25.

Through the efforts of his parents and Bill Shinn, Newcomb Mott finally left the Soviet Union on Friday, January 28, 1966, aboard an Air India flight bound for London. The fare to the Motts was 214 roubles. Pan American flew the body from London to Boston for no charge.

In the week following his death the press was full of reports and speculation on the manner in which Newcomb Mott had died. Most of these reports originated in Moscow and "unnamed Embassy spokesmen" supplied background and developments.

Unfortunately, there were three major errors in fact and a grave breach of privacy which permeated the bulk of these reports, and they gave support to the Soviet contention of suicide by razor blade while the prisoner was traveling on a train.

In his January 25 story from Moscow, New York *Times* correspondent Theodore Shabad wrote: "The Embassy confirmed today that a recent gift package sent to Mr. Mott contained both jars of marmalade and razor blades."

No jars of marmalade had been sent to Newcomb Mott, and as already noted, razor blades were only in the packages of November 24 and the prisoner had requested a supply of same in his letter of December 12.

The story of recently sent razor blades was repeated in papers throughout the U.S. and elsewhere.

In the *Herald Tribune* of January 25, Moscow correspondent, Stuart H. Loory wrote: "Last night the Embassy acknowledged that it had sent Mr. Mott razor blades among other things in one of several packages. All of them passed through the hands of Soviet authorities and were approved by them."

Also in his report of the same date, Mr. Loory reported: "An American Embassy spokesman said bruises were also found on Mr. Mott's body and that they were apparently caused after his death. He said, however, that they were minor and of the sort made by normal handling of a body."

This statement was also widely reported. There was one thing incorrect about it. After death a body *cannot* be bruised in any way, "minor" or major.

The third error followed a Novosti report on the twenty-seventh for foreign consumption and an English-language broadcast on the same day by Radio Moscow. Both reports declared that Newcomb Mott had grown depressed because he had been abandoned by his family and his government, neither having done anything to obtain his release by bail. Novosti also maintained that Newcomb Mott had taken pills the day of his death, suggesting that they had affected him mentally. Both contentions, of course, were totally untrue, but while John Guthrie personally protested the first lie to the Soviet Ministry of Foreign Affairs, an "Embassy spokesman" was quoted as saying that indeed penicillin and tranquilizers had been sent to the prisoner at the request of his parents.

The only penicillin to reach Murmansk, it will be recalled, was hand carried by Bill Shinn and turned over to KGB Captain Androv. The prisoner never saw it. No tranquilizers were ever sent him.

Some reporters did point out that all packages had to pass close inspection by prison and KGB officials. Aside from a small amount of aspirin, even the subsequent Russian autopsy report found no evidence of drugs. But by then the contention had been generally accepted.

So there it was, handed out from Embassy sources unknown: *razor blades* that were not sent; *bruises* that were not made after death; *drugs* that were never taken.

The breach of privacy, which also reflects directly on an Embassy source, was the passing on to newsmen information that was strictly confidential between the Motts and the United States Government.

New York *Times* dispatches referred to details of the four-hour family meeting in Murmansk. After the meeting Bill Shinn had correctly made a confidential report of it to his Embassy superiors.

"According to sources Mr. Mott was depressed recently because the Embassy allegedly turned down a suggestion he made to Mr. Shinn for obtaining his release by such methods as a prisoner exchange and the payment of bail."

The Berkshire Eagle, in its headline story of January 22, 1966, was able to quote from Newcomb Mott's last letter to Bill Shinn, a letter his parents were not to see until a month later. And the day after the *Eagle* made its reference, Loory of the *Herald Tribune* wrote: "The American [probably Bill Shinn] would not answer a question about whether the six to eight page letter, which contained information about books Mr. Mott had been reading, his thoughts, and some requests, had shown any despondency. The letter was addressed to a consular official *and as such was considered a private communication.*" [Italics added.]

Private to some in the U. S. Government but not so private to others.

On the day Newcomb Mott's body departed the Soviet Union, John Guthrie requested that the Soviet Ministry of Foreign Affairs leave off with telling lies and get on with supplying a full report of just how Newcomb Mott had died. His contact in the Ministry, Valentin I. Oberenko, agreed that a prompt report was desirable, and subsequent press communications from Moscow, quoting "reliable sources," said the Soviets would probably comply with the demand by Monday, January 31.

Howard and Phyllis Mott (along with a good many of their fellow Americans) had not for one minute accepted the unofficial and confusing Soviet explanation of their son's death. They wanted a second autopsy performed by American doctors, and the Medical Examiner for Suffolk County,

Massachusetts, Dr. Michael A. Luongo, agreed to take on the assignment. As a result, directly after the Pan Am flight from London landed at Boston's Logan Airport, the sealed wooden container bearing Newcomb Mott's body was taken to the Medical Examiner's office in Boston's Mallory Institute of Pathology. There in the laboratory, assisted by five colleagues, Dr. Luongo conducted the second autopsy.

Before the casket was opened, documents accompanying it were read by the Examiner and the death certificate was "found to give no specific information regarding the cause and manner of death."

The body was now dressed in new clothing, all of Soviet make, none of the original clothing worn at the time of death, accompanying it. During the course of the examination, thirty-five 35-mm. Kodachrome slides were made under Dr. Luongo's supervision "to record the general appearance of the body and the anatomical findings observed." Before sending Newcomb Mott's remains home, Soviet doctors had neatly *removed* the area in the neck where the fatal wound had been made. They had also removed many of the internal organs and a portion of others, including a third of the brain, none of which made the examining doctor's task any easier. In the course of the autopsy, suitable tissue for histological and toxicological examination was retained. The latter was of particular interest because of the Soviet claim that Newcomb Mott had taken drugs. This examination revealed no drugs, only "a small amount of salicylate [usually indicating therapeutic amounts of aspirin]."

The autopsy report, signed by Drs. Luongo, Katsas, and O'Dea, noted in conclusion: ". . . some bruises of a type not typical of self-infliction . . . most of the wounds which remained were of a type compatible with self-infliction. However, it must be emphasized that any wound consistent with self-infliction may also be consistent with infliction by other persons. Furthermore, the opinions formed by a pathologist usually take into consideration much more information than is available from the body alone."

This information was listed as the scene of death, the clothing and instruments which caused injury, and the events surrounding the death. Without these the examiners could come to no final conclusion.

Before the autopsy, Dr. Luongo had told the Motts the photographs would cost a dollar apiece. But the doctor did not send them a bill for the photos, nor did he and his colleagues charge for the examination. However, when it was over, Dr. Luongo called again in a state of some excitement and said, "What am I going to do? The reporters are knocking down the door. I'm besieged!"

Drawing on her own medical experience, Phyllis Mott suggested that he delay the press, saying that the toxicological tests had yet to be made. Her major purpose in wanting to delay was so that she and her husband and Rusty could be out of the country when the press came asking questions.

News stories the next day quoted the Medical Examiner as saying there was nothing surprising in what he and his colleagues had found, but they had been "limited" in drawing conclusions because of the prior Soviet autopsy. He could not release details of the findings until the Mott family had given permission; also the toxicological tests were not complete. Dr. McBay of the department was quoted as saying the tests would take several days and that tissue from the body would also undergo extensive examination.

On Monday, January 31, 1966, Newcomb Mott was buried amid the snow-shrouded New England landscape. There had been a blizzard the night before which had continued on into the early morning. Now the wind blew down over the flank of Mount Everett, driving the drifting snow in biting swirls. It huffed and pummeled against Sheffield's Old Parish

Congregational Church where two hundred mourners had gathered in brokenhearted farewell. It supplied an angry, elemental counterpart to the Reverend Phillip C. Hammond's eulogy, spoken out of friendship and love for Newcomb and his family.

"And then we, his closest friends, and the world in general were shocked by the report of his death; and well we should be, for by his death Newcomb Mott has shown us what we seemingly did not realize from almost half a century of dealing with the heirs of the Bolshevik Revolution, where there is no room for trust, where there is no concern for human life, where there is no place for interhuman faith, where truth, no matter how peculiar, cannot be taken for granted, there can only be annihilation.

"Hence, by the loss of his own life, he reminded us once again that man has no value unless there be some faith in the value of every individual life.

"When he crossed the border into Russia, he bore an American passport, one of the proudest privileges granted to citizens of the free world.

"Perhaps the time has come for us to raise the question as to whether or not we, as citizens of the United States, can any longer expect the respect and trust from certain nations which our passport once brought us and whether or not we in this age of distrust and injustice need to begin to do something as individuals and as a nation to restore the prestige of our country abroad and to insure ourselves and our fellow Americans against harsh treatment and lack of personal protection."

Among those who heard the service was Brigadier General Timothy J. Regan, Massachusetts Governor John Volpe's personal representative. Three who failed to hear it, arriving late, were a trio of Polish-Americans, onetime refugees. They had driven all the way from Boston over snow-blocked highways simply to come and pay their respects and present a small wreath.

Later, at Center Cemetery, within sight of the Mott home, Phyllis, Howard, Rusty, and other members of the family stood at the graveside and said their silent good-bys to Newcomb. The bitter winter wind lashed and hissed among the pines and rocked the naked elm branches, making them twist and crack in anguish.

On that sad Monday the U. S. Embassy in Moscow waited in vain for the expected Soviet report.

The wait continued. Three times in February, on the seventh, fourteenth, and twenty-fourth, Deputy Chief of Mission Guthrie requested from the Soviet Ministry the forthcoming report. On March 7 he expressed to the Ministry "mounting U.S. concern over the Soviet failure to offer the results of its investigation."

Then on March 10 the long-awaited document was passed on to the U. S. Embassy. It consisted of a one-page explanation of how Newcomb Mott had died and a twenty-six-page autopsy report. No instrument of death accompanied it; no clothing, no photographs, no report of the guards, and no permission for American officials to question anyone connected with the case.

This is the Soviet explanation of how Newcomb Mott met his death:

> The convicted Mott, traveling in solitary compartment No. 9 of the special railroad car to the place where he was to serve his sentence, during the latter part of the day, January 20, 1966, began to show signs of abnormal behavior: having placed on the shelf a picture postcard of the Madonna, he spread out playing cards before it, began to talk to himself, wrung his hands, loudly shouted some words, and then with a sudden movement gathered up the cards and tore them up. After this he began to look for something among his belongings, and threw out canned goods and other things from three boxes that were in his compartment.

> Having noticed blood on N. Mott's body, the guards tried to enter his compartment, but N. Mott, being in a state of very nervous agitation, prevented access to the compartment and threw three glass jars of canned goods at the guards.
>
> In spite of this the convoy personnel entered the compartment and gave N. Mott first-aid treatment, which he resisted. Then N. Mott became weak from the great loss of blood and although steps were taken to save his life, died soon thereafter.
>
> An inquest conducted in Moscow on January 24, 1966, and in which participated a board of forensic medicine experts of the Ministry of Health of the USSR, headed by the Chief Forensic Medicine Expert, Professor V. I. Procorovski, Doctor of Medical Sciences, established that the death of N. Mott, who ended his life by suicide, resulted from loss of blood and the accompanying aspiration of blood into the respiratory passages, caused by a deep cut in his throat made by a safety razor blade.
>
> In examining the scene where the incident took place, in compartment No. 9 of the special railroad car in which N. Mott was traveling, a Gillette razor and four Wilkinson razor blades were found.

A month before the Soviets turned over this document, Attorney Francis W. H. Adams, acting for the Motts, issued a press release in which he made certain demands of the Soviet Government:

> 1. A careful examination of the pathological findings considered in relation to the background and temperament of Newcomb Mott casts serious doubt on the claim of the Soviet officials that Mr. Mott's death was a suicide.
>
> 2. The failure of the Soviet Government to send the clothing which Mr. Mott wore at the time of his death

with his body suggests a desire on the part of the Soviet Government to prevent full investigation of the death.

3. The failure of the Soviet Government to produce the instrument said to have caused death is highly suspicious.

4. The failure of the Soviet Government to supply a copy of an official Soviet post-mortem report or to make any other report of the circumstances has not been explained.

In view of the brutal and heartless manner in which this young man's life and death were dealt with by the Soviet Government, it is Mr. Adams' belief that the Soviet Government should be called upon to do the following:

1. Produce the alleged weapon.

2. Produce for questioning the security guards who are said to have permitted this alleged suicide in a small washroom on a moving train.

3. Produce for chemical and other analysis the clothing worn at the time of death.

4. Produce for questioning the doctors and prison and all other officials who in any manner were responsible for the health and physical and emotional well-being of Mr. Mott up to the time of his death.

5. Provide a full explanation from competent witnesses of every fact in any way relating to the death and permit examination of such witnesses by American officials.

Mr. Adams pointed out that the suppression of evidence and the many questions unanswered by the Soviet Government raised serious doubts concerning the good faith of the unsupported allegation of the Soviet Government that Mr. Mott committed suicide.

On March 19, after a thorough examination of the Soviet documents, the U. S. Embassy requested the Soviets to supply essentially the same basic information that former New York

Police Commissioner Adams had demanded. These requests continued until April 19, when the Soviet Foreign Ministry announced there would be no more information and the material it had handed over was "an act of good will" on the Kremlin's part.

In offering background on Newcomb Mott's death, the Soviet autopsy report, under the heading of "Preliminary Information," gave some additional points of interest. The train the prisoner was on, it said, was number 94 on the Leningrad-Sverdlovsk run and that "from the report drawn up on January 20, 1966 by the chief escort, Selivanov, with the participation of escort Murodyan and the conductor Aububakirov, it is evident that the prisoner Newcomb Mott cut his own throat and died."

Later it was reported that Selivanov, Murodyan, and conductor Aububakirov were disciplined. Why, if they were trying to save a demented man's life?

The Soviet story of how Newcomb Mott died bears scrutiny. He possessed no picture of the Madonna; he was an agnostic. His mother believes that when the version was concocted the KGB had confused the good-luck charm she had offered her son in Murmansk with a religious token such as the supposed card. As for playing cards, his parents had included a pack in their gifts, but he had told them he was sure he would not be permitted to have them. With respect to the three boxes said to be in his possession on the train, neither they nor any of their contents—food, clothing, books, newspapers, magazines, *et al*—were returned because, according to the Soviets, they were blood soaked and the health authorities ordered their destruction. In addition, there was a notebook in which it had been suggested that the prisoner record his experiences. Of it Bill Shinn told the Motts: "We did specifically ask the Foreign Ministry if the Soviet authorities had found any writing of Newcomb's among his effects and their reply was negative."

To have expected any other reply would be, to say the least, naïve, almost as naïve as a Soviet prisoner's attempting to write his experiences while in prison.

Among Newcomb Mott's few effects that were eventually returned were his passport, wallet, driver's license, a number of personal cards one would put in a wallet, and his wristwatch. All were said to have been in his possession at the time of his death. A laboratory examination of these effects and others, such as his reading glasses and a pair of sunglasses, showed they could not have been.

The Soviets offer for public consumption the spectacle of two armed guards and a conductor unable to enter a prisoner's barred compartment because he was throwing jars at them. It is reasonable to ask then just at what point did the prisoner take the time to systematically carve up his wrists, arms, elbows, stomach, and neck, while stamping on his feet, kicking himself in the groin, and bruising his neck, wrists, hands, and elbows.

The story is not credible from any aspect, perhaps because the people who invented it couldn't have cared less. What is puzzling, however, is why the Embassy and the State Department didn't check on the details.

Train number 94 from Leningrad was due in station Shar'ya at 4:37 P.M. January 20. From Shar'ya train number 94 proceeds to Kotelnich, a main junction on the line which is over fifty miles west of Kirov. Had Newcomb Mott been on train 94, or any train, he would have been traveling under the authority of the Transportation Department of the KGB which takes it orders from Moscow. Had he died on the train which the Soviets said was in the vicinity of Shar'ya "late in the day," meaning closer to midnight than 4:37 P.M., his body would have been taken to Kotelnich and not to Kirov. This is so *not* just for reasons of proximity, but because to take the body to Kirov would have been to place it under the authority of Kirov Oblast Regional Administration. The guards and conductor were under Moscow's command. They would have notified their superior there of what had happened, and been told to take the body off the train at Kotelnich. Those who know Soviet bureaucracy know that this is how it works—one authority never quickly or willingly yielding its power and direction to another. How Newcomb Mott's body may have reached Kirov will subsequently be explored, but this Soviet administrative difference indicates that it did not come by train from Shar'ya.

While the State Department was in the process of "requesting" the Soviet investigation report, Mr. Adams took action on his own. Late in February he contacted Dr. Ephraim J. Felderman, Chief of Pathology at Central General and Hempstead General Hospitals on Long Island. He asked the pathologist if he would have a look at the existing evidence, which at that time consisted of the autopsy slides and Dr. Luongo's report. Felderman—a short, peppery, straight-talking physician and former New York City Assistant Medical Examiner—paid a visit to the noted attorney's law office in Manhattan. There he was filled in on Newcomb Mott's background and the case. He read Dr. Luongo's material, and then he and Adams went over the slides together. Dr. Felderman left the meeting highly skeptical of suicide. When in April he received a copy of the twenty-six-page Soviet document he was able to substantiate his suspicions and produce medical proof for them.

In the Soviet report he recorded forty-six points that required clarification or further investigation, but more important than all else, he proved to fellow physicians, to Francis Adams, and to the author that Newcomb Mott could not have cut his throat under any conceivable circumstance with a double-edged Wilkinson razor blade—or any razor blade—as described by the Soviets. This is so because by neither its length nor its width is a razor blade capable of making the kind of death wound detailed by the Soviets and revealed in the slides. The cutting length of a Wilkinson double-edged blade is 1½ inches, its width is ⅞ of an inch. The depth of the wound was approximately 2½ inches, more than *twice* the width of the blade. The Soviets described a wound, which the autopsy slides show, that penetrated the pharyngeal cavity severing the epiglottis deep in the center of the throat. To the layman this is the area of the Adam's apple, and Dr. Felderman, using laboratory specimens of the area in question, was unable to duplicate the fatal wound even while holding the razor blade by a protective piece of cardboard. It takes a sharp object both stronger and longer than a razor blade to penetrate through these neck organs even if the head is thrown back at the time.

Dr. Felderman did not know and would not speculate on how Newcomb Mott had died, but he knew he had not met death from a razor blade in his own hand.

In his written evaluation of the autopsy slides, Dr. Felderman made some additional observations: "The many incisions of the right antecubital fossa [inner arm at the joint] should be explained. Many of the incisions are almost horizontal. They seem to go outward. The position and direction of these incisions do not seem to be consistent with use of the left hand.

"The left wrist. There are approximately fifteen incised wounds there. These wounds are not consistent with self-infliction and are in a different direction.

"The fingers of the right hand show incisions going in the same direction as the fingers and not transversely. It is not possible to hold a razor to inflict wounds and at the same time cut the fingers in this manner.

"There are sixteen incised wounds on the left and right lateral aspect of the neck. It would appear that these could not have been self-inflicted because their direction is such that it would be almost impossible to be self-inflicted."

On April 25, 1966, the U. S. Embassy delivered its final

note on the case to the Soviet Ministry of Foreign Affairs. The note said: "The United States Government has found it impossible to arrive at meaningful conclusions about the events leading up to Mr. Mott's death and the means by which his death came about."

It then went on to repeat the Soviet failure to supply specific information, citing four major omissions in the Soviet documents but by implication accepting the story of the prisoner on the train going berserk.

The note concluded:

"The Soviet Government's refusal to provide those vital elements of information which must be available to the Soviet authorities and which are essential to an objective judgment as to the cause of Mr. Mott's death is scarcely responsive to the Ambassador's request of January 22, 1966, for a most thorough investigation of the circumstances of Mr. Mott's death and a full report. Moreover, the failure of the Soviet Government to be more forthcoming in this matter obviously will be a source of major concern to Mr. and Mrs. Mott, who have an indisputable right to full information on the tragic death of their son. Finally, it must be obvious to the Soviet Government that only by a full disclosure of all the relevant information could it be demonstrated that the Soviet authorities do not bear responsibility in connection with the tragic death of Newcomb Mott while he was in their custody."

One need hardly consider the Soviet reaction to a demand based not so much on the power and prestige of a mighty nation as on the peace of mind of two of its disillusioned citizens.

On the same day that this "formal request" was sent forth, Francis Adams called a press conference in New York and issued a protest of a different sort. In it he revealed Dr. Felderman's findings and stated, ". . . it must be concluded from clear evidence of the physical facts that Mr. Mott was murdered."

Referring further to the report from the Soviet Government, Mr. Adams made the following points:

1. There is no explanation as to how Mr. Mott was confined or how he was protected, if at all, from possible assailants.

2. The razor blade alleged to have been used has not been produced.

3. The Soviet Government has refused to turn over Mr. Mott's clothing.

4. The Soviet Government has refused to produce photographs alleged to have been taken during the Soviet autopsy.

5. The Soviet Government has refused to produce the report of January 20, 1966 by the chief escort on the train, Selivanov, with the participation of escort Murodyan and conductor Aububakirov. The failure to do so leads to the inescapable conclusion that the Soviet Government is afraid to reveal the statements of those who were actually on the scene.

6. The refusal of the Soviet Government to produce the alleged security guards is highly significant and suspicious.

7. The fact that there were over sixty-five separate wounds on Mr. Mott's body has not been explained. In this respect it is to be noted that the Soviet report concedes that there were multiple wounds on the body.

8. The suggestion that Soviet guards were unable to enter the compartment in which Mr. Mott was confined while he was allegedly making sixty-five wounds on his own body is unbelievable.

9. There is no explanation as to why Mr. Mott was being sent into the interior to begin to serve his sentence before his appeal for clemency was determined. In the

absence of such explanation it is fair to suggest that this was a part of a plan to cause Mr. Mott's death.

Little press coverage was given to Dr. Felderman's findings and Mr. Adams' serious accusations, and there are at least two known reasons why the State Department and U.S. officialdom did not choose to take the accusations seriously and have never done so.

The first reason was based on the twin evaluation reports of the Soviet autopsy performed on the body of Newcomb Mott as recorded by Embassy observer, Captain (Doctor) James W. Bizzell. The reports are dated January 27 and February 3, 1966, and offer four conclusions:

"1. There was no evidence that restraint was placed upon the victim nor that there were any contusions inflicted prior to death.

"2. All lacerations could feasibly have been self-inflicted.

"3. The case was most likely suicide in nature.

"4. It is conceivable that the powders taken from the victim's clothing for analysis may have been a drug, in which case it could have played a part in his frame of mind at the time of his death."

Photographic evidence, plus the medical opinion of leading pathologists, completely refute Captain Bizzell's first point. In point two, if all lacerations could have been self-inflicted, they also could have been inflicted by others. But more specifically, Captain Bizzell unknowingly contradicted his own assumption by observing that the principal wound across the throat was "two to two and one half inches in depth." As noted, a razor blade could not have inflicted such a wound, which not only gives the lie to the Soviet explanation of Newcomb Mott's death, but also destroys the credibility of the Captain's apparent case for suicide, which he repeated in point number three. The final assumption is extremely slanted and was later invalidated by Doctor Luongo's findings.

Captain Bizzell's observations of the autopsy are open to further question. He reports "multiple deep lacerations on both sides of the face . . ." and there were none. He maintains ". . . all of the victim's fingers were individually examined and there was no evidence of lacerations or cuts, as from a double-edged razor blade." The autopsy photographs show cuts on two of the fingers of the right hand. He refers to "necrosis points" being made *after* death, and such points can only occur during life.

According to the State Department, "It was concluded by the Soviet examiners and Dr. Bizzell . . . that Mott was not bruised before death." As already medically stated: a human body cannot be bruised *after* death.

As to the Captain's expertise in pathology, he was graduated from Baylor Medical School in 1962. During 1962–63 he interned at Presbyterian St. Luke's Hospital in Chicago, planning to practice Internal Medicine. Following his entry into the Air Force he was posted to the Embassy in Moscow on September 11, 1964. At the time he was called upon to make a highly charged judgment as to whether Newcomb Mott had been murdered or had committed suicide, he was not known to have had any practical experience in the highly specialized and delicate fields of Pathology and Forensic Medicine. Dr. Bizzell refused to discuss the case with the author, declaring his reports were "secret."

There is another far more prestigious reason why the State Department "off the record" accepts Newcomb Mott's death as suicide. On March 31, 1966, Dr. Lewis K. Woodward, State Department Medical Director, contacted Brigadier General Joseph M. Blumberg, Director of the Armed Forces Institute of Pathology in Washington, D.C. Dr. Woodward asked Dr. Blumberg if the AFIOP would make an evaluation of the Soviet autopsy report as well as Dr. Luongo's and the toxicological examination signed by Dr. McBay.

The senior staff of AFIOP did so and a two-page summary was written which General Blumberg "finalized."

ARMED FORCES INSTITUTE OF PATHOLOGY
Washington, D.C. 20305

Address reply to the Director
Attn: MEDEM-PE
JMB/CJS/djk
6 April 1966

Lewis K. Woodward, Jr., M.D.
Director, Medical Division
Room 2906
Department of State
Washington, D.C. 20520

Dear Doctor Woodward:

The report in the case of *Newcomb Mott,* containing the Soviet report of autopsy, report of autopsy performed at Boston, comments of the Mott attorney, and background information, has been reviewed at the Armed Forces Institute of Pathology. The opinions rendered in this case are based only upon these records, for neither photographs nor pathologic materials have been provided for review.

It is noted the pathologists who performed the second autopsy at Boston did not have the Soviet records for review. The report of these pathologists does not include a microscopic examination of tissues, but it has been implied they retained tissues for these studies.

The medicolegal post-mortem examination performed in the Soviet Union is complete and adequate. There are no discrepancies between the findings of the Soviet and American pathologists. Based upon the Soviet report, the manner of death is compatible with suicide. The incised wounds of the neck, upper extremities, and abdomen could have been produced by a safety razor blade, or any sharp instrument similar to a safety razor blade.

The allegations of the Mott attorney, Mr. F. W. H. Adams, concerning the manner of death is not consistent with the findings of both the Soviet and American pathologists. These pathologists are in essential agreement the incised wounds are compatible with self-inflicted injuries. A report of the post-mortem and toxicological examinations has been provided by the Soviet Government. It is agreed, however, it would be desirable to have the clothing of the Subject and the alleged weapon available for further examination.

It is not possible to render an opinion concerning the Soviet inquest since records of this inquest are not available for review. The conclusions of the board of forensic medicine experts, dated 14 February 1966, seem valid and are compatible with the records provided for review. Without further knowledge of the scene, the circumstances of death, and observations of prison train personnel, it cannot be determined whether or not the Subject was temporarily deranged at the time of his death.

Concerning the question of maltreatment or homicide, the absence of defense injuries, the presence of hesitation-type incised wounds, and the anatomic locations of the incised wounds, compatible with a self-inflicted pattern, would not tend to support this allegation. Furthermore, the toxicologic studies performed in the Soviet Union indicate the Subject had ingested an excessive quantity of salicylates prior to death. Although a therapeutic level of salicylates was detected in the liver during analysis by the Massachusetts State Police, the Subject probably did not survive long enough to attain a toxic level in the blood or tissues. These toxicologic studies suggests [sic] intent for suicide by another method, that is, overdose of salicylates. The toxicologic analysis of the white powder contained in his trouser pocket revealed salicylates and tends to support this opinion.

In summary, the records indicate the Subject had been nervous during his confinement and had requested tranquilizers. Death resulted from an incised wound of the neck which resulted in aspiration of blood and hemorrhage. There are no significant discrepancies between the Soviet and American post-mortem examination. Although it would be desirable to have the alleged weapon, clothing, photographs, report of scene investigation, and statements of guards for examination or review, the manner of death, based upon available information, is compatible with suicide.

JOE M. BLUMBERG
Brigadier General, MC, U.S.A.
The Director

Thus although the State Department and particularly the Office of Soviet Union Affairs have never publicly accepted Newcomb Mott's death as suicide, taking the comfortable public position of doubt, inside the Department suicide has been bought by some officials on the strength of Dr. Bizzell's reports and AFIOP's two-page evaluation. This evaluation, even from the layman's point of view, is an incredible official document and, from the opinions of a number of physicians who have studied it and the pertaining material out of which it was fashioned, "the worst kind of medical supposition."

Paragraph one: ". . . neither photographs nor pathological materials have been provided for review."

The autopsy photographs were the most important medical evidence available to U.S. investigators. Since Dr. Luongo's report was made available to AFIOP by the State Department, why weren't photographs? Or why did not Dr. Blumberg's senior staff request them?

Paragraph three: The medicolegal post-mortem examination prepared by the Soviet doctors is *not* complete and adequate. It makes no mention of the two-inch bruise over the victim's trachea, nor the bruises on the rest of his body, and even Dr. Luongo's report refers to "cutaneous abrasions and contusions on both wrists . . . and some bruises of a type not typical of self-infliction."

The AFIOP letter next states: "The incised wounds of the neck, upper extremities, and abdomen could have been produced by a safety razor blade, *or any sharp instrument similar to a safety razor blade.*"

Dr. Felderman's experiments proved that the fatal wound could not have been produced by a safety razor blade. For the Armed Forces Institute of Pathology to suggest that death was caused by "any sharp instrument similar to a safety razor blade" is grotesquely slipshod. The statement is carelessly thrown in, yet if taken seriously it refutes the entire Soviet case. Either the instrument was a Wilkinson razor blade or it was not.

Paragraph four: It is true that "The allegations of the Mott attorney" are not consistent with the Soviet findings, but as for "the American pathologists," murder was not ruled out.

Paragraph five: Here admitting they lack the necessary evidence to make a determination, the authors of this evaluation then proceed to speculate that Newcomb Mott may have been deranged at the time of his death.

Paragraph six: "Concerning the question of maltreatment or homicide, the absence of defense injuries [etc.], would not tend to support this allegation."

As already noted, and as will be further demonstrated, there *were* defense injuries and definite evidence of maltreatment. The remainder of this paragraph not only is pure speculation but also contradicts Dr. Luongo's evaluation of the small amount of salicylates that had been ingested.

The final paragraph: Newcomb Mott's nervousness was never more than a normal reaction to what he was undergoing. His letters illustrate his ability to keep his balance. Furthermore, anyone who knows anything about arctic Russia and particularly Murmansk knows that as soon as one departs the general area for the south, he experiences a great mental and physical uplift—just the opposite from depression. The dreadful climate is one reason why the Soviets pay workers in Murmansk 40 per cent more than anywhere else in the USSR.

The speculations, assumptions, contradictions, evaluations, and failure to examine *all* the evidence at hand indicate that this supposedly authoritative and official summary on the death of Newcomb Mott is a document almost completely lacking validity.

In seeking independent backing or refutation of Dr. Felderman's conclusions, the author approached eight physicians. Two are pathologists for a large metropolitan hospital. One is a neurosurgeon. One is considered by his colleagues a leading world authority in the field of neuropathology. One is director of the department of pathology in the school of medicine at an Ivy League university. The remaining three are practicing M.D.s who in the course of their careers have been engaged in pathology and forensic medicine.

For the most part they were approached independently, and five of them made a study of the autopsy slides which the AFIOP did not ask to see. Each offered his own evaluation based on the evidence at hand, and all supported Dr. Felderman. As one summed it up, "I do not think it possible that a razor blade could inflict such a wound in the throat." This same pathologist, using a Wilkinson double-edged razor blade, attempted to duplicate Newcomb Mott's throat wound on laboratory cadavers and could not.

The five doctors who saw the slides conceded they had never observed a suicide case with so many so-called hesitation wounds on both wrists and both sides of the neck. They felt these slashes—one right beside the other—might have been made to cover up other marks such as bruises on the wrists and neck, the former caused by rope, the latter by thumbs.

But incredible as it may seem, it was an extract from the Soviet autopsy report which Dr. Felderman had seized on with surprise, that all eight physicians accepted as medical proof that Newcomb Mott had been beaten about the head, "over a period of weeks" before he died!

The extract is found on page 2 of the Soviet Forensic Histological Examination, and its findings are completely at variance with the Soviet external examination of the same area. The extract deals with the tissue analysis of Newcomb Mott's brain: "The pia-arachnoid is swollen and disintegrated. Its inner layers contain, in a limited area, accumulations of fresh loose erythrocytes. In certain places, small accumulations of yellowish-brown masses are visible near the blood vessels. The blood vessels of the pia-arachnoid are plethoric. The erythrocytes in the blood vessels are partially hemolyzed.

"The brain substance is plethoric throughout. Thc capillary network looks as if it had been injected. In various parts of the brain, in the cortex and in the subcortical areas, there are loose erythrocytes in the perivascular spaces. There is a moderate pericellular and pericapillary edema. In the brain substance, as well as in the pia-arachnoid, near some of the blood vessels, grains of yellowish-brown color are visible. In the cortex, there are individual small arteries with swollen walls."

To the laymen such medical terminology requires translation. As one of the neurosurgeons put it: "Accumulations of the fresh loose erythrocytes in the layer of the pia-arachnoid indicate hemorrhage before death. Small yellowish-brown masses visible near blood vessels are the pigment from disintegrated blood cells, such disintegration having occurred during life, in other words the late result of capillary hemorrhages."

This interpretation of the extract was supported by the other seven doctors. In answer to the question of how long before death hemorrhages took place, the over-all estimation was not a matter of hours, or even a few days, but at least two weeks. The brain of a prize fighter reveals similar hemorrhages, as does the brain of anyone beaten with a rubber truncheon.

Another physician, the neuropathologist, stated: "From the information on the cerebral findings, I am inclined to suspect murder. This is because of the presence of cerebral vascular congestion and extravascular hemorrhages together with cerebral edema, a strong suspicion of trauma and/or asphyxia exists. I cannot conceive these changes having occurred as the result of a person cutting his own throat."

The questions arise out of the surprising Soviet admission, which is actually repeated at the conclusion of the particular report. Why did the KGB let it pass, and why was it not detected by Dr. Blumberg and staff?

The first answer is that probably those in the KGB who read the document knew nothing of medical terminology, and as for the Soviet doctors, they were following orders, possibly knowing little and caring less about the case, which had gotten the barest kind of coverage in the Soviet press. These, after all, were tissue slides and the examining doctors, who made their studies between January 31 and February 10, did not associate them with the identity of any particular individual. That, or they did what they did for reasons unknown.

With regard to the answer to the second question—there is none. Dr. Blumberg personally told the author that nothing unusual had been noted in the Soviet report. Evidently Dr. Blumberg and his senior staff did not request to see the tissue slides. Dr. Felderman did, and he eventually received two slides of brain tissue, sent from Dr. Luongo's Boston office. Although the slides at best failed to present Dr. Felderman with all the medical information he sought, his laboratory analysis revealed some positive evidence of previous brain hemorrhage. The doctor refused to accept this evidence as conclusive, however, saying the Soviet autopsy report gave much more detailed proof of the same thing.

Answers to why and how Newcomb Mott died remain in the realm of speculation, but there are two major schools of thought on the latter. Shortly after his death, *Newsweek* magazine reported that some were saying he could have been a victim of Stalinists in the Soviet Government wishing to *embarrass* the Foreign Ministry in its desire to pursue coexistence and détente. A variation on this was that the KGB had ordered his death for the same reason, and also as a pointed illustration of what could happen to those who do not take the USSR's borders and regulations to heart.

U. S. Sovietologists questioned on the matter have mixed opinions on this line of possibility, some saying it does not take into account the structure of the Communist bureaucracy, and others offering their own variations on the same theme.

However, the most likely supposition which fits the pattern of circumstances is that Newcomb Mott was sent to a labor camp sometime shortly after January 2, and while there was attacked by other prisoners. Aside from medical evidence, several facts give support to this contention. There are many prison compounds in the Kirov area. Two are at Shekshema and Ponzyrevo, and at both are found the kind of correctional camp to which the prisoner had been sentenced. These camps come under control of the Ministry of Maintenance of Social Order with an administrative office in Kirov. If Newcomb Mott died at either camp, his body would have been taken to Kirov, and this would have explained its presence there and not at Kotelnich as earlier described. In accepting this theory, several former Soviet prisoners and two noted Sovietologists agree on one further point: although Russian convicts are noted for their bestiality, they would not have attacked the prisoner without a green light from higher authority.

In examining motivation behind this line of thought there are several unexplained facts that warrant close attention. One, at least an hour of Newcomb Mott's time, following his crossing the Soviet border, has never been accounted for. Two, Norwegian authorities later reported to U.S. officials that Mott had not told the truth when he declared he had been told by some individuals that he could visit Boris Gleb without a visa. Mott did tell the truth, and the Norwegian report is incorrect, either deliberately or through error. Three, had the information given the author by Birger Kvammen, concerning the broadcast he'd heard from Murmansk inviting anyone to visit Boris Gleb, been introduced at the trial, the Soviets would have had a far more difficult time handing down a rigged verdict.

But the most important fact of all centers on the safety razor Mott was permitted to keep in his cell. For a prisoner in the USSR, no matter his nationality, to be in possession of any object that could be used as a weapon, or a device with which to kill himself, is against all Soviet prison regulations. Yet a safety razor was given to Newcomb Mott shortly after his arrival in Murmansk. So far as can be determined, no American before Mott's imprisonment, and none since, has been granted this privilege. It will be recalled that Newcomb himself was puzzled by what can only be termed an incredible breach of regulations.

The question is—why was it granted?

The possible answer is—that the KGB learned that while Newcomb Mott was lost he had stumbled onto something of a top secret nature or had accidentally met someone whose identity must remain secret, and that although he did not realize the significance of what he had seen, intelligence officers in the United States would have extracted the information from him. Therefore the decision was made by the KGB to break the prisoner down mentally, so that he would use the razor to take his own life. And this they failed to do.

There are, of course, other theories as to how and why Newcomb Mott died. His parents believe he never left Murmansk alive. Others have suggested that wherever he was, he might have tried to escape. This last does not seem credible, but at this time there is simply no telling.

Only two things appear certain. Newcomb Mott did not kill himself. He was slaughtered by Soviet persons unknown for reasons unknown and for over a period of time before his death he had been beaten on the head.

THE WHITE HOUSE
Washington
June 2, 1966

Dear Mr. Adams:

The President has asked me to reply to your letter regarding the tragic death of Newcomb Mott.

After a careful review of the efforts of the U.S. Government on Newcomb Mott's behalf, the President continues to believe that the actions taken by the Administration were those appropriate and most effective in the situation as it developed.

You are familiar with the actions which this Government took in an effort to bring about the release of Newcomb Mott. The representations made by Secretary Rusk, Ambassador Kohler and other officials of this Government to the Soviet Government, including their chief of state, carried the full support of this Administration. The death of Newcomb Mott did not ensue from any failure by the U.S. Government to take appropriate action. It is a matter of deepest regret to the President that official representations failed to evoke the desired response from the Soviet Government.

As to this Government's responsibility to caution American citizens traveling abroad of the hazards to their personal safety, you may recall that on Febraury 14, 1966 a Department of State spokesman announced that our advice to those intending to travel to the Soviet Union had been revised. Our new statement is designed to reflect our changed appreciation of the treatment which American tourists accused of violating Soviet laws can expect to receive in the USSR.

Sincerely,

Harry C. McPherson, Jr.
Special Counsel to the President

Mr. Francis W. H. Adams
Attorney at Law
Satterlee, Warfield & Stephens
277 Park Avenue
New York, N.Y. 10017

Chapter Fourteen

On February 1, 1966, within two weeks after Newcomb Mott's death, Senator Edward M. Kennedy delivered a speech on the floor of the Senate, giving a detailed account of the case. In it he declared: "One of two things must be true: Either Newcomb Mott met with foul play while in the custody and full control of Soviet officials, or he took his own life while in the custody and full control of Soviet officials. In either case the Government of the Soviet Union is to blame for his death."

In placing the blame the Senator from Massachusetts went on to make six demands of the Soviet Government, adding, "I feel that our Government and his family deserve these courtesies from the Soviet Union. As I said, they are no more no less than what the Soviets would ask if this tragedy had occurred to one of their innocent citizens on our soil. I intend to press for them, to keep pressing until satisfactory answers are forthcoming and until those responsible are punished.

"I think the Soviets have handled the case badly from the beginning until now. But I have no desire that the case damage the relations between our two Governments in the very difficult matter of international relations in which we share a mutual concern. I make this speech not to embarrass the Russians but to see that justice can be done in the future."

Although Senator Kennedy's somewhat stunning suggestion that a Soviet citizen on U.S. soil could be put through the same ordeal and meet with the same fate as Newcomb Mott was ignored by the U.S. press, the Soviets, in taking into account the Senator's six demands, made succinct reply via Tass.

"Senator Edward Kennedy spoke in the U. S. Senate and tried to whitewash Mott and to prove that he crossed the border 'by accident.' But Mott's guilt was fully established in court and he himself did not deny the fact that he had violated the border intentionally.

"Edward Kennedy has gone so far as to blame the Soviet Government for Mott's death. His six demands of the Soviet Government are an unconcealed attempt to interfere in the international affairs of a sovereign state. It is pertinent to ask what Kennedy's stand would be if such demands were put to the U. S. Government. Although Kennedy has said in the Senate that he did not wish to put the Soviet Government in the difficult position by his speech, it can hardly contribute to normalizing Soviet-American relations."

As to Senator Edward M. Kennedy's desire not to "embarrass" the Soviet Government, he was repeating the State Department policy line, earlier indicated. Since 1965 the American public has been belabored with this line about Soviet "embarrassment." Spokesmen, columnists, commentators, educators, clergymen, a veritable host of spoken and written word experts have pressed it home. In the new lexicon we no longer find the Soviets aggressive, unprincipled, or barbaric; they are now only embarrassed, having evolved from that earlier more primitive state through the most remarkable evolution in the history of mankind made not in Moscow but in Washington.

For instance, Joseph Alsop writing in his column "Matter of Fact" on April 27, 1966, with regard to normalizing Russian relations, said: "If the consular convention were now ratified for instance, the Soviets would no doubt be pleased; but they would also be embarrassed for exactly the same reason that some congressmen are obstructive. Because of Viet Nam, they would probably have to forbid a Leningrad consulate at this time."

Less than a year later the Consular Convention was ratified. The situation in Viet Nam was if anything worse from the Soviet point of view.

Policy lines notwithstanding, the State Department knows there are two sources of economic benefit the Soviet Union seeks from the United States. They are tourism and *valuta* foreign exchange. As shown, threats of a possible decrease in the former, rising out of the treatment of Newcomb Mott, had no effect on bringing his release, and shortly after his death the Soviets put on a campaign to attract American travelers. In this they had on March 5, 1966, the assistance of NBC News.

MACNEIL

"The Soviet Union has just launched an expensive campaign to attract American tourists—and apparently to repair the damage to Russia's image as a tourist paradise caused by the Newcomb Mott case.

"Mott was a young booksalesman from Massachusetts who strayed across the Russian border, was sentenced to eighteen months imprisonment, and allegedly committed suicide on a Soviet train.

"Two weeks ago the State Department warned Americans that in view of the Mott incident, travel to Russia was now risky.

"At the same time the Soviet Travel Agency Intourist came out for the first time with a glossy supplement to the Sunday New York *Times*. For $80,000 Intourist got twelve pages of enticing color photos and ads from airlines. The response according to the Russians has already been heavy. Last year twenty-two thousand Americans went to see sights like Moscow's Red Square and the Kremlin and the number is expected to go to twenty-five thousand this year. Intourist is expanding tourist facilities so that tourists can travel farther in Russia.

(to film)

"Intourist operations are run from a pleasant, skyscraper office in Manhattan. Until this year, the advertising budget was modest, too modest for Sunday supplements. But the Russians deny they are trying to answer State Department warnings. The Intourist director is Anatoly Slavnov, a former Olympic oarsman. We asked how he felt about the warnings that travel to Russia was risky.

[strip of film]

SOF SLAVNOV

runs: 1:58

ENDS: ". . . they found it very interesting."

"When asked for clarification of the U.S. position, the State Department spokesman, Robert McCloskey, repeated the warning about dangers in Russian travel, but said the Department was not discouraging Americans from going."
Robert MacNeil, NBC News, New York.

RAY SCHERER

. . . and Ray Scherer. NBC News, Washington. Good night."

On April 26, 1966, the State Department issued its final "angry" protest to the Soviet Government for its failure to give an adequate explanation of how Newcomb Mott had met his death. An Embassy spokesman in Moscow was quoted as saying, "It looks like the end of the road now. We can't force them to divulge more information."

But that was not the end of the road as far as the Soviets were concerned. On May 27, 1966, *Newsweek*'s Stockholm correspondent cabled: "Newcomb Mott case has further repercussions here as Norway refused to open its northern Norway border to Boris Gleb again this summer. Stop. This was where Mott supposedly slipped over. Stop. Also heard reliably that USSR made great mistake, transporting Mott on same train with common criminals, that they were actually prepared to set him free, that they returned his belongings to him on train, and that he was jumped by criminals resulting in injuries covered by suicide."

In tracking down the "reliable sources," it was learned that information had come to the correspondent from Swedish officials who were passing on diplomatic cocktail talk held with a Soviet. The Soviet did not explain why or how Newcomb Mott was being sent home via a train said to be heading east toward the Urals.

Throughout the spring and summer of 1966 the name of Newcomb Mott continued to appear in print in the United States and Europe. Always, of course, reference to him was in respect to U.S.-Soviet relations, but then on September 11, almost exactly a year after he had crossed at Boris Gleb, the Thomas J. Dawson case broke. Dawson, a twenty-four-year-old Peace Corps member in Iran, had inadvertently wandered over the Soviet border near the Caspian Sea. Unlike Newcomb Mott, he was not looking for a border control point but sea shells. Soviet guards jumped him, and for the next few weeks it looked like a repeat of the events of a year ago. Dawson was held in solitary confinement and questioned intensively by the KGB, while the State Department again began making contacts and protests.

Three days before Dawson's arrest, Peter Kalitenko, like

Gregory Sarapushkin before him, called the Soviet Embassy in Washington and said it was now time for him to go home, too. Kalitenko and Sarapushkin were the Russian pair who had gotten lost at sea, come ashore in Alaska, and had asked for asylum in the U.S. in August 1965. Meetings were arranged between U.S. and Soviet representatives with Kalitenko present, and on September 19, just like his comrade from Lavrentiya, Kalitenko was bundled on to an aircraft and shipped east. The Washington *Post* made absolutely no reference to the interlocking connection between Newcomb Mott and Gregory Sarapushkin, and Thomas Dawson and Peter Kalitenko.

The New York *Times* in its story mentioned the four but failed to link them together in what can only be described as a most incredible coincidence. Fortunately, in the latter case, Dawson, after being held a month, was released by the KGB and sent home. His mother did not believe her son's freedom had anything to do with Peter Kalitenko's return to Siberia. In a letter to Phyllis Mott she said, "I know if it weren't for your son, my son would never have been freed."

The Soviets had slain Newcomb Mott, but he had come to haunt them.

This was further borne out in the joint case of Craddock M. Gilmour, Jr., and Buel Ray Wortham, Jr., both arrested on October 1, 1966, at the Soviet-Finnish border. The two, former Army lieutenants discharged in Germany, had been touring the Soviet Union. They were arrested for exchanging money on the black market and Wortham for stealing a statue of a bear from his Leningrad hotel as a souvenir. These crimes, minor as they were, were certainly more serious than Newcomb Mott's. Furthermore, both should have known better. As one long-time career officer in the field of Soviet affairs bewailed, "Would you tell me what is the matter with these young people who think they can fool around Soviet borders and break their laws? Has no one taught them any better, that the Soviets play rough?"

In handling both cases, the Soviets set some new precedents. First they granted Gilmour bail for $11,000, then they tried him, found him guilty of illegal currency exchange, fined him $1111, and let him go home. With Wortham it took longer. They found him guilty as charged, and sentenced him to three years in a labor camp. Then they let him out of prison on bail amounting to $22,222.22, raised by the people of his hometown of North Little Rock, Arkansas. Finally on March 21, 1967, the Soviets sold Wortham into freedom for *valuta* in the amount of $5,555. There had been no bail for Newcomb Mott, no purchase price.

When Gilmour was released by the Soviets on December 2, 1966, he was believed by the State Department to be the first foreigner to have been permitted bail before being tried. Wortham became the first foreigner ever known to have gotten bail in the USSR after being convicted.

Although Newcomb Mott's name was mentioned by writers and commentators reporting the dual cases, few saw that his death had a direct bearing on the fate of Gilmour and Wortham. But there is no doubt that it did. The Soviets are anxious for the American public to forget Newcomb Mott, and by their treatment of Dawson and the two former lieutenants they have gone a long way toward succeeding.

At the end of 1966 another incident occurred which deserves mention not because Newcomb Mott's memory played any part in its development, but because of the reason for its successful resolution. U.S. travel agent Vladimir Kazan-Komarek, a former anti-Communist resistance leader in Czechoslovakia, had gone to the Soviet Union on a tour. In November he returned west via a Soviet Aeroflot plane. The plane diverted from its regular course and made an unscheduled stop in Prague, whereupon Kazan-Komarek was arrested by the Czech SBD and charged with espionage and assorted crimes. The United States Government vehemently protested the Soviet-Czech kidnaping. In late January a Czech court sentenced American citizen Kazan-Komarek to eight years in jail. The victim was, like Newcomb Mott, a resident of Massachusetts, and as in Mott's case, Senator Edward M. Kennedy took an active role. He wrote a letter to the Czech President Antonin Novotny, reportedly invoking his late brother's efforts to improve East-West relations. But just as something more than letters was needed to free Newcomb Mott, something more was needed to free Kazan-Komarek, and something more was forthcoming.

Writing in the Los Angeles *Times* on February 6, 1967, Robert J. Donovan reported: "Speaker of the House John W. McCormack, D. of Mass., and other members from Massachusetts put pressure on Secretary of State Dean Rusk to twist Prague's arm.

"The twisting soon began with the action of the U. S. Embassy in Prague in withholding between 50 and 100 visas from trade-hungry Czechs who wanted to come to the United States on business.

"In unofficial talks at cocktail parties and other gatherings American diplomats lamented to Czech diplomats that U.S.-Czech trade relations, unfortunately, were not susceptible to improvement because of the Kazan incident."

On February 4, Kazan-Komarek was released from a Czech prison and sent home. Senator Kennedy's letter was used by some editorial writers as the basic reason for his constituent's release, but, as Donovan's article pointed out, it was simply a device instituted by the Czechs to save face and hide the reality, which was that direct, quiet economic persuasion brought results.

A year after Newcomb Mott's death the Senate was involved in debate over the ratification of the Consular Convention, signed between the U.S. and Soviet Governments in 1964. Proponents for ratification sought out Phyllis and Howard Mott and asked them to make statements in favor of it, declaring in effect that had there been a ratified pact at the time of Newcomb's arrest he might never have been brought to trial and thus would have survived. But the Motts declined to become involved in the debate, refusing to speculate on what might have happened if something had been different. It had happened, and they were not about to have their son's memory used as a pawn in any argument over U.S.-Soviet relations.

It was actually Senator J. William Fulbright, Chairman of the Senate Foreign Relations Committee, who had first used the case of Newcomb Mott as a reason for ratification of the Consular Convention. This had happened at the time of Newcomb's trial in November 1965. The Senator had written a letter to the Washington *Post,* attacking opponents of ratification, and maintaining that it had been "weeks" before any word of Newcomb's arrest was heard by the U. S. Government and by then Soviet officials had decided to make a case of it. The Senator was, of course, totally misinformed.

The most blatant political use of the case of Newcomb Mott was made by Bernard Gwertzman, also writing in support of the Consular Convention. Gwertzman, a foreign affairs writer for the Washington *Star,* had done a considerable amount of interpretive reporting on Newcomb Mott during his imprisonment and even after his death. Through his State Department contacts he was more conversant with the case than most of his fellow newspapermen.

In the January 27, 1967, edition of the *Star* he wrote a column titled "Interpretive Report, The Case for Consular Pact." Commenting on the pact's opponents, Gwertzman stated: "The recent case of Newcomb Mott, who was arrested in November 1965 and kept in virtual solitary confinement for ten weeks except for three spread-out interviews with a U.S. consular official, hardly seems to register on the opponents.

"It is quite possible that Mott would have pulled through his ordeal, *and not committed suicide,* if he had felt less isolated, and if the U.S. officials had had more access to him." (Italics added.)

The facts were that Newcomb was arrested in September,

that he spent eleven weeks in "virtual solitary confinement" before his trial and at least seven after it. The horror was that Gwertzman, reflecting unpublicized acceptance at State, had openly and unequivocally bought the Soviet line of suicide.

We have had letters from all over the U.S. and Europe about Newcomb's thoughtfulness for others, the kindness he performed, and the gifts he sent after visits. Most of these letters are from people we do not know at all; they are from people of all races, colors and creeds, and all walks of life. We feel that these messages are a fitting memorial for our son.

We walk in pride that we have had the privilege of knowing such a fine son for twenty-seven years.

From a public statement written by Phyllis and Howard Mott

Chapter Fifteen

Between September 1965 and January 21, 1966, for Phyllis and Howard Mott their son's ordeal became their own, but always with the belief that he would return to them soon or late.

His death shattered them. After its initial numbing impact a few things sustained them. There was Rusty. There were friends and family who rallied around to give them what protection they could. And then over a long period of time there were hundreds upon hundreds of letters from strangers. They came from all across the country and the globe. They offered their sorrow for a son cruelly slain in the bright morning of his life. The writers sent of themselves, affording a glimpse of the human spirit, and by their numbers firmly re-established the essential goodness of man to a bereft family who most sorely needed such affirmation. These strangers sent their faith and prayers and in so doing gave sustenance. Some who had heard of the memorial scholarship enclosed small donations, one or two or five dollars. Others who knew Soviet behavior, or had been imprisoned in Russia, were sure Newcomb had not taken his own life. All showed their kindness. And although today the flood tide of mail has ebbed to a trickle, it has never altogether ceased. It was, and is, to Phyllis and Howard Mott a source of light in the darkness of their loss.

There is no way to measure the effect of personal tragedy on the recipient of the blow. There is no total recovery from it either, nothing can ever be quite the same. There is, however, with inner courage, with strength of will, the ability to mend together the wreckage of self and continue on. This the Mott family has been able to do.

They have done so under difficult conditions. For a period of months Rusty served on a destroyer, patroling off the North Viet Nam coast. Over and over the Motts have had to read inaccurate news stories about Newcomb. For example, a year after his trial the Boston *Globe* referred to him as having been arrested as a spy.

In the firm belief that the State Department, the United States Government, and President Lyndon B. Johnson let their son down badly, Phyllis and Howard Mott recognize that one country does not threaten another with atomic war over the jailing of a single citizen, no matter the circumstances. Nor do they or millions of their fellow citizens believe that over the handling of one unimportant citizen, diplomatic relations should be broken. But they do believe, and rightly, that their son's case was handled with diplomatic gloves when bare knuckles were in order.

Frank W. Knowlton, Jr., of Grafton, Massachusetts, expressed this sentiment aptly in the Boston *Globe* when he wrote: "International tension brought on by Viet Nam, and the exigencies of the Cold War, bring into sharp focus the widespread doubts that our aggressive military efforts, on the grounds of social justice, are matched by an attitude of more than righteous indignation through 'protocol' levels of our government when civilian citizens of this country are detained, humiliated, even subject to mental and physical torture by Communist-bloc countries."

Support for this contention was supplied in reverse by a Political Affairs officer in the Office of Soviet Union Affairs, when commenting on Newcomb Mott, he stated flatly, "I don't care what anyone says, we handled the case right, and if I had to do it over again, I'd do it just the same way."

Another State Department official, on a much higher policy-making level, laid bare another aspect of official attitude in such matters. He saw no comparison between the kidnaping of former Czech underground agent Kazan-Komarek and the detention of Newcomb Mott, because the charges in the former case were far more serious than in the latter. In other words, the degree of pressure brought to bear by the U. S. Government depends not so much on the fact that an American citizen is being held by the Communists as on the charges placed against him.

Such a policy gives little support to President Johnson's statement that wherever the American citizen goes the American flag goes to protect him.

Phyllis and Howard Mott, of course, have good and sound reasons not to accept any of these contentions, and because they cannot, the hurt of Newcomb's death has been that much more painful. Neither they nor anyone else they know who wrote to the President asking him to bring the strength of his office to bear has ever received a personal acknowledgment from him. Members of the White House staff did reply. Furthermore, the State Department permitted privileged reporters to see the "classified" case files and then denied to the Motts that it had done so.

In all of the thousands of dollars of expense to them, there was only one item the Motts contested. For seventeen months, through their own efforts, the State Department's and the Embassy's in Moscow, they fought to get refunded the $200 Intourist had cheated them out of while they were in Russia. In April 1967 they finally succeeded, but in pursuing this goal they learned that any American tourist filched of his money by Intourist stands very little chance of ever seeing it again and that some so cheated have taken their case to the courts unsuccessfully.

SAS rendered the Motts one final service. In February 1966, a month after Newcomb's death, upon learning from Carroll Woods that the State Department had made no plans, and was not contemplating any, for bringing home their son's bags from the U. S. Embassy in Oslo, they contacted SAS. But even in this small matter there was a snafu. Howard Mott had given an SAS representative a special letter of authority to claim the luggage, but an Embassy official refused to turn it over until the Embassy had also received a letter of authority. Finally their son's luggage came home.

At a much later date he and his wife noticed that the principal bag had been carefully searched, and the inner lining expertly pulled loose. Evidently someone had checked to see if Newcomb Mott "had possessions worth looking into at international frontiers."

In the spring of 1967 the State Department again issued a warning to tourists planning to visit the Soviet Union. In a revised bulletin on "Travel to the Soviet Union" the Department said: "There have been indications of Soviet interest in exchanging imprisoned American tourists for Soviet citizens convicted of espionage in the United States."

Also in the spring of 1967 after the New York *Times* announced that the border at Boris Gleb was again going to be opened to tourists and *no one* would need a visa to get in, the Norwegian Parliament following a hot debate rejected the Soviet overture on the grounds that there wasn't enough to see in Boris Gleb to attract tourists. The *Times* dispatch said that in 1965 the Soviets had used Boris Gleb as "a mailbox for Soviet agents" and a place to scout for new recruits.

On a day in September, in the time of *ruska aika,* Newcomb Mott went on a walk from which he never returned. The memory of his walk remains in the minds of most because of what the Soviets did to him. But there are others who remember him for what he was, for although a man may walk alone, he leaves the imprint of himself in his passage, and, as the hunter's boots bend the tall grass, often the imprint remains.

Index